Jennie Greene

CHRISSIE

My Own Story

By Chris Evert Lloyd

with Neil Amdur

SIMON AND SCHUSTER

NEW YORK

SIMON AND SCHUSTER and colophon are trademarks of Simon & Schuster.
Designed by Eve Kirch
Manufactured in the United States of America

10 9 8 7 6 5 4 3 2 1

Library of Congress Cataloging in Publication Data

Lloyd, Chris Evert.
  Chrissie, my own story.
    1. Lloyd, Chris Evert. 2. Tennis players—
United States—Biography. I. Amdur, Neil.
II. Title.
GV994.L58A33   796.342′092′4 [B]   82-867
ISBN 0-671-44376-3   AACR2

ACKNOWLEDGMENTS

Many people have participated in the preparation of this book.

Special thanks must go to Stephanie Tolleson, Ingrid Bentzer, Rosie Casals, Connie Spooner, Billie Jean King, Jeanie Brinkman Evans, Janet Haas, Brenda Bricklin, Lynda and Ron Samuels, Phillis Flotow, and Laurie Fleming Rowley. All contributed time and insight into the project.

A very special thanks to Steve Flink, Cynthia McGinnes, and Bob Kain, who have been longtime supporters in different ways.

And especially to my best friend, Ana Leaird.

—C. E. L.

To my parents
  for their love, encouragement, and values;

To Drew, Jeanne, John, and Clare
  for their support and individuality;

and

To John
  whom I'm crazy about

Contents

Photo sections follow pages 32, 96, and 192.

Introduction

No athlete, female or male, has lived more of her life in the public eye than Chris Evert Lloyd. The world has literally watched her grow up—on and off the tennis court. For someone who has always professed to be such a "private person," Chrissie's career was seldom away from the scrutiny of the public. And over the years, her social activities often attracted as much attention from photographers and the media as her tournament successes—at a time when women's tennis was becoming synonymous with sports liberation.

This is a story about growing up. It is also a story about family, friends, relationships and a woman who dominated a sport for a decade with a won—lost record that may go unmatched.

I first approached Chris Evert Lloyd about her interest in writing a book after she had won the United States Open singles title for a third consecutive year in 1977. I had known Chrissie and the Evert family as far back as the early 1960s when I was a reporter for the *Miami Herald*. The south Florida tennis community was alive with promising young players, and Holiday Park in Fort Lauderdale, where Jimmy Evert was the teaching pro, remained one of the area hotbeds.

"I'd like to write a book," Chrissie said in 1977, "but I don't know if this is the right time." After consulting with her mom and dad, everyone agreed that a book about a twenty-two-year-old woman tennis player seemed premature.

Nothing further was said about the project until after the 1980 U.S. Open. In the course of a general discussion about her career and priorities, Chrissie and I again discussed the project. Her interest seemed considerably more positive, and I offered reasons why the timing of the book now was appropriate: Her life was in order, she was married, had gone through a series of challenging hills and valleys, and she understood herself and might have something to say to women, men and sports followers. Several months later, again after listening to input from her husband, parents and close friends, she came back ready, willing and eager to tell her story.

As you will see in the following pages, writing has always been an intimate form of expression for Chrissie, whether it was informal notes to friends slipped under a hotel-room door or intensely personal comments to herself during the years when she kept a diary. Her decision to expand these thoughts into a complete narrative is simply an extension of this interest.

Chrissie's family and friends, who have played such an integral part in her life, were unusually responsive during interviews. That many of her closest friends, like Janet Haas and Jeanie Brinkman Evans, who is married and now lives in Australia, still retained actual notes, tapes and letters from important occasions years later underscores their strong attachment to her despite being separated by time and distance. They wanted to help, not only in reliving the highs and lows of Chrissie's life but in providing her with as much background material as possible.

The contribution of John Lloyd, Chrissie's husband, deserves special mention. John's wholehearted support for the project alleviated many of Chrissie's initial concerns about discussing previously private relationships. Without John's encouragement and advice, the fabric of the book might have lacked its emotional intensity and honesty.

John remains a far more important figure in Chrissie's success and happiness—on and off the court—than he has been given credit for. Their marriage works because John has allowed Chrissie to be herself, a consideration that reflects his warm, sensitive qualities as a human being.

The Everts remain an extraordinary family—consistent in their beliefs, unspoiled by success. If there has been a touch of the American dream to Chrissie's life, perhaps she has earned that trip. She has survived the various initiations that test the spirit and will and seems to have emerged a stronger, more mature person from this experience. And, of course, all of this initiation came under the microscope of a public that had prepared its own impressionable focus of her.

In extensive taping and editing sessions with Chrissie, I tried to stress that this book should tell people who she is and how she came to be this person, not project an image that she might want the public to see. Having had the experience of working with Vince Matthews, the 1972 Olympic 400-meter champion, and Arthur Ashe, the tennis professional, on their autobiographies, I believe Chrissie has been faithful to herself and her fans.

Her legacy to tennis is assured. She certainly merits a place on any all-time list, probably in the top five because of her amazing consistency over such a long stretch. If women's tennis now is as tough as its supporters say, with more depth than ever and the pressure of prize money, travel and a variety of surfaces, her success is multidimensional.

Suzanne Lenglen and Helen Wills brought women's tennis from the social arena to the center stage of sports. Maureen Connolly introduced the youthful spirit, and Billie Jean King proved that women could be winners. Chris Evert Lloyd proved that winners could be women.

Neil Amdur
October 1981

1 • One More Time

I hung up the phone in the room at the Berkshire Place hotel in New York and started to cry. Not tears of pain, fear or sorrow specifically, just emotion.

"What's the matter, lovey?" John asked, a husband sensing his wife's uneasiness on the night before the most important tennis match of her life. "Everything all right at home?"

I wiped away the tears and nodded. But in the back of my mind, I still felt frustrated by the long-distance phone conversation with my father. "I really want to win for him tomorrow," I said.

"Why didn't you tell him then?" John asked. "I'm sure he would have wanted to know that."

I knew he would. But it had taken me a painfully long time to convince myself that I was ready to face Tracy Austin in the semifinals of the 1980 United States Open championships. Until a few minutes before, I wasn't so sure I could.

I sat on the bed, too weak to stand. John put his arm around me, but I couldn't stop sobbing. Lynda Carter walked into the room and sat down next to me.

"It's okay," she said, realizing how shaken I was. "Don't worry. It's okay."

Lynda Carter and Ron Samuels, her husband, are two of our closest friends. Lynda is familiar to millions of television viewers as "Wonder Woman" and, more recently, as a versatile entertainer. She and I have been close friends for several years and share many interests. She understood what was happening to me.

I had phoned my dad in Fort Lauderdale to catch up on family news and talk about the match with Tracy. My dad was his usual self during the call. "Just hang in there," he said. It was one of his pet phrases that I came to appreciate during the years when I had to "hang in there" by myself on the tour.

"I feel good," I said.

"Just stay out there and be prepared for a tough competitor," he continued. "Tracy is a tough player, but you're playing really well and I think you can do it if you hang in there. I think you're ready to be there now."

My dad's faith choked me up. I wanted to tell him how wonderful he and my mom have been throughout my career, always taking everything in stride. I wanted to tell him that, after two years of wondering whether tennis really mattered in my life, I was prepared to do whatever it took to beat Tracy.

I had conveyed these feelings to John after we finished dinner in our room earlier that night. As always, John asked me how I felt about my next match. I knew what he wanted to hear and could read the hopeful expression on his face. I thought for a moment, stared at him and felt a sudden surge in my stomach. "I'm prepared to stay out there all day to win if I have to," I said.

I was surprised at how easily the words came out. Had they been stored somewhere, waiting until I could handle their implications? "To stay out there all day" meant that I might have to play minutes to win one point, possibly hours to even qualify for the final. Yet somehow, after phoning my father from the bedroom of Ron and Lynda's suite, I couldn't bring myself to tell my dad how I felt.

"Why don't you just call him back?" Lynda said, echoing John's sentiments. She knew my father and teasingly called him "Jimbo." My dad may be a "Jim" or "Jimmy," but "Jimbo" was Lynda's creation.

"I don't know if it'll make any difference," I said, too uneasy to even look at Lynda. I was frightened by my insecurities. Where was the strength?

"Did you tell your father that you love him?" Lynda asked.

"No, but he knows it," I said.

Lynda handed me a towel and grabbed my shoulders. "Why don't you just call him back, ask him to come up and tell him that you love him?"

"I can't," I stammered. "He wouldn't understand."

"Well, how do you know he wouldn't understand? Have you ever done it? What does it cost you?"

Lynda was playing devil's advocate. Parental approval had produced long, tearful conversations between us. Lynda said that it had been hard for her to talk to her father until after she was married. She felt that my dad held back certain emotions from me as a teaching pro because he wanted to show strength and discipline that I could carry onto the court.

"I told you he's never seen me win a major tournament." My emotions were teetering. Was I coming apart completely?

Lynda would not let up. "I don't understand. Do you think that if he were here, you might be nervous or something? Do you *NOT* want him to come?" Her voice hardened on the word "not."

Lynda and I trusted each other enough to probe. I had been the No. 1 women's tennis player for five of the last eight years, earned several million dollars and met many famous people. Yet tennis often became a secondary consideration in my life because it wasn't enough to make me happy. For five years, Lynda had been a popular television heroine. Just as I had grown tired of tennis, Lynda wanted out of "Wonder Woman." But after the initial joy of leaving the show wore off, Lynda admitted she was climbing the walls again and frustrated.

I was trapped in a no-man's-land. "No, I would love for him to come," I said.

"Well, why don't you tell him that?"

"I can't."

"Yes, you can. Just pick up the phone and say, 'Hey, Dad, I love you. I need you to be here. I want you to be here. You're not a jinx.' "

Lynda left the bedroom and closed the door. Her words had touched me more than any of Martina Navratilova's serves, Tracy's ground strokes or those chilling stories about "Chris Evert —The Ice Maiden." Sometimes it takes a friend to lead you out of the forest. John had done that for me as a husband. He had given me stability, enthusiasm and confidence when those qualities seemed gone in 1978. John had said it was okay to quit and take time off, okay to get angry without sacrificing what I believed in. Lynda had watched my computer ranking drop from one to three, behind Tracy and Martina in 1980, but still had faith in me.

"There really is a delicate balance," she once told me, "between trying to be a good wife and trying to be successful in your career. And there aren't that many people who can pull it off."

Lynda is one of the most normal people in her business I've ever met. The pressures that an actress and an athlete face are very different. I can play a match for two hours, be competitive and work right through pressure. But Lynda can't go to the supermarket without wearing makeup. As one of the world's most beautiful women, with a dazzling figure and striking features, she has to be "on" all the time. John and I agree that Ron and Lynda have pulled it off. They value their privacy, as we do, and manage to keep their relationship in one piece.

John knew how much winning the Open meant to me, but he never applied an ounce of pressure. It was always, "You're playing well," even after I lost the Wimbledon final earlier in the summer to Evonne Goolagong Cawley or struggled before beating Mima Jausovec, 7–6, 6–2, in the quarterfinals of the Open.

My dad was the same way. He instilled a sense of hard work in his five children but never made tennis a chore. "If I can't beat her tomorrow," I told him, after calling Florida a second time, "then she's a better tennis player than I am."

I told him how much I wanted to win, how I had peaked emotionally for this tournament. He seemed surprised and moved by my call. And I got him to promise—sort of—that he would fly up for the final if I beat Tracy.

"If I win this match, you're going to come up, right?" I said.

My dad had taken off time from work and flown up for the 1971 U.S. Open semifinals at Forest Hills, New York. He also came to Wimbldeon in 1975, but I didn't win there either.

"Okay, well, we won't think about it now," he said, on the phone. But I knew that if I beat Tracy, he would have to come up. Calling him again relieved some of my anxieties. I had been honest with myself.

"You can do anything you set your mind to," John reminded me as we left Ron and Lynda's room at 10:45, after playing Tiles, a gin rummy–type game, and watching Lynda's television special. "But first you have to believe in yourself."

• • •

Earlier that afternoon, with a rest day before the semis, John and I had practiced at the National Tennis Center in Flushing Meadow. But it's difficult to be yourself when two hundred spectators are watching every stroke. After about an hour and twenty minutes, I was playing well enough to quit. I didn't want to leave my eagerness on a practice court.

I don't play perfectly in practice. In fact, I'm a terrible person to practice with. I let out all my frustrations in practice—throwing my racquet, talking to myself, complaining, cursing. I've actually cracked a few Wilson wooden racquets by throwing them to the ground. I won't do it at Wimbledon or the National Tennis Center in front of several hundred people. But those who have watched me over the years at Holiday Park near my home in Fort Lauderdale know how I get after myself.

Most of my bad practice sessions have been with family and friends. My sister Jeanne and I used to practice together. When I was fifteen and Jeanne thirteen, she was competitive with me in practice. I didn't like that, so I would hit the ball into the corners on her serves or mutter things like "How can you lose a point to her?" I would talk loud enough for her to hear. One day, after about thirty minutes, Jeanne stopped, stared at me and snapped, "Chrissie, just listen to yourself!" I felt about an inch high. She is my sister, I love her dearly, and yet I was taking it out on her. My brother John got so fed up with my antics one day that he yelled out, "I don't need this," stalked off the court and walked home. I've never done that with my husband, and John's patience has made me a more considerate practice partner.

There are only a few married couples on the women's circuit —Kerry and Raz Reid, Evonne and Roger Cawley. Since the woman is the tennis pro, the man has the role of supporting, caring and looking out for the wife. It's the reverse on the men's circuit.

When John comes to a tournament with me, he makes certain that I eat right, wake up at the right time and get to practice. The nonplayer for that week has to be unselfish and giving. When I go to a tournament with John, the roles are reversed. It's difficult when two people each have a career in tennis. With the commitments for travel, practice and appearances, at least one person in the relationship has to be more flexible. In some of the marriages that did not work in tennis, both people may have been demanding in their own ways. For the first three years of our marriage, John has been more flexible. He has given so much to my career, and I've been more demanding in our relationship. I've often felt it would have been difficult to have married a man who was very demanding, because I put so much into my tennis when I'm playing that I know my husband would also have to participate. John saw what kind of person I was—how disciplined and determined, how serious I was about my career. He knew I wouldn't be happy just giving up my career for his even though I was willing to do it. John wanted me to be happy, knew playing tennis would make me the happiest, and grasped enough of life on the men's and women's circuits to understand where the line had to be drawn.

I'm a perfectionist and get a little moody. John knows how much I have to give to my tennis in energy and emotion. So during a tournament, he doesn't want to wreck my concentration and does everything to help me reach my goal for the week. If there are reporters around, for example, he'll work as a buffer and field them off for me. It's important to know that the reverse is true when I'm with him.

When I was single, tennis was the focal point of my life. On the day of a match, I became quiet and internalized my emotions. I wasn't responsive to anyone else. Now I'm more aware of other responsibilities. John knows what to expect before a big match, what to say and how to say it.

At Wimbledon earlier that summer, my attitude was negative, even after I had beaten Martina in the semifinals. "You're playing great," John told me after that match. "You can really win this one."

I was hesitant. I wanted to say, "Yeah, I played great. It was a great match to win." But somehow the words weren't there. "I played pretty well," I said. That night, John and I rehashed the match with Martina, but I still didn't feel any confidence oozing from my voice, and John picked up the negative feedback. I lost the final to Evonne the following day.

The uncertainty continued over the summer. I won the U.S. Clay Court championship in Indianapolis and the Canadian Open in Toronto and played well in beating Kim Sands, 6–0, 6–0, in the first round at the U.S. Open. But at the postmatch news conference, a reporter asked, "Are you fearless enough to win this tournament?"

Deep inside, I didn't feel I was. But I couldn't say "no" with all those journalists sitting there because then it's as if I've lost the Open before it's really begun. So I kind of hedged a bit, paused and said, "Yeah, I think so."

I was not fearless. And every day, while beating Peanut Louie, Wendy White, JoAnne Russell and Mima Jausovec in straight sets to reach the semis, I thought about that question. When I made up my mind that I could beat Tracy, after having lost to her the last five times, I could answer that question.

Our semifinal was scheduled for eleven o'clock. John and I went right to sleep around eleven the night before, and I slept beautifully. I don't like to rush on the day of a match, so I give myself plenty of time to wake up, order breakfast, read the papers, shower, dress and pack my tennis bag. As usual, I found some candy bars in it. My mother has been putting candy bars in my tennis bags since junior days. If we had to play two matches a day then, she would buy them and tell me to eat a bar before my second match. Now, she will put four or five in my bags during the Open or Wimbledon.

I also picked out my "lucky dress" for the match. It was the same dress I wore when I won the Italian and French Open titles and also wore against Martina in the semifinals at Wimbledon.

I've never worn the same dress in two straight matches, even when the matches were important. I could have washed out a "lucky dress" after a semifinal and then worn it again for a final, and maybe I would have won a Wimbledon title in 1978, 1979 or 1980, but I would be conscious of having worn the same dress in the last match, even if it was a lucky dress.

Apparel manufacturers like Ellesse, with whom I have my current contract, want you to wear as many different outfits as possible during a tournament. My lucky dress was plain white and fitted at the waist. At the top, it had pink satin, with a pink border on the neck and sleeves. Around the neck, along the pink borders, were little flowers. It was a simple dress that fit me nicely, and I had never lost in it.

Lucky dresses were an integral part of the tour until blouses and skirts became fashionable and commercial. It's not the same anymore. Martina Navratilova had a lucky dress designed by Ted Tinling that she always wore for big matches. When she lost to Tracy one year, she threw the dress away. I had one so-called lucky yellow dress that I had worn in some important matches. After I lost to Evonne in the dress, one of my friends told me to burn it. I didn't burn the dress, but I never wore it again. It just hangs in my closet in Fort Lauderdale. Every time I look at the dress, it still brings back a bad memory.

John was amazed that someone like myself who had won so many times had so little confidence as a player. "If I were the best in the world, or even in the top five," he once told me, "I would never think that I could lose to anyone."

John never told me how nervous he was about my match with Tracy until afterward. But on the ride to the National Tennis Center with Don Barbera, our regular limousine driver for the Open, John was thinking about the match. His lips were pursed, and he had that familiar controlled anxious boyish look. Even Don was not his normally lively self.

John is more than a calming influence on me. I respect him and look up to him, and these are two of the basic ingredients in our marriage. I've respected many tennis players over the years for their ability—Billie Jean King, Martina, Tracy, to name just a few—and I've respected people for their leadership qualities, like Billie Jean and Arthur Ashe. But to respect people for their values, you have to reach their core, their roots. I know John so well and have watched him respond to pressure situations. He has so much patience and is consistent—not high-strung one day and mellow the next. He's very at peace with himself and calms me down with his presence. I couldn't be with someone who was fidgety or nervous because it would rub off on me. Just looking into John's eyes and seeing the faith and belief he has in me and knowing that if I do my best, that's all I can demand of myself, is wonderfully reassuring.

John helps me face the reality of problems. If either of us is deep in thought, we know each other well enough to say, "What's on your mind?" or "What's bothering you?" or "C'mon, tell me, you've got to get it out in the open; it's not healthy to let it fester." Every little point is worth talking about, and John has a wisdom and practicality that soothes.

I hate it when someone asks questions and talks while I'm trying to prepare for a match, but it happens all the time. "Oh, isn't that a beautiful building over there?" someone will say, bringing up ridiculous bits of trivia to hold your attention. Having played Tracy so often, I basically knew what I had to do, but wanted to hear how John felt. It's more ritualistic than strategic; he heightens my nervous energy and makes me aware of what I should do. "You have to be patient and just stay out there all day if necessary," he said. "And you really have to try to move well."

Before marriage, I felt pressure to win because that's where I thought happiness was based: If I won matches, I was supposed to be happy; if I lost, I was unhappy. Wimbledon 1978 changed my attitude; win or lose, I know John loves me and gives me belief in myself. And that inspires me.

I felt the same positive atmosphere at the National Tennis Center. Walking from the limo to the locker room, some of the early arriving spectators at nine-thirty smiled, waved and shouted, "Good luck, Chris." I was the underdog now, had lost a few matches, and people could understand what I had been through. At long last, as No. 3 in the world, I was human to them.

Entering the women's locker room, the first person I saw was Rosie Casals. Rosie is a dear friend and former doubles partner who would give you the shirt off her back. She's not the hard, tough person people think she is; she is sensitive, warm, totally unselfish.

"I didn't wake up this early to see you lose," she said. Rosie rarely gets out of bed before noon.

As usual, Connie Spooner was also in the locker room. Tall and trim with long flowing hair, Connie has been the trainer for the Women's Tennis Association since 1975. She has been treating me for various ailments since I suffered tendinitis in my right hand in the summer of '76. Connie still tapes my wrist before matches. Somehow, taping keeps my wrist firmer; since I always play with a wristband, few people were even aware that I had an injury. But I had been feeling twinges during the Open, taped the wrist for matches and then applied ice on it during the evening to minimize swelling.

Connie dispenses more than medical advice in the locker room. She has a lively sense of humor. In Boston earlier in the year, she had brought a new puppy, Patches, on the circuit. The dog was only eight weeks old, and Connie and Rosie had been trying to housebreak her.

"We're really having trouble," Connie said, "because she seems to like clothing to go to the bathroom on."

I happened to be changing clothes in the locker room before a match one day when Connie and Rosie were talking about how cute the puppy was. I had put my shirt and skirt on a shelf, but when I went to find the clothes, they were gone.

"What happened to my shirt?" I asked. Before anyone could answer, I saw my shirt on the floor covered with a brown pile.

I let out a scream that must have been heard in nearby Cambridge. Rosie picked up the shirt, shook it, and the brown pile flew toward me. That brought another scream, until I saw Rosie laughing. She picked up the pile and handed it to me. It was plastic. She and Connie had bought it as a joke earlier in the day.

During an earlier U.S. Open, I had just showered after a doubles match with Rosie, and was standing there wearing a bra and panties. Rosie had nothing on but panties.

"You guys better get dressed," Connie warned. "We're taking pictures now."

I felt frisky. "Go ahead and take a picture," I challenged. Connie took the picture. A year later, she and Rosie were leafing through some old photos, found the picture and brought it to a tournament.

"I'm going to sell this to the papers and make a fortune off it, Chrissie Poo," Rosie teased. Rosie has been calling me "Chrissie Poo" for years.

"Let me see it," I said, forgetting what the picture even looked like. Rosie playfully held up the photo, baiting me to grab it.

"You can't show anybody that picture," I said.

"I thought that's what you were going to say," Rosie fired back. "Why not?"

"I don't care about the bra and panties," I said. "But I look ten pounds heavier there." Rosie was floored by that rationale.

Tennis differs from team sports like football, basketball and baseball in that opponents must share locker rooms. It's almost impossible to hide all emotions, before and after a match, when your opponent or your opponent's friend might be changing clothes five feet away. Allowing an opponent who looks and sounds confident in the locker room to carry this onto the court can be devastating.

Most players practice before a match to sharpen their strokes. I hit with John from ten to ten-thirty, showered for the second time and then let Connie tape my wrist. The locker room was deserted with the exception of Connie, myself, Tracy, and Jeanne Austin, Tracy's mother. Mrs. Austin was whispering to her daughter while Tracy changed clothes in another corner. Everything had been professionally cordial between Tracy and myself that morning, but I felt uncomfortable with Mrs. Austin in the locker room. My mom has been in the locker room on occasion, but she knows how sensitive I am about her spending more than routine moments there. And my mom made it a rule never to talk about tactics in the locker room before a match. Mrs. Austin is always in the locker room before Tracy's matches.

I sat alone and tried to clear my mind. Before a match, I want to block out all distractions; if the mind is strong, you can do almost anything you want. It's a form of hypnotism. If you look at an object long enough and think you're suspended in midair, you might feel as if you're floating. My eyes were open, and I wasn't into any space flights, but I checked my racquets, adjusted my dress and washed my hands—prematch rituals.

I felt nervous, but it wasn't one of those I-dread-going-out-there numbers, which had terrified me earlier that year when Tracy had gotten the only career edge on me of any player; I was excited, wanted to get onto the court and into the match. For me, eagerness is an assertive sign. Over and over, I told myself, "I'm prepared, I'm ready to play. If I win, it will be a great moment. If I lose, I hope I'm not disappointed because I gave it my all, I put myself on the line."

A No. 1 ranking for the year hinged on the outcome. I had won the Italian, French and U.S. Clay Court championships and was runner-up at Wimbledon. Tracy had taken the Avon Series championship and had the head-to-head edge. World rankings are more important to me than dollars. If a player wants to make more money, he or she can always do a commercial or sign another endorsement of a product. I would rather play less and win less prize money, but wind up No. 1. The public identifies with No. 1 and so do the players. Those players who deny that No. 1 means anything only cop a plea because they can't be No. 1 or won't try for it. Some people go through life and don't set out to achieve anything. Being No. 1 means you've conquered something.

I had no idea whether Tracy was thinking about a ranking as we left the locker room and the indoor complex and walked toward the stadium court. Sometimes you can look into an opponent's eyes and read uncertainty or fear; if her voice shakes a bit when she talks, she's nervous.

Tracy had been upset by fifteen-year-old Andrea Jaeger in the Volvo Women's Cup at Mahwah, New Jersey, the week before the Open. It was the first time she had ever lost to a younger player, and John and I reasoned that the loss might shake her confidence and saddle her with additional pressure as the top-seeded player in the Open. She struggled with Anne Smith in her opening match before winning, 6–2, 7–5, then rolled through Rosie, Sylvia Hanika, Virginia Ruzici and Pam Shriver in straight sets.

Walking from the locker room to the stadium at the National Tennis Center is a waltz compared to sitting in the Players' Waiting Room before being ushered onto the Centre Court at Wimbledon. The Open has a brisk carnival atmosphere, with vendors hawking programs, and souvenir stands outside the facility and underneath Louis Armstrong Stadium. The waiting room at Wimbledon is a sanctuary; it's you, an opponent, the attendant and a few historic pictures on the walls. At the Open, you can feel New York's pulse, even if you can't hear yourself think sometimes because of the planes flying around LaGuardia Airport.

Tracy and I walked into the stadium without speaking. I wondered whether it was the first day of the tournament or the women's semis. Only about one-quarter of the nineteen thousand stadium seats were filled. At Wimbledon, when the first semifinal begins, as always at two o'clock, the Centre Court is filled, with thousands more standing.

The DecoTurf asphalt court was still wet from an early morning drizzle. It started to drizzle again when Tracy and I took our places on the court for the warm-up. Would rain delay us one day? I didn't want to lose any enthusiasm; I wanted to play.

It takes me a while to develop a rhythm and pace before a match; Tracy hit the ball solidly and confidently during the warm-up. "If she's going to hit the ball that way, it's going to be tough," I thought, as one of Tracy's two-handed backhand cross-courts nicked the sideline paint.

The longer we rallied, the more thoughtfully determined I became. We had similar styles, down to our two-handed backhands, and I had to be stronger mentally. There could be no letdown, no loss of patience as in our 1979 Open final, which Tracy won, 6–4, 6–3.

I won the toss and elected to receive. It would give me an extra game to settle into stride, a few more balls to hit before I served. Let Tracy deal with serving the opening game. I was ready. Or was I?

2 • The Family

I wanted to crawl into a hole. I hated that feeling of everyone staring at me, but I was late for the first day of school, and the thought of being singled out, as the center of attention, made me uncomfortable.

My mother had taken me into the class at St. Anthony's School in Fort Lauderdale, kissed me and waved a sentimental good-bye. I stood in front of the whole class, petrified. The first-grade teacher, a nun, walked behind me, held my shoulders back and introduced me to the class, as she had done with other new students that day. "This is Christine Evert, everyone," she said. "Remember her now. This is Christine Evert."

I wasn't special, and I was very, very shy. Some girls are born beautiful, some are born ugly and others are simply born plain. I was plain looking, insecure about my looks and too reserved to raise these issues with my mother and father at the time.

It's difficult to explain how shyness can shape a personality. I stayed in the background and observed, a quiet child who hated arguments and accepted discipline. My mom liked to say that I was a peacemaker. "While the others might pick a big twelve-ounce glass from the cabinet for milk or juice," she recalled, discussing some of the habits of her five children, "you always picked the small orange juice glass."

My teachers saw me in the same way. "Chrissie is a very good student," they would report to my parents, "and she excels on tests and paper work, but she really should volunteer. She should raise her hand more and speak up."

I was a dreamer, my own best friend. After school, I came home, ate dinner, finished my homework and went to sleep in a room that I shared with my younger sister, Jeanne. Because I stored so much from the day's activities, life would blossom in my dreams: I was the beautiful fashion model that I read about in a magazine, an actress, a successful tennis player.

Before ever hitting a ball, tennis took me out of my shell. My father was the teaching pro at Holiday Park, a municipal facility in the northeast section of Fort Lauderdale. The twenty courts were only a five-block walk from our house, and they were convenient to hang out at and create my world around. Phillis Flotow recalled that I sat on the wooden step across from the office and playfully pulled the hair on the legs of some of the men after they finished their matches and came off the courts.

"You do that one more time and I'm gonna kill you!" the men would shout. Of course, I did it again until they complained to Phillis, who was an assistant in the office.

Phillis was a friend, someone who combed my hair, saved bobby pins, drew creative pictures and took me to lunch and to Sears for chocolate marshmallows. My dad taught me how to play tennis, but Phillis made it fun. She started as a part-time employee with summer junior clinics in 1960. The following year, the city approved my dad's request to retain her as a permanent assistant. Phillis and her husband, who died in 1974, had no children, but she liked to tell people that "all my tennis kids" were her children. At Holiday Park, with the Everts, Flemings, Gfroerers and other families of that period, Phillis had a flock.

"I have always felt that children need one adult who is a good friend and not in their family," she would say.

Phillis became my dad's designated hitter after he finished

Enjoying the Florida sunshine at age one.

My parents had me working at a very young age.

I'm getting down low, but the racquet definitely looks too big for me!

*My first big tournament—
the Orange Bowl—and,
would you believe it,
Bonnie Smith, my tall
partner, and I won the
doubles.*

*Laurie Fleming and I (at age fourteen) shaking hands
after another one of our highly competitive junior
matches.*

My mother and I after church one Sunday when I was ten. The ribbons and bows were her idea!

The clock has struck well past midnight and Billie Jean King has ended my Cinderella streak in my first U.S. Open. I am sixteen years old.

My whole high school, including the school band, greeted me at the airport after my good showing in that Open.

*From the airport, a limo whisked me to school, where I had to
stand up and tell my experiences at my first U.S. Open.*

A family picture.

Camera 5

Action shots on grass courts in England.

Art Seitz

Accepting the Virginia Slims championship trophy after beating Martina in the finals. Here I am nineteen.

his daily instruction. "I'll watch the office if you want to hit with Chrissie," he would say. Anxious to please and enjoying time away from scheduling courts, Phillis readily obliged. She even tossed out enticing challenges.

"I'll give you a penny for every ball you hit over the net," she proclaimed one afternoon.

Phillis felt comfortable making that offer to a small, skinny six year old who had just started taking lessons and could barely hold a wooden racquet with both hands. But as my strokes improved, I collected dimes, quarters and dollars from our workouts. In later years, Phillis raised the stakes to a dime for each game I could win. When I started taking sets from her, she gave me a bag of dimes and told me to forget it.

I'll never forget Phillis' love and patience. I bought her a gold pin with the word "Special" on it a few years ago, brought back a silk fan from one trip to Japan and invited her to Wimbledon in 1980 and 1981, all expenses paid. She wasn't sure she could take the time off and told me she was saving quarters for a future trip to Wimbledon. I'll keep inviting her as long as I play there, and she's even starting to bend a little. She went to the 1980 U.S. Open, and I heard her cheering at all my matches.

My father involved all his children in tennis. Participation in sports was a healthy, positive experience that could be shared as a family, he stressed. Tennis offered incentives that extended beyond childhood.

"There are great people associated with tennis," he would tell us. "And you need goals. Kids without goals come home from school and just wander. It's not healthy."

As the third of four brothers growing up in Chicago, my father had no time for wandering. When he wasn't in school, attending Mass or singing in a church choir, he played tennis. He even rode the streetcar for ninety minutes every day during the winter to get to an indoor court.

My father's family roots are in Luxembourg, a tiny independent country in northwest Europe, squeezed into an area bounded by West Germany, France and Belgium. It is smaller than the state of Rhode Island and has about one-third as many people but was founded as far back as A.D. 900.

In 1973, my father's oldest brother, Chuck, traveled to Grosbus, a tiny rural community in Luxembourg with a population of about four hundred, to explore what he called the "House of Evert." He found a beautifully manicured farming area and a group of independent people who practice what they preach in their national anthem: "Mir welle beiwe wat mir sin," or "We want to remain what we are."

"I went to a church in Grosbus," he later told us, "and found the church directory. Sure enough, that's where the Everts must have come from, although there were no addresses. I couldn't understand why anyone would want to leave this beautiful place for Chicago, so I asked one of the farmers in the town. He said, 'If you one day had Germans come in and take over your home, and the next day you had Italians come in and take over your home, you would leave.'"

The way my uncle pieced our saga together, my father's grandparents came to Chicago in the late 1800s, settled on Chicago's North Shore and bought some land for farming. Instead of holding the land, however, which now is worth about $100,000 an acre, they sold it and invested in stocks. My grandfather started in the banking business but lost almost everything in the Great Depression and never quite recovered.

The Depression became a dominant influence on my dad's values. If we complained about needing a new dress or shoes, he would say, "When I was your age, we had to eat food from cans, and they were rationed. We would get a little sliver of meat once a month, and that was a luxury."

One of the qualities I admire most about my parents is that they didn't change their life style after I became successful. My father was offered many lucrative jobs as a consultant and teaching pro at private clubs in Florida and California and turned them all down. He had no desire to cash in on my fame or seek any fame for himself. We never had a maid while I was growing up, and my mother still cleans, does all the laundry, cooks and serves food in the cafeteria at St. Anthony's. We also still have only one car, although it's in much better shape than the 1954 black Comet that frequently shook up the whole school.

My dad never believed in buying a new car until the old one fell apart. Even when I won cars at pro tournaments—and I guess I've won anywhere from twelve to fourteen over the years—we always took their cash value. When John and I come home on visits, my dad prefers to rent a car and let my mom drive. He figures that if I drive and have an accident, the other party will use my name as an excuse to chase a large settlement, even if the damage is only minor.

No one worried about our black Comet. I could always tell when my dad was coming to pick us up at school because you could hear the muffler six blocks away. In the morning, the whole school would line up outside, salute the flag and recite the Pledge of Allegiance. We usually arrived when all these events were happening, and our good ole black Comet would break up the ceremony. The car had a hole on the floor of the back seat, so if you looked down you could see the road. My brother Drew, Jeanne and I would bend over and stick a long pencil through the hole and scrape the road like scouts leaving a trail.

I finally asked my dad if he could please drop us off two blocks away to avoid the embarrassing arrivals. "Chrissie, you shouldn't care what other people think," he said. Meanwhile, Jeanne, Drew and I sank lower in our seats whenever we approached school.

My dad is such a good, wholesome man that I often wondered if there was a rebellious streak in him. "Did Dad ever do anything wild when he was younger?" I once asked my uncle Chuck.

"Yes, he's a lot more of a leader than he'll let on," my uncle said. "When the kids in the street would light firecrackers, he was always there. But he had a mind of his own and wasn't influenced or swayed."

Geography can be a strong influence on a child's interests. Arthur Ashe had tennis courts virtually outside his door while growing up in Richmond, Virginia, because his father was a park police officer. Bjorn Borg was about four blocks from the Sodertalje Tennis Club in Sweden where he began his training at the age of nine. My husband John is from Leigh-on-Sea on the English coast; his father coached tennis on the weekends and coaxed John, his older brother, David, and Tony, his younger brother, into tennis, in addition to soccer, their first love.

My father lived in a house across the street from the Chicago Town and Tennis Club. He and his brothers weren't members of the club, but they watched some of the better players of the 1920s and '30s and then went outside, stretched a net across the street, put down lines on their "court" and imitated the strokes of the stars.

Chuck was the first brother who enjoyed any success. At the age of 12, he entered a 15-and-under summer-long tournament sponsored by a Chicago newspaper. He won, and it inspired Jack, Jimmy and Jerry to try qualifying for various events.

"I don't think all four brothers ever sat down at a meal together in our entire life," my uncle Chuck recalled of their busy schedule. "Grandma washed white clothes until they came out of the chimney."

During the winter, there were only two places to play indoors in the Chicago area, the Broadway Armory on the north side of town and the Southside Armory near Comiskey Park, the home of the White Sox. The Broadway Armory was closer, but it was usually overcrowded and too expensive, so my dad rode the streetcar after school to Southside where he ballboyed and practiced on the wooden floor with George O'Connell, the pro. My dad waited for hours just to get on a court, which explains why he hates anyone who loafs or fools around at Holiday Park.

My dad was short and sturdy and worked hard, and his persistence and patience paid off. In 1940, he won the National 18-and-under Indoor title. He was captain of the Notre Dame tennis team, won a national title in Canada, and reached the last sixteen of the 1942 National Championships at Forest Hills before losing to Ted Schroeder, the eventual champion, in four sets.

Tennis indirectly brought my mom and dad together. My dad had gone to school with Bill Tully, a well-known squash and tennis player in Westchester County, just north of New York City. Bill's wife, Kay, was a close friend of my mother's sister, Angela Thompson. The youngest of ten children, Colette Thompson was a trim, vivacious blue-eyed brunette who had to assert herself at an early age. "I never even thought twice if I thought I knew the answer to something," she would tell me. "The hand would go up instantly."

Life with the Thompsons, in New Rochelle, New York, contrasted considerably with that of the Everts in Chicago. My mom likes to say that growing up in her house was "Life With Father," a happy, carefree suburban experience. But Joseph Thompson, after a week of operating his oyster business, also held regular Saturday roundups with his children to hash out who was good and who was naughty and what punishments would be given.

People still tease about how John and I met for the first time at the 1978 Wimbledon tournament. But my mom and dad first hooked up over the telephone, after my dad called to verify what time he would pick up Angela for a party preceding Bill Tully's wedding. My mom answered the phone and immediately flipped over Jimmy Evert's deep voice.

"Who's the smoothie?" she asked her sister. Angela explained that he was a tennis pro from Florida. Colette thought tennis pros were sophisticated and worldly.

"When I first met your dad," she later recounted, "I had a streak in my hair that I had just put in. My brother George told me to take the streak out because I looked like a chorus girl. But I couldn't take it out unless I dyed my hair, so I had to have a beautician dye it, except that the rinse looked so terrible the next day that I went to the wedding wearing this big hat. When your dad cut in and asked me to dance, he must have thought I was straight off the chorus line."

As different as they were, two years later, on September 20,

1952, my mom and dad were married. My brother Drew was born on September 8, 1953, and I followed on December 21, 1954, named after my two grandmothers, Christine Evert and Marie Thompson.

My father's mother was firm, strong-willed and extremely religious. My dad believes that my determination and commitment came from her. "Grandma was a little more outspoken than you," he recalled. "When she had something on her mind, she would tell you."

My dad was a planner. He saved $8,000 before the wedding and used much of the money as a down payment for a small two-bedroom house in the Wilton Manor section of Fort Lauderdale. He never bought anything on time. If he couldn't pay cash, we didn't buy it. When it came to a choice of rugs or an air conditioner for the house, the air conditioner won. In south Florida, especially in the summer, air conditioning is a necessity.

After Jeanne and John were born, my parents realized that the family had outgrown the first house, so in August 1961 we moved to a modest, three-bedroom, green-and-white, ranch-style home at 1628 Northeast Seventh Place. We're still there.

My father was strict. We were reprimanded for messy rooms and spanked for fighting. I was neat with my schoolwork, but the room I shared with Jeanne was a disaster area that not even a sharp hand to the behind could shape up for more than a day or two.

I enjoyed making my parents happy. Jeanne and I, along with Sandra Campbell, a neighbor, put on our own Broadway shows in the garage and backyard. Sandra was a born actress who went on to major in drama. We sang and danced and acted out roles. On one occasion, the three of us put on cute dresses and sang "Baby Face." I loved to tell jokes and make my audience laugh. There were two sides of me even then, but it would be years before I was relaxed enough to let more than a few friends into my world.

My dad also had two sides. At the courts, his nickname was "Lash," an ominous tag that Robert (Red) Reid, one of the assistants, humorously dreamed up because of my dad's no-nonsense habits. Red even made up a stamp with the word "Lash" on it to sign office mail. Alex Cmaylo, another local tennis enthusiast, called my dad "The Penguin," because of the way he walked. Alex, whose son, Mike, was a ranking player, had nicknames for everyone around Holiday Park: Phillis was "The Water Buffalo" (she didn't like that too much); Red, because of his hair and freckles, was "The Rooster"; and I was "The Minnow," probably because I was so tiny.

If my dad was a drill instructor during the day, after work he would come into our room, put his arms around Jeanne and me and read us poems—from nursery rhymes to Kipling's "If," his favorite. He also sang to us, songs like "A, you're adorable, B, you're so beautiful . . ." He knew all the words from A to Z, and wandering through the alphabet with him was a treat. No one saw this tender, sensitive side of my father except his children.

My dad's bark often was louder than his bite on issues like long hair or practice. Phillis Flotow once showed up at the courts with her ears pierced. "Why?" my dad pleaded. "Now the girls will only want their ears pierced."

Of course, we did. Naturally, my dad turned us down, but not totally. Several months later, after much prodding, he said we could have our ears pierced, if this were done under medical supervision. Dr. David Johnsen, a family friend, performed the procedure.

"You have to realize that your dad doesn't understand girls," my mom would say, trying to rationalize some of his decisions. "He never had a sister, he had three brothers, and the only woman in his life was his mother, who was very strong-minded."

My mom worked on the theory that any compromise was a victory. If I wanted to go to a movie, football game or some other weekend function, and I had a tournament or practice the next day, my mom would say "yes," and my dad would usually say "absolutely not." My mom then would say "Okay, what about if Chrissie's home by ten?" My dad then would mutter something like, "Oh, all right."

My father worked seven days a week, usually from eight in the morning until about six, seven or eight at night, depending on when it got dark. During the week, the children ate dinner in the kitchen between seven and seven-thirty. My parents ate later, around nine or nine-thirty. On the weekends, we ate together; sometimes, on Sundays after Mass, we splurged on a family meal at the International House of Pancakes. But with my dad at the courts all the time, we almost never went out for large family dinners.

My mom believes I would have turned out entirely differently if I hadn't been exposed to tennis. I was a hard child to know, she said, because I seldom displayed emotions; she still recalls that I asked her not to cry at my eighth-grade graduation because it might look mushy. From the time I was six years old, however, my father drilled in me the importance of being controlled on the court, and I carried this attitude, consciously or otherwise, to my off-court life as well, although the emotions were always there. I cried when I gave up cheerleading for tennis and also when I couldn't go to my first slumber party because of practice the next morning.

"Don't worry, Chrissie, there will be other times," my mom would say. "Your father just feels there are more important things now than staying up all night at slumber parties."

Some parents prefer to leave their children alone on the premise that permissiveness expands a child's growth. They encourage their children to play at other children's homes or become independent. However, parenting was a twenty-four-hour-a-day endeavor for my mother and father: They drove us to school, my mom served lunches in the cafeteria and was a room mother. We spent three or four hours at the tennis courts with my dad after school, and we went to church. The family was the core of our lives, my parents protected us, and we looked out for each other.

Drew was the oldest and quietest—husky, dark haired, even more internal than I. At the age of ten, Drew wanted to be a priest and set up an altar in the living room. Jeanne and I, who were about nine and six, became his altar "boys," and Drew performed the "Mass" in Latin, with prayer books. He didn't need the books because he had memorized all the prayers; since Jeanne and I were interested in possibly becoming nuns, we enjoyed the ceremony. But Drew was the leader: Once a week, usually on a Saturday or Sunday, he put on a robe, with all the ornaments of a priest. He even had a chalice and served communion, and I rang the bell.

There is something about being close in age to a sister that makes you feel as one. Because we shared a bedroom, Jeanne and I were very close. We had separate twin beds but sometimes held hands at night. Jeanne was a leader—creative, spontaneous and always the first to spot a trend or wear certain clothes. Her nickname was "Bubbles," because she was bubbly and spoke up, even when it might be painful.

At the 1976 U.S. Open, for example, Jeanne gave a poignant interview to Tony Kornheiser, a reporter, who was then working for the *New York Times*. Jeanne was not playing that well at the time, had lost in the second round to Wendy Overton and bared her soul, describing how some people had expected her to be something she wasn't and how it affected her to be what Tony penned "The Other Evert."

"Sometimes my father says it," Tony quoted Jeanne. "He tells me that he's sorry that I haven't done any better. He tells me that I have to have a goal. You see, my father doesn't believe in doing things halfway. Neither does Chris. When I tell him that my goal is to be happy, it blows his mind; it's too vague. I always end up crying with my father. Always. I feel so much for him. I just wish I could hold him and hug him and say to him, 'Dad, stick with me.' But I can't."

My mom and I thought the article was very moving, to the point of tears. Jeanne had been totally honest and revealing, but my dad felt burned.

As you go down the line in our family, the children become more outgoing and fearless of authority. John was the most rebellious. He was five years old when my dad first admonished him for not concentrating on the court.

"When I was your age, I could hit every ball over the net," my dad shouted to him.

John stared and then shouted back, "Yeah, but you had a

gooder teacher." I was never bold enough to try those kinds of verbal passing shots on my parents.

My mom, who believes in astrological signs, calls John "the perfect Aries." Aries people have to try everything and learn the hard way, often by themselves, she says. They have minds of their own. That was John—he even ran away from home for a few days once and wound up at the apartment of Jeanne's boyfriend. I've heard that nine out of ten women marry men who have the same sun sign as their fathers. My dad is a Virgo and so is my husband, John.

In some respects, my brother John and I are alike. Now at Vanderbilt University, he's very serious, competitive and plays tennis at 100 percent. That's why our practice sessions were always brutal—we both wanted to win so badly. John always said what was on his mind, like the time he told my dad that a nun in the school had slapped him. It wouldn't have been so bad, but Judy Klemesrud, a reporter, happened to be in the house.

Judy was one of the first journalists who was allowed to spend a significant amount of time with the family, and that included the first time we'd eaten by candlelight in the dining room in almost three years. During the meal, we were discussing how classmates had treated us since my success.

"Most kids are nice about it," I said, "but I can tell that some are jealous. They'll say, 'Oh, tennis, that's not so important.' Others come up and say, 'Oh, can I walk with Chris Evert?' or they just want to talk tennis. I can't tell if they're interested in tennis or me."

My dad grew uneasy. "Chris, I don't see why you have to say things like that about your schoolmates."

"Well, it's true, dad," John piped in. "People do say things. One nun in my school said, 'Oh, you're living on your sister's glory,' and then hit me across the face five times."

"John, you're a wise guy!" my dad snapped. "You're no angel, and I agree with the discipline." Looking at Judy, he continued, "He's tired, he's never been this way before. They've never said anything bad about parochial schools before." John started to cry. "John, leave the table right now!" my dad said. "Do you hear me?"

"But it *is* true, dad." Jeanne said. "That nun does hit children. She hit some kids in my class when we were that age."

"I don't want to hear any more about it."

Judy recounted that scene in her article for the *New York Times Magazine*. My dad immediately put the house off-limits to the media. The less pressure focused on members of family, the better, he believed; what happened within the family should be kept private. At the time I agreed with him because I saw how disappointed and hurt he and mom were reading about the family in detail. Now, each time I reread Judy's article, I just laugh; that particular episode was funny, spontaneous and very realistic. We were just being ourselves.

There's no question that my success adversely affected my brothers and sisters. Drew and John were singled out at local and college tournaments. Some hecklers at college matches would shout "C'mon Chris" when they played, which was unfair. Local radio and television stations requested interviews, even when my brothers weren't the No. 1 players on their teams. The interviewers, of course, were more interested in whether I was going to win the Open or Wimbledon.

My sister Clare was born on October 8, 1967. She has benefited from the trial and error that went into raising the other children. She's bright, uninhibited, happy, and my father is much more flexible with her. He'll say, "Go to bed, Clare," and Clare will counter with "But I don't have school tomorrow. Can't I stay up and watch this movie? I'll sleep until nine o'clock." Sometimes, she actually persuades him. There was no way that could have happened with me. I loved watching "The Ed Sullivan Show" on Sunday nights, and was especially looking forward to seeing the Beatles make their famous appearance. But we had to go to bed at eighty-thirty every night, even on Sunday, so I always missed the last half of the show. We went to bed the earliest of all of our friends, but my parents sincerely believed that eleven or twelve hours sleep were essential when you were growing up.

For a long time, when I was single and traveling on the tour, Clare was the highlight of my life. I loved to come home and see her and actually felt as if I helped raise her. I changed diapers, baby-sat, took care of her, talked to her on the phone every day from tournaments and felt as if she were my daughter. We practiced together, and enjoyed turning the tables on my dad. During practices, he drilled her to move, the same way he had with me. I would yell out "Great shot, Clare," and start clapping, knowing that my dad seldom gave out compliments.

"Thanks, Chrissie," Clare would shout back. "Dad, did you hear that?"

If my dad was fairly chauvinistic in his early attitudes, having the world's No. 1 women's player for a daughter opened his eyes to the whims and ways of a career woman. Now, he's all for women's rights and the role of the modern woman. Throughout my childhood, he was a father who gave us love and devotion. And as a teacher, he understood me, the game, how it should be played and what it would take to win.

3 · Happy Days

There is no magic formula for teaching tennis. My uncle Chuck had a theory that if you could keep your head absolutely motionless and your feet solidly based on the court, you could do anything with a tennis ball. Quiet head, set feet, explode on the ball, never lose eye contact, never wonder where the ball is going became Evert teaching doctrine. My uncle says no one learned to execute that formula better than I did, but I'm still not totally aware of each nuance, perhaps because the routine has become so mechanical.

I wasn't that crazy about starting tennis. It meant giving up swimming at Kara Bennett's house on weekends, and hitting tennis balls didn't seem as much fun as cannonballing into the water. But I didn't question my dad's decisions at the time, and the more balls that cleared the net, the prouder I became; tennis emerged as a form of self-expression, an outlet that I lacked within the structure of a classroom.

In Florida during the 1960s, many young players achieved national rankings at 12 years old and then disappeared just as quickly. Sheryl Smith of North Miami Beach was a national 11-and-under champion in 1961 and soon left the sport. Patty Anne Reese of St. Petersburg won the National 12s in 1964.

How far do you push someone until they respond or resist? Tracy Austin was the national 12-and-under champion in 1974. She had several splits with her longtime coach, Robert Lansdorp, and the most recent, in 1981, produced a lawsuit over their contractual dealings. Did Tracy outgrow Lansdorp? Did Lansdorp feel he was entitled to a bigger cut because of Tracy's No. 1 ranking at one point in 1980? It's a very sensitive issue.

Jean Hoxie was a famous tennis teacher from Hamtramck, Michigan, who was credited with the early success of Peaches and Plums Bartkowicz. Legend has it that Peaches once hit 950 volleys in a row off a practice wall and 1,775 consecutive shots with only one bounce. In 1966, at the age of seventeen, Peaches was ranked fifth nationally among U.S. women and won a record number of national junior titles. But by 1972, when she should have been in the prime of her career, Peaches already was gone from the top ten, with her best tennis behind her.

I don't think I could have stood up to the intense training and expectations that Jean Hoxie put on Peaches. My father was a disciplinarian, but in a sensitive, loving way. If he had ever yelled at me after a match or spanked me for a tennis-related problem, I definitely would have rebelled.

My dad never tried to influence my playing style. I was skinny and small-boned, so I was more comfortable at the baseline. Since most of the courts in Florida were composition clay, the slowest of all major surfaces, serve-and-volley was risky.

There has always been speculation about the origin of my two-handed backhand, especially since my father was a former player. Two-handed players have been around tennis for decades, with a variety of styles. Pancho Segura hit a two-handed forehand that became his pet shot. At the time I was growing up in Florida, Mike Belkin was a Miami Beach clay-court specialist who had made the top ten in the U.S. using a two-handed backhand.

I never took up a two-handed backhand to copy Belkin, Peaches Bartkowicz or Eddie Dibbs, another Floridian. My father stood at the net and threw balls to me. I was on the other side, in the middle of the court, when he would say, "Racquet back, turn sideways, watch the ball, follow through." He said those same lines every day for years. The more proficient I became, the farther back I moved on the court. There was no way I could hit balls over the net on my left side with one hand. The racquet was too heavy.

My dad tried one experiment at converting me to a one-handed backhand. I was nine years old, and the experiment lasted about a week. In the evening, he hit balls to my back-hand and had me return one-handed. I got the balls back accu-rately with slightly less pace. But the next afternoon, my dad saw me back on the court hitting two-handed again; finally he got discouraged and just said the heck with it.

There are advantages and disadvantages to the two-handed backhand. Because both hands are involved, it forces a player to prepare earlier and bend the knees; a player thus has better racquet preparation, steadier body position, more time for dis-guise and pace and more control over the shot. The backswing also can be stylized: Bjorn Borg, for example, has a long, exag-gerated swing, in which he brings the racquet back slightly below his knees and close to his side with a small loop on the way back and both wrists cocked downward for topspin; Jimmy Connors brings his racquet straight back, with a firm straight wrist; I also hit a flatter stroke than Borg, with my racquet almost parallel to the court on the backswing.

The presence of the left hand above the right (the situation is reversed for left-handers) gives the two-handed backhand stability and power. But the key factor is flexibility: With the two-handed backhand, even if a ball is behind you, the early racquet preparation allows for sufficient recovery to lob offen-sively, or hit a reflex ground stroke.

The disadvantages of the two-handed shot involve technical adjustments. Players who become too dependent on two hands never learn how to volley under stress. It's also more difficult to dig out short balls hit to the backhand because the instinct of the two-handed player on ground strokes is to drive rather than slice. Anticipation is essential for getting to low balls before they are unplayable. With two hands, lifting over low balls on surfaces like grass and clay can be troublesome.

Recently, some doctors have suggested that the two-handed backhand can put greater strain on back muscles because the shot stresses such a sharp, swiveling sideways movement. But the one-handed backhand has an unnatural crossover, and some players have developed tennis elbow from hitting one-handed backhands too early, too late, or with too much arm and not enough body.

There is no mystical element behind the current popularity of the two-handed backhand. With the availability of more courts and large indoor complexes, children are playing tennis earlier, sometimes at the ages of two and three. Obviously, younger players will have more difficulty gripping the racquet. The success of so many two-handed players has rubbed out notions that a two-handed backhand is an outlaw shot or liability. Teachers will always stress the one-handed technique. But even Alex Mayer, a longtime textbook teaching pro, decided that if his son, Gene, won and felt more comfortable hitting two-handed from both sides, it was futile to change that. Now Gene is among the world's top ten, and teachers have to explain his double formula.

My first serve has never been a weapon on the court. But nobody has ever attacked it either, and my serve may be the most underrated phase of my game. A hard, fast serve can be a plus or a minus depending on how it fits into your game. Many players hit their first serve at ninety miles an hour, their second serve at forty-five miles per hour and wonder why they lose a point. You're better off slowing down your first serve and speeding up your second.

My dad always stressed the importance of getting in 70 to 80 percent of my first serves. "When you get your first ball in," he would tell me, "it means you're loose and playing with confidence. When you start missing that first ball, other things will start going wrong."

Much of my dad's early instruction involved common sense.

"Keep the ball deep" was a constant reminder during our rallies. Don't try anything you're not capable of executing. You can't make players into something they're not supposed to be.

My dad felt I lacked the aggressive temperament to be a good net player. Young California players were trained on faster hard court, where aggressive serve-and-volley was stressed. But these players generally made more errors than winners during their matches. On clay, if you were steady, you didn't have to be strong, you didn't have to hit winners all the time. If you just got the balls back, you would eventually win the point, induce your opponent into the error and destroy his or her confidence.

My dad believed I was born with certain skills. "I don't know if you can really teach a person the kind of discipline that you have on the court," he once told me. "Your mom and I can help bring out some of your inherent qualities, like concentration and discipline. But you can't teach somebody to block everything out of his or her mind. Some people can and some people can't."

My attention span was longer than that of most children. I could sit for hours and let Phillis comb my hair in the office. On rainy days, I played Flinch, Kings Corner or Hearts on the floor with Drew, Jeanne, and Laurie and Carrie Fleming. Fred Fleming, their father, still recalls a match I played in the Orange Bowl Junior Championships one year. Someone had left a chair near a back fence, but it had been pushed forward. Several times during the game I ran back and bumped into the chair. Mr. Fleming became angry and moved the chair during a changeover.

"Why didn't you move the chair back against the fence?" he asked me after the match.

"What chair?" I said.

My dad had a simple teaching philosophy. Once I learned the basic strokes, he focused on moving. Movement was the one area where all good players succeeded, he said. Some people are born with the knack of moving and getting into position; others must learn sound footwork, being alert and staying on their toes. A quick mind, quick hands and quick feet would give me a head start on my opponents.

Jumping rope is a good drill for improving footwork, but I jumped more for fun than training. Anticipation, standing on the balls of the feet, not the heels, and staying alert were more important.

Phillis Flotow still talks about one of the first tournaments I ever played. I was 10 and had gone to Miami to play in a 12-and-under event. When I returned home later that day, I snuck into the office and told Phillis to "hide me."

"What did you do?"

"Mr. Jones is going to snitch on me," I said. Mr. Jones was not his real name, but his daughter was one of the top-ranking players in Florida at the time.

"Well, what did you do?" Phillis persisted.

"I really didn't do anything wrong," I said. "But I know he's going to snitch on me."

Phillis and I didn't have time to talk because my dad was coming off the courts and Mr. Jones was walking from his car, so she told me to hide in the ball box and then pushed the box against the desk.

Mr. Jones was angry. "You ought to go to all of Chrissie's matches," he told my dad. "She hits the same shots over and over and keeps making the same mistakes. If you try to tell her something, even when she wins, she doesn't listen. She keeps repeating the same errors."

From inside the wooden box, I could hear Mr. Jones criticizing me for not taking his advice during my match. I was inconsiderate and too stubborn.

"Well, I'm sure if Chrissie did anything wrong, she knows what she did," my dad said. "I'm not going to follow my children around the tennis courts. I don't believe in it. She gets enough coaching during the week. When she's playing in a match, if she makes a mistake, a stupid mistake over and over, she deserves to lose."

"But she won't listen," Mr. Jones said.

"Well she didn't lose—she won, right?" my dad countered.

"So she must have figured it out for herself." My dad never knew I was hiding in the ball box all that time.

• • •

I'm very stubborn. Once I make up my mind, I don't budge, though I may take longer than usual to think through a question and will study both sides before making a decision. I took a debate course in high school and was outstanding at whatever position I took, but my aims come from within, not from outside prodding.

My father was serious about our tennis but was never obsessed with it. Schoolwork was more important than forehands and backhands, and report cards came before the results of my matches. Karin Benson was the 12-and-under queen in Florida then. She was a couple of years older and sometimes beat me, 6–0, 6–0 or 6–0, 6–1. But I never felt angry or humiliated after my losses. I came off the court with a little smile on my face, determined to work harder. I wanted approval of my tennis and equated perfection with goodness. In some ways I wasn't playing as much for myself as for my father because he spent such a great deal of time with us. I wanted to win for him.

You can have the best coach in the world, someone who knows the game inside out and is an excellent teacher. But he or she can only help to a certain point. After that, it's up to you to produce the mental side, to carry out what the coach has said. My dad taught me how to play the game, but I taught myself to win. Embracing his belief that the one who works the hardest will do the best started me on the road.

I was fortunate to win early with my type of game, so the confidence came quickly. Other coaches conceive elaborate tactical plans about percentage approach shots, sliced forehands, topspin lobs and other techniques. I developed a very simple understanding of my game, and my father felt playing the best I could was more important than concerning myself with too many fine points of strategy. Many coaches are always analyzing other people's games. I'm not knocking people who do their homework, but if you watch someone a lot, especially if that person is playing well, you start to think, "Gee, this one's tough." You start to have doubts about beating him or her and wonder if that player's weakness is your strength, and can you hit to that side of the court? So you stop playing your own game, start changing a few things and wind up less efficient.

I have always tried to use my strength to the maximum. Maneuvering my opponents side-to-side, not letting them take control of the rally so that they could drop shot, slice or hit short balls were my keys. Take away the strength of their game.

When you're not playing your best game, when your opponent is making you play a different type of game, you're in trouble. You've got to take the initiative and play your game whether it's serve-and-volley or from the baseline. You've got to put your best game forward, especially at the club level. If Martina Navratilova's serve-and-volley game is off, she can stay back and play a few games from the baseline and see if that works for her. But the club player hasn't really practiced every single aspect of the game, so you have to play the best you can and then practice another type of game to fall back on later.

I was blessed with living in a favorable climate that allowed me to play tennis year-round. If you don't think weather counts, consider the significantly large number of successful players that have come from California and Florida.

My husband, John, is amazed at the amount of tennis young people can play in this country. He watches my sister Clare come home from school, go straight to Holiday Park and play two hours a day, perhaps three or four hours on the weekend. He felt lucky to play two hours a week on the one floodlit court in his town, and that clay court invariably was unfit during the winter.

John has compared his career with that of Brian Teacher, who is the same age but grew up in California. Both started on the circuit at the same time, but Brian probably played fifteen to twenty times the amount of hours. In England, unless you live five minutes from Queen's Club or can afford to play indoors, it's almost impossible to play during the winter.

John also sees a difference in competitive attitudes, which may explain why so many young Americans have crashed the international scene. In England, losing wasn't the end of the world, he has told me; if you lost well, that was okay as long as you tried. In the United States, young Americans have been taught that number one is the only thing that matters: It doesn't matter how you do it as long as you do it. "Sometimes I think it would have been better if my parents had pushed me a little more," John once told me. "I played soccer and hockey and cricket. If my father had maybe said, 'Well, don't play any of those sports, just play tennis,' maybe I could have gotten four extra hours a week, which might have made a difference between being top twenty-five in the world and top ten. Then again, I enjoyed doing all those things."

I had another advantage that was not available to John in England—competition. Laurie Fleming and Susan Epstein, two other south Florida players, pushed me for about six years in the juniors. I could not afford to let up without losing to them.

Laurie's family moved to Florida from Pennsylvania when she was eight years old. During the next eight years, our families were car-pool close, and we became best friends, practice partners and rivals on the court. Playing and practicing with Laurie were major reasons why I won the national 14-and-under singles in 1968 (she won in 1969).

Laurie and I competed at everything—how we looked, dressed, our grades, boyfriends. Laurie was a better athlete, better looking, a little better student and married my first boyfriend, Pike Rowley. Tennis was the one area where I felt secure; I never lost to her but my dominance did not affect our relationship. The mornings of our matches, we warmed up with other people and wouldn't socialize. One hour after the match, everything would be back to normal again. If the shoe had been on the other foot and I had started losing to Laurie, I honestly don't know if I could have been that flexible and gracious. But Laurie took the losses very, very well, never dwelled on them and was mature about our friendship. We realized that we helped each other and enjoyed our fun times more than our rivalry.

When my dad wasn't looking, we would sometimes play left-handed on his lesson court, goofing around and laughing.

"You look out for my dad and I'll look out for your dad," Laurie would say. As soon as she spotted my dad leaving the office and coming down the walk, we'd announce "30-all," switch hands and start playing right-handed. On other occasions in the summer, when my dad went home for lunch, we played "crazy doubles," which usually involved standing on the shoulders of boys from the high school team. Lobbing there was a feat.

Of course, we always prayed for rain. Rain meant no practice, a day off, the chance to socialize, gossip with Phillis, play cards. As soon as the slightest drops hit the court, Laurie and I would run off the court, babbling in "IV language" to Phillis. "IV" was our own concoction around Holiday Park, so that nobody could understand us. We put two letters in the middle of all words and then just rivambivled on. Even Laurie's husband, Pike, learned to speak and understand it, and Laurie and I still toss out a few lines when we see each other.

It's a lot different on the junior circuit now. The rivalry among the clothing and racquet manufacturers is intense, agents mill around junior tournaments studying potential prospects, and the pressure to turn pro is much greater because of the money.

Kathy Rinaldi of Jensen Beach, Florida, turned pro only a few months after her fourteenth birthday in 1981. I thought she moved too quickly, and it showed later in the year when she had trouble winning first-round matches in some tournaments.

It's one thing to turn pro if you're No. 4 in the world. But a young player who is struggling with a computer ranking in the twenties, thirties or forties faces the prospect of having to win every match just to avoid playing qualifying matches for the bigger tournaments. Young players should finish the juniors— win the 18-and-under national title, turn pro at 18 and then go on the tour seriously after they finish high school.

I learned some things the hard way when I was a teen-ager. At one tournament in Tulsa in 1971, my sister Jeanne and I were staying at a private home. I beat Mary Ann Eisel in the final; that night, feeling grown up, when the hostess at a cocktail party offered us a drink, I accepted. I downed four gin and tonics in about thirty minutes. They tasted great, but after another hour, I started throwing up and passed out. The next day I got sick on the flight home. At the airport, my mom asked what was wrong and I told her I had the flu; I couldn't admit that I was totally hung over from drinking.

That episode turned me off hard liquor for good. I may have an occasional glass of wine now but nothing stiffer. No way. I'm glad I had that experience then because I was still young enough to profit from my mistake.

Laurie Fleming and Susan Epstein extended me all through the juniors. In 1970, I surprised Margaret Court at a women's tournament in Charlotte, North Carolina. By the time I was ready to play the U.S. Open for the first time in 1971, I didn't feel any pressure. I had faced competition better than some of the women pros and was ready and eager. That's what made the summer of '71 so special.

4 · The Endless Summer

Triple match point. Mary Ann Eisel had the situation under control, serving at 6–4, 6–5, 40–0. On a slick grass court, where the balls seldom bounce the same way twice, there seemed no way I could win. Against the fourth-ranking women's player in the United States, whose serve-and-volley reputation had been established on faster surfaces, my hopes were even slimmer.

Mary Ann delivered a flat first serve to my backhand. In my mind, the match was over. We were already shaking hands at the net, and I wondered how the 10,233 spectators at the West Side Tennis Club in Forest Hills would treat a second-round loser in the 1971 U.S. Open Championships. Would they see me as cute, sad, tired? Would they appreciate my efforts?

Mary Ann's serve bounced a foot inside the service line. But instead of skidding like a pellet, the ball suddenly came up 10 times larger, a huge balloon waiting to be popped. Mary Ann rushed the net, eager for one finishing shot, so I aimed a two-handed backhand at a spot down the line. The angle of the return eluded her outstretched racquet and landed several feet inside the baseline. 40–15.

The crowd broke the silence inside the stadium with applause that reverberated off the concrete. I walked to the deuce court. Mary Ann had served to my backhand and I had hit a winner. Would she go wide to the forehand and move in? Would it even make any difference at double match point?

Her first serve spun into the net. I moved in several steps. The second serve was short, almost tentative, and begged to be put away. With more than enough time to prepare my racquet, I whipped a forehand cross-court placement. 40–30. The roar of the crowd this time was almost deafening. I had never played a match in front of so many people.

The week before the Open, I had won the Eastern grass-court championships. But the Orange Lawn Tennis Club in New Jersey was smaller, and its spectators were more staid than the large galleries that flocked to Forest Hills after tennis opened its gates to amateurs and professionals in 1968.

At the age of sixteen, entering my junior year in high school, the Open was a bonus to my summer. I had played primarily junior tournaments, won the National 18s on grass, played an intersectional junior competition, and beat Winnie Shaw and Virginia Wade in Cleveland to help the United States edge Britain, 4–3, in the Wightman Cup. Even if I lost to Mary Ann, after an easy first-round win over Edda Buding of West Germany, my summer had been rewarding.

The noise of the crowd shook Mary Ann's confidence. She double-faulted for the sixth time in the match. The score was deuce, and the vibrations from the crowd were inside me. I could feel their energy. Was Mary Ann choking, after having played so well? I couldn't believe I still had a chance. Just hit out, I told myself: If you break back to 6–all, fine; if you lose, at least you went down with your best shots. Impatient, I over-hit a backhand and gave Mary Ann a fourth match point. She attacked, but I drove another angled forehand return low at her shoe tops. Deuce again.

Mary Ann snapped a crisp first serve to my backhand. Guessing that she would stay wide to the forehand with another twist serve in the deuce court, I reacted late and drove the return into the net. Match point number five. The percentages were building against me.

Mary Ann was an attractive, accomplished player who had been ranked among the top ten American women every year since 1964. No one questioned her spirit and strokes, but an inability to finish off rivals sometimes caught up with her in long three-set matches. How much more could I survive?

She should have put everything into her fifth match point. But instead of serve-and-volley, which was the heart of her game, Mary Ann tried to win the point and the match from the baseline. A backhand drifted wide. Deuce again.

Mary Ann returned to serve-and-volley and reached match point for a sixth time. But her serves were falling shorter and the first volleys became tentative. She lifted a forehand volley wide and then pushed a backhand volley into the net at deuce. I broke serve with a forehand cross-court passing shot that brought the crowd to its feet. After six match points, I had a new crisis—"sudden death."

Tiebreakers were adopted by the United States Tennis Association (USTA) the previous summer to shorten sets and enliven matches. Some tournaments opted for best-of-12-point playoffs, but the U.S. Open chose a 9-point playoff known as "sudden death," because at 4–all, the next point was decisive. Spectators loved "sudden death," but players treated it as tennis's equivalent of Russian roulette.

"Sudden death" catered to the player who was steadiest and luckiest at that moment, not necessarily the best. The sound of ball against racquet was all you could hear in the stadium. I served and won the first two points; Mary Ann closed to 1–2 but then pushed a backhand half-volley into the net. She had converted that shot with uncanny touch and accuracy earlier. I drove a backhand pass down the line for 4–1, and then outrallied her on set point. After having written myself off, our match was even.

Confidence is the difference in a decisive set. I had not lost a match since February and spent six weeks of intense training that summer in Florida. For three hours in the morning, I had hit with Laurie, Jeanne and my dad at Holiday Park; in the afternoon, I played three sets with a Bolivian pro, Oscar Chirella, at a local club. The workouts were designed for stressful situations in long matches. By contrast, Mary Ann had not won a tournament all season, had lost to Kerry Melville in three sets at Wimbledon and to Rosie Casals in the U.S. Professional Championships. With the crowd in my corner, sometimes cheering her faults, Mary Ann managed only one game in the last set.

"I've never played in front of a crowd like that," she told reporters afterward.

There had been no pressure on me. Mary Ann had the ranking and credentials, so the crowd rooted for the underdog. If it had been the National-18 tournament and I were the top seed, the fans would have cheered for Mary Ann. There was more pressure on me when I played Marita Redondo and Janet Newberry in the semis and finals of the 18s than when I faced Mary Ann.

I left the court to a rousing ovation, but the women's locker room in the Tudor-style clubhouse might as well have been a morgue. Rosie Casals, then No. 2 behind Billie Jean King in the American rankings, gave me a dirty look. Other players tried to console Mary Ann. Valerie Ziegenfuss walked past my locker and said, "Good match," but she was the only player who congratulated me. It was a familiar chill. At several earlier tournaments in Florida, I had lost to Nancy Richey and Denise Carter, and the other players sat together and cheered for Nancy and Denise as if I were the enemy.

I felt resentment. A more casual, open person could have gone to some of the players and said, "Hi, I'm Chris Evert, I'd like to get to know you a little better." But kids were the exception rather than the rule in women's tennis in 1971. I hadn't spent enough time on the circuit for them to understand me and was too shy to reach out. As an amateur ineligible for prize money, I was a threat to their livelihood. I played only a handful of women's tournaments, and most were on clay, which was another source of annoyance to them. "Wait till we get her on grass or hard court," they would whisper among themselves.

In 1971, the women were just forming the basis of what

would emerge as a $10-million-a-year pro tour by the end of the decade; but few women earned significant sums then, and even Margaret Court, while sweeping the Grand Slam in 1970, had banked less than $70,000 from tournament winnings. In 1980, a total of nineteen players earned over $100,000, excluding endorsements.

The frustration of the women was understandable. Open tennis was approved in 1968, but tournament prize-money breakdowns still stigmatized women as second-class citizens. At the first U.S. Open, Tom Okker of the Netherlands collected $14,000 as a runner-up because Arthur Ashe was then an amateur attached to the U.S. Army. Virginia Wade, a "registered player" as Okker was at the time, got only $6,000 for beating Billie Jean King in the women's final. The distribution ratio went from bad to worse in 1969. Stan Smith won $4,000 and a new Renault car as the men's champion at the Eastern grass-courts. Patti Hogan, the women's champion, earned just $1,000.

The Pacific Southwest Championships ignited the torch for a revolution by announcing a meager $7,500 purse for the women and $60,000 to the men in 1970. At Forest Hills that year, two players, Ceci Martinez and Esme Emanuel, circulated a questionnaire in the stands to see if spectators would support a separate women's circuit. The response was surprisingly favorable. Behind the scenes at the Open, Billie Jean and Rosie asked Gladys Heldman, then editor and publisher of *World Tennis* magazine, if she would convince Jack Kramer, the tournament director of the Pacific Southwest, to increase the women's prize money.

Although a former top-ranking player, Kramer had little sensitivity for the women's game and refused to budge. Gladys, who was the mother of Julie Heldman, a top-ten American, decided to swing into action by herself and set up an eight-player women's event at the Houston Racquet Club the same week as the Pacific Southwest. The prize money was $5,000—from the sale of 100 tickets priced at $50 that entitled the purchaser to attend special instruction clinics. Another $2,500 came from Virginia Slims cigarettes, which entered the sponsorship market mostly because of Gladys' personal friendship with Joseph F. Cullman III, the chairman of the board of Philip Morris.

The rest is history. The women who agreed to sign symbolic one-dollar-a-year contracts for that event were Billie Jean, Rosie, Nancy Richey, Julie Heldman, Kerry Melville, Judy Dalton, Val Ziegenfuss, Peaches Bartkowicz and Kristy Pigeon. On the second day of the tournament, which Rosie eventually won, the players were informed by telegram that they had been suspended by the USTA. "Women's Lob" was born on September 23, 1970.

The new tour created special problems for my parents and me, but it had nothing to do with New Feminism. If I played USTA-sanctioned events instead of the Women's Lob circuit, I was considered a scab outside the union. If I agreed to play the Slims events as an amateur, I risked being suspended from all future USTA junior events and was ridiculed for robbing the pros of their prize money. It was a no-win situation, and I was a pawn in the power game between the USTA and the women. As long as the USTA felt it had enough quality independent players like Evonne Goolagong, Virginia Wade and myself to maintain a legitimate circuit, it had leverage to continue suspensions against Billie Jean, Rosie and other contract pros. But what the USTA did not bargain for was Gladys Heldman's fierce determination to make women's pro tennis a marketable commodity. By the first four months of 1971, Gladys had organized fourteen tournaments with combined prize money of $189,100. Trapped at the net, the USTA had no choice but to play ball with Women's Lob or risk losing everything. On February 13, 1971, while Billie Jean, Rosie and others were playing a pro tournament in Philadelphia, they were reinstated by the USTA. I remained an outsider, adored by spectators because of my youth but unwelcome in the sorority.

Beating me became a community project. Some of the pros agreed the most logical way to send me home for the summer was to keep the ball short and "down the middle," to minimize the angle on my drives. Francoise Durr of France followed these tactics skillfully and won the first set, 6–2, in our third-round match at the Open. But I found my rhythm and timing, and with the crowd again creating its own loyalties, I took the next two sets, 6–2, 6–3. "You theenk thees is fair?" Frankie complained in the locker room afterward, disgusted that spectators were cheering her double faults.

Lesley Hunt underwent an even more bizarre reaction. Lesley was staying with Phil and Pat Fellman in Harrington Park, New Jersey. Like many tennis-minded families, the Fellmans enjoyed housing players during the Open.

Over breakfast the morning of our match, Lesley told the Fellmans that she had dreamed that spectators were throwing champagne glasses onto the court during points. "It was weird because the whole court was covered with glasses and cases of champagne," she said.

I don't know if Lesley thought about her dream during our match. Like Frankie and Mary Ann, she won the first set, 6–4, only to lose, 6–2, 6–3. Lesley entered the locker room sobbing, after telling reporters, "Maybe I can beat Chris Evert, but not twelve thousand people at once."

The buildup by the women bordered on vengeance. I wasn't inciting the crowds the way some players could with gestures or gamesmanship. I wasn't hitting balls behind my back or being cutesy. If the crowd had been the other way around and treated me the way they treated Mary Ann, Frankie or Lesley, I might have been in tears too. But why take it out on me? I was just being myself, playing my game and trying to deal with my own personal problem—menstruation.

My period was the furthest thing from my mind during the Open. I had almost given up hope of ever having a menstrual cycle. All my friends had gotten their periods for the first time when they were eleven or twelve years old. I was a late developer—three months shy of my seventeenth birthday and still hadn't experienced it. Even when blood stains first appeared the day after the match with Mary Ann, I thought they were the result of a cut. I didn't realize my period had started until days later, before my semifinal with Billie Jean. At first I was embarrassed and worried because I didn't want an accident on the court. My mom was excited and offered reassurance. "It's great. You should feel pleased and relieved," she said.

"Why did I have to get it now?" I said, treating it more as a distraction than a discovery. "Why couldn't I get it next week?"

Menstruation affects athletes differently. At least one day a month, your timing is off and you're slower from cramps, swelling and bloating. I'm completely hopeless on that one day. I'll trip over things or walk into walls. Usually, my "one bad day" will occur two or three days before my period actually arrives. Once my period starts, I'm fine and I play better when I have it because I'm more or less relieved. But three or four days before, my energy level drops, I feel a little swelling, my timing goes, and I don't anticipate or move as well. During the 1980 U.S. Open, that "one bad day" came the afternoon that I played Mima Jausovec in the quarterfinals. I had no movement, energy or feelings; my period didn't actually start until Sunday, the day after the final.

With two-week tournaments like Wimbledon and the U.S. Open, there's a 50 percent chance that you will get your period during the tournament. I just pray that it doesn't affect me to the point of costing me a match. Sometimes, I will look at the date of an event and decide whether I want to play it based on what I know about my period. Given a choice, I would rather be 100 percent for a tournament in Switzerland than 70 percent for another one in West Germany. Obviously, you can't schedule around your period, but some players get bad cramps and nausea, and I've lost matches because of it. So has Martina Navratilova.

During the 1980 Wightman Cup, I struggled from 1–5 down and two match points against Virginia Wade in the third set before winning. In the press room, British journalists wondered what was wrong with my game.

"Well, it's that time of the month," I said. "You know, it's difficult for you men to understand, but a woman has days like that." I tried to explain what was happening, but I don't think the writers printed my reason. Maybe they were trying to protect me or maybe sports writers just don't print this type of information. But after skirting the issue for so long, I just decided to bring it up.

The day that I played Billie Jean in the 1971 Open semifinals, I was conscious of having my period for the first time. But I felt fine physically and overriding that was my awe at the prospect of playing someone who had become a symbol of the sport before the largest crowd of the tournament, which included Vice-President Spiro T. Agnew.

The sky was overcast, and a gentle breeze only wrinkled the flags above the stadium as Billie Jean and I walked onto the court after shaking hands with the Vice-President, who was seated in the marquee.

"You're on the crest of a wave, so enjoy it while you can," Billie Jean said. At the time, I thought her comment was a very intellectual point to make to a sixteen-year-old girl walking out to play her biggest match. She didn't say it in any concerted attempt at psyching me out or shaking my confidence at a winning streak that had reached forty-six in a row. Photographers, officials, linesmen and ball boys were crowding around us for pictures. Billie Jean had made the comment simply and directly.

I had played Billie Jean earlier in the year at a Virginia Slims clay-court tournament in St. Petersburg, but the match ended abruptly after we split sets. Billie Jean won the first, 7–6, and then retired with cramps after I won the second, 6–3. I beat Julie Heldman in the final.

I had no chance to talk with Billie Jean in St. Petersburg. But while most of the women resented my presence at the Open, Billie Jean was among the few who spoke up and said, "Hey, Chrissie's good for women's tennis. Let's give her a chance. Let's take advantage of the publicity."

A new face was what the Open needed in 1971. Margaret Court had decided to skip the tournament because of pregnancy. Evonne Goolagong won Wimbledon earlier that summer but was talked out of trying New York by her Australian coach, Vic Edwards. Rod Laver and Ken Rosewall, the top men pros, cited battle fatigue as their reason for not entering.

Timing is so important, not only in coordinating your tennis stroke, but in being in the right place at the right time. It was a transitional period for tennis as a sport, especially for the women, who were attempting to change an image, to prove that they could compete without forever being labeled as freaks.

From the time she achieved her first top-ten U.S. ranking in 1960 as a seventeen year old, Billie Jean defended women as athletes. The first thing that struck me about her in St. Petersburg was her energy. When she talked, her eyes were always lit up, intense, full of fire. It was as if she had a plan or dream and wanted to share it with everyone. Her energy made Billie Jean's physical appearance seem bigger. I had grown to 5 feet 4 inches, and she was 5 feet 6, but her physicality could overwhelm you.

It was also difficult to concentrate against her on the court because you wanted to see what she was doing. Billie Jean was expressive—always moving, yelling, screaming, demanding attention. This attitude intimidated players, including me, and even a telegram signed by seven hundred classmates from St. Thomas Aquinas High School was only meager moral support at the Open that day.

Billie Jean's determination was legendary. I had a 0–30 lead on her serve in the second game, but she held and never granted me even a break point in seven other service games.

The crowd of 13,647 was demonstrative and noisy. But unlike Mary Ann, Frankie and Lesley, Billie Jean called for passion from the stands and won her share of supporters. She also knew concentration was essential: If she allowed herself to become emotionally untied, anything could happen.

As a tactician, Billie Jean had few peers. She faulted twenty-one out of fifty first serves, but used a spinning second serve to move me around so she could establish a comfortable volleying position. She varied her volleys to disrupt my anticipation at the baseline, mixed drops with drives, sliced some strokes and topspinned others. She won, 6–3, 6–2; some writers said they had never seen Billie Jean play a more complete match.

"If you had wound up winning that tournament as an amateur," she told me afterward, discussing the significance of our match, "it would have been a step backward for us. The public and press wouldn't have understood but I knew what that could do if I lost. I had been an advocate of getting rid of the words 'amateur' and 'professional.' To me, professionals were the highly skilled players. How would that have looked for a new tour if a sixteen-year-old amateur had won?"

Billie Jean is a missionary. No frontier is too wide, no challenge too intimidating. Billie Jean had a big-match temperament, and her so-called "Battle of the Sexes" with Bobby Riggs in 1973 dramatized this point. Billie Jean used the occasion to fire cannons for the women's movement. Margaret Court was physically stronger than Billie Jean with better reach and a good volley, a great backhand and a technically sounder game. Billie Jean's second serve and forehand are weaknesses, but if it came down to 6–all in the third set, with both players fit, I would still put my money on Billie Jean.

In Billie Jean's mind, we had to remain cohesive as a group to succeed. We could not create tiny power fiefdoms, as the men had. My early success, she said, divided the women. They did not resent me personally but what I stood for: I was young, uncommitted and had been spared the political hassles, suspensions and identity struggle. Billie Jean had to beat me to prove a point: Women professionals were professionals.

Billie Jean and I are different—in playing style, religion, and personality—but our family backgrounds are strangely similar. "The first time I walked into your house," she once said, "I thought, 'Oh my God, it's like home.'"

I never understood Billie Jean until we played doubles and practiced together a few years later. Other players sometimes whispered uncomplimentary things like "I don't agree with her" or "Hasn't Billie Jean gone a little bit too far this time?" But I found a gentle, giving person who would spend hours discussing motivation, success, tennis, marriage, children. When I had personal problems, Billie Jean offered input. As a perfectionist, she understood the pressure, loneliness and responsibilities of being No. 1 and shared those thoughts with me.

Two qualities I admire in people are intelligence and the

ability to deal with people. At the 1971 Open, reporters were struck by my self-awareness. I knew who I was, where I wanted to go and what I thought it would take for me to reach that goal, but I needed others to help me explore my self-doubts about the personal side of my life.

• • •

I beat Margaret Court in front of a handful of journalists. But at the Open, my first match against Edda Buding was played in the stadium. No one prepared me for that occasion, so my answers before hundreds of members of the media were understandably short and cautious. But what would you expect from a sixteen year old? I was the first young face who emerged in the open era, the youngest talent on the tour since Maureen Connolly. Maureen got her No. 1 national ranking in 1951, at the age of sixteen, but back then tennis was followed by the classes, not the masses. In the last decade, the Women's Tennis Association has made media relations a top priority. Tracy Austin, Andrea Jaeger and Kathy Rinaldi have benefited from what happened to me. Now the women welcome new blood with open arms, teach newcomers how to deal with the press and assist in their social maturity. I was out there alone and didn't want to speak up and regret sounding foolish. Once you are quoted in the newspapers, on radio or television, there's no way you can take back those words. If you're talking to friends, you can always apologize with, "No, I'm sorry, I didn't mean it that way." But if you offer an opinion to the press, they're going to print it.

In 1979, Tracy Austin was being interviewed after a Family Circle Magazine Cup match on Hilton Head Island, South Carolina. The subject came up about Pam Shriver trying to complete two years of high school in one, and the burden it placed on her schoolwork and tennis less than a year after she had lost to me in the 1978 U.S. Open final. How could Shriver handle such a load, the journalists wondered? And wasn't it a tribute to her intelligence?

"Did anyone ask what her grades are?" said Tracy, who was

an A student at Rolling Hills High School in California. The following day, newspapers carried Tracy's quote, with the suggestion that she might have been sniping at an old junior rival. One week later, a letter from the headmaster of Shriver's school in Maryland was published in a newspaper defending her academic record.

I always paused when reporters asked me questions at those early news conferences. I wanted to sort out replies: "How would the quote seem if I answered this way? How would people react to it?" Journalists were not looking out for me; they were out for themselves and good press. Now that I'm older and more comfortable, I'll say what I feel, take the consequences, and try to help some of the younger players with their problems.

I feel close to Andrea Jaeger despite our age difference. After she lost to Peanut Louie at the Chicago Avon indoor tournament in 1981, I phoned her.

"I always call you after a big win," I said, "so I felt as if I should call you after you lost to show that I don't think of you as a friend just because you're a winner."

Andrea laughed, but I could tell she was upset. "I'm fifteen, I'm from Chicago and the crowds were against me," she lamented.

"Listen," I said, "the crowds have been against me lots and lots of times, and you really have to block it out of your mind. They're going to be for you at times and against you at times, and don't let it affect your play."

Andrea is a thoughtful, sensitive person. She has sent me cards when I have been sick and a telegram on my birthday. During the Colgate Series finals in Washington, D.C., in January 1981, when John and I were confined to our hotel room with viruses, she brought me comic books and electronic games.

Conditions have changed on the tour since 1971. My mother and I stayed with relatives, Merrill and Joe Sinnott, in Larchmont, New York, during the 1971 Open, and often practiced on grass courts in Westchester County. I wasn't that exposed to other players and the media. Most of the players now stay at hotels for major tournaments, practice whenever and wherever they can and must contend with the possibility of matches in the late morning, afternoon and evening.

The novelty of young kids creating a fuss in major championships has also worn off. Each year, it seems, women's tennis has a new face. When I returned home after the 1971 Open, my hometown treated me as if I had won the tournament. "Would the Evert family please wait until the last people get off the plane?" the Northeast Airlines flight attendant announced as we prepared to land that evening in Fort Lauderdale. I was the last person to step out of the doorway of the plane. At the bottom of the metal stairs, the St. Thomas Aquinas band was playing the school song and 850 students were waving handmade signs that read "Welcome Home, Chris," and "We're Proud of You, Chris." I was so stunned by the attention and the appearances of the mayor of Fort Lauderdale and Florida Governor Rubin Askew that I wanted to cry. A limousine whisked us to the club room at school, and there was another ceremony and speeches by the president of the student council and the governor. Then I was asked to speak.

"It was great to do so well in the U.S. Open," I began, still slightly dazed by the reception. "I didn't expect to reach the semifinals, and playing Billie Jean King was an honor, but now I'm just happy to be home and starting school again."

The students applauded. Then I turned to my older brother, Drew, and said, "Do you want to say anything?" I totally embarrassed him, because Drew didn't want to make a public speech. But he went up to the microphone and said how much fun it had been to fly to New York and see the large crowds at the tournament.

After the ceremony, I apologized to Drew. "I feel like a jerk for doing it," I said. "I shouldn't have done it, but I was so nervous up there that I wanted somebody else to speak."

I tried to talk my parents into letting me skip school on Monday because we had arrived home so late on Sunday night, but skipping school would look bad, they said. What I didn't realize was that a *Life* magazine photographer and several newspaper photographers would follow me to all my classes that day, and Father Vincent Kelly, the principal, had bought a large cake that was devoured in the cafeteria at lunch. St. Thomas didn't have many occasions for sports celebrations. The school received recognition as the home of Brian Piccolo, the late pro-football player with the Chicago Bears, but it was small alongside the public giants like Fort Lauderdale and Stranahan High Schools. Our county rival was Cardinal Gibbons; we called them "Cardinal Garbage."

I should have savored all the ceremonies, plus the special "Chris Evert Day" that was proclaimed the following week. But Billie Jean's advice to "enjoy it while you can" never seemed to work for me; I never looked back, always ahead and said, "Okay, I've done well here, but I can't start enjoying it or I'll suffer in the future." I don't know why I embraced this attitude: Was I too frightened of losing what I had worked so hard for? Was I basically insecure without tennis? Was tennis a crutch for social identity? Too often, players score upsets one day and then flatten out against someone they should beat because they are still riding the crest of a wave. I didn't want to reach the semifinals at the U.S. Open and then fall off the surfboard. And yet I was still so unsure of myself socially that I always tried to sit in the last seat of the last row in classes. It made me less conspicuous.

I was taking a course called Comparative Society and showed up for the first time that Monday after the Open followed by the camera crews. The teacher finally asked the photographers to leave, but since I had been at the Open, I had no books.

"Do you want to share my book?" a girl in front of me asked, turning and extending her book. The girl was dark haired and attractive. I was so surprised by the offer that I didn't even react, but wound up sharing the book. After class, I asked her name. "Ana Leaird," she said.

During the next few weeks, I borrowed Ana's notes and walked with her after class. She offered to drive Drew, Jeanne and me home from school one afternoon, after we were waiting in the parking lot for my dad. Ana owned a Mustang convertible. When she put down the top that day, some of her classmates thought she was trying to score points with me, but that night, I called Ana and said that my mom and dad would agree to pay her $5 a week if she would car-pool us to and from school. Ana accepted and a long friendship began.

One month later, Lele Forood, who also became a pro tennis player, joined the car pool. Lele's mother drove her to our house, and then all of us would pile into Ana's car. We were some crazy group: Lele was always late, Jeanne and I fought over borrowing makeup, and Drew, the first one out of the house, would sit in the front seat, turn on the radio, tune out everyone and try to avoid getting hit by the flying mascara.

Ana and I hit it off well, even though we were a class apart. We went to the same church, spent free time together in school, and she even convinced me to attend two rush parties for Exchangettes, a national high school sorority. Ana's real selling job began after I was voted into the club. As vice-president of Exchangettes and my "big sister," she had to call my mom and inform her about the initiation procedures. The way Ana recalled, the conversation went this way:

Ana: "Mrs. Evert, my name is Ana Leaird. We haven't met yet, but I'm the girl who drives Chrissie and your other children to and from school every day."

Mom: "Oh yes, Ana. Chrissie's mentioned you quite a few times."

Ana: "I'm calling as vice-president of Exchangettes. I don't know if you've ever heard of us, but we're a national sorority. I thought you'd like to know that Chrissie has been voted in by the other sisters."

Mom: "Oh, that's wonderful. I'm so happy for Chrissie."

Ana: "I thought you would be. Chrissie won more votes than anyone else. It's a real prestigious organization, and as Chrissie's 'big sister,' I think it's quite an honor."

Mom: "That's just great, Ana. I'm very happy that Chrissie's been accepted by her classmates. What does she have to do?"

Ana: "Well, we're going to come by and pick her up on Sunday night. Traditionally, the way girls find out they have been voted into the club is that we come in the middle of the night, wake them up, put them into a car, go around to all the houses and take them to the beach for breakfast. It's really a lot of fun. I remember I was asleep and the girls came to get me about one-thirty in the morning. We always call the mothers ahead of time so that they can have a little bag packed for their daughters."

(Silence on the line.)

Mom: "Oh, dear."

Ana: "What's the matter?"

Mom: "Well, I'm just not going to be able to tell my husband about this."

Ana: "Why?"

Mom: "Well, you see, if I tell my husband, he's not going to let Chrissie do it, and he's going to forbid me to allow this to happen. So I think I'm just going to have to forget that you and I had this conversation."

Ana: "Okay, fine."

Mom: "Now when are you going to pick Chrissie up though I don't know that you're going to pick her up?"

Ana: "We're going to come on Sunday night because there is no school on Monday."

Mom: "Okay, but remember, I've forgotten our conversation."

Ana: "Sure, Mrs. Evert. Anything you say."

About fourteen girls were to be initiated that night. Ana had a map of the city and put dots on the map to designate the houses. My house was third on the list.

That night, as always during initiations, the girls wrapped toilet paper around the radio antennae of the cars in the procession. They drove into the front yard of the first two houses, honked their horns, jumped out of the cars and then went into the routine of hand clapping, singing the club song, spelling out the name of the club, knocking on the door, waking up the new sister and bundling her up and out into the next car. I was supposed to be asleep but heard the horns blowing about a block away from my house. Then came the screams, claps and the knock at the door. Lying in bed, I looked at the new watch I had received as a sportsmanship winner at the Open. It read 12:45.

My mom answered the door, but it was my dad's deep voice that caught my attention. "Sweetie, sweetie, what's going on around here? Sweetie, what's happening?" he said.

"Oh, honey, I forgot to tell you," my mom said, as Ana and the other girls paraded through the house. "They're coming to get Chrissie."

My dad could not believe what was happening. "Chrissie? She has to play tomorrow. What are you talking about? It's quarter to one in the morning."

I wasn't sleeping and wore a new nightgown for the occasion. On the way out of the door, my mom handed Ana a bag. I was too excited to say anything.

"Where are they going?" my dad asked, still bleary after having been awakened in the middle of the night. "Where are they taking Chrissie? What's happening? Wait a minute."

My mom, normally the more emotional, was calm. "Don't worry, honey, I'll explain it to you later."

But my dad still wasn't satisfied. "Colette, what is going on around here?" By this time, however, everyone was gone.

I had an unforgettable time, eating breakfast at 6:30 in the morning on the beach with the sun coming up in front of me. Ana drove me home at 9:45, and it wasn't until we approached the house that it suddenly dawned on me. "What am I going to tell my dad?" I said. "I have a game at eleven, and I haven't slept all night."

Ana was more concerned about making a fast exit. "I'll see you later," she said.

Later that night, Ana called for an update. I told her that my dad had been furious about my missing so much sleep, that I hadn't been able to practice, but that my mom thought it was important to be accepted by friends.

"Was it all worth it?" Ana asked.

I had no hesitation. The episode had opened my eyes. In later years, it would become even more important to my decision making.

5 · Wimbledon I

The toss was clean, at head height, and the wooden racquet moved into an easy rhythmic swing before making contact with the ball. The entire motion flowed smoothly and in harmony, and even the follow-through seemed flawless, with the body weight forward, balanced and the eyes riveted on the ball.

The first time I watched Evonne Goolagong play tennis, my dad and I marveled at what a great first serve she had, how well she glided to the ball and how naturally she moved. Seeing Evonne only reaffirmed my dad's notion about how important movement was to all phases of the game; after I saw her that day in Dallas, I felt even more mechanical because everything she did was instinctive, with feel and touch.

I'm a product of hard work. I might have been a reasonably good swimmer if I had stayed in the sport, but I would not have done too well in soccer, field hockey or figure skating. Andrea Jaeger is a jock who enjoys kicking around a soccer ball with the boys after her matches; Evonne probably would have excelled in soccer and field hockey too.

My game is placements and timing, deep ground strokes, stepping into the ball. Training the body to obey the mind, as I've done, differs from the more conventional method of getting the mind to obey the body. Spectators can appreciate the grace, fluency and beauty of serve-and-volley because there is a certain rhythmic pattern, a logical flow that has a beginning (the serve), middle (return) and potential end (volley). A baseline game has definition only in the mind of the executioner. "Even if you have to take some of your power off," my dad would remind me, "hit it deep because your opponent can't do anything if your shot is deep." Wise words, but hardly designed to light fires for spectators who view long rallies as boring and without purpose.

Contrasting playing styles, our differing backgrounds and, of course, our youth made the first match between Evonne and myself a heralded event. When it finally occurred, at Wimbledon in 1972, most people had forgotten that we almost met earlier that year at the T-Bar-M Racquet Club in Dallas. The draw for that Virginia Slims event even seemed rigged when Evonne, Billie Jean and I wound up in the same half.

That tournament convinced me that you can't judge all tennis players by their strokes. On opening day, Evonne was eating lunch with Vic Edwards, her coach, and listening to music from a tiny transistor radio on the table in the coffee shop. Her hair was messy and curly, she wore a T-shirt and I could tell she had nothing on underneath it. The extent of our conversation after our introduction was "hello." I was a seventeen-year-old schoolgirl, she was a twenty-one-year-old Wimbledon champion from the Australian countryside; we were on different wavelengths—or so I thought until later that week.

The draw had Evonne and me paired for the semifinals, but someone forgot to tell Billie Jean, and all the talk about an Evert-Goolagong show only created another challenge for her. Billie Jean and I met in the quarters, and I led, 7–6, 3–1, but she took the last two sets, 6–3, 7–5. Players patted her on the back in the locker room as if she had just won Wimbledon. I walked into the locker room alone and crushed. I had smoked her, 6–1, 6–0, at the Women's International tournament in Fort Lauderdale, but one month later, on a different surface and with that combative spirit, Billie Jean had exacted revenge. "Bad luck," Julie Heldman said. "Billie just played well."

I walked into the lavatory and broke into tears, disappointed over the close loss and distraught over the continued indifference from the players. I had never done anything to hurt them, but they were making every effort to rub my nose in it. I splashed cold water on my face and tried to keep from throwing up. I felt a hand on my shoulder and spun around instinctively.

"Don't worry, it's all right," Evonne said, patting me softly and putting an arm around my shoulder. "It's just a tennis match, don't worry, don't be upset."

I always think about that incident when I see Evonne. It was a side of her I had not expected. She seemed so predictably casual eating lunch that first day and listening to music before our match at Wimbledon. I remember looking at her and thinking, "Here I am a nervous wreck and she's singing." Under duress, Evonne had shown me another side—soft, caring and tender—which I appreciated even more than her delicate touch volleys.

I'm sensitive about how people judge me. It's not so much whether they like me or not; I only ask to be treated fairly. Judge me as I am, not how you think I am.

At the 1971 U.S. Open, I was "Cinderella in Sneakers" to some American writers. I didn't necessarily feel like Cinderella, Alice in Wonderland or other heroines from nursery rhymes, but at least the reference was complimentary. After I beat Britain's No. 1 player, Virginia Wade, and Joyce Williams in the Wightman Cup matches that preceded the 1972 Wimbledon fortnight, I suddenly became "Little Miss Cool," "The Ice Maiden," and "The Ice Dolly" to the British media. None of the nicknames were flattering.

I'm not cold and indifferent. During my first U.S. Open and Wimbledon, I was shy and defensive. When someone asked a personal question such as "Do you have a boyfriend at home?" I felt threatened. My privacy was being invaded for the first time, I didn't want everyone to know everything about me, and I wasn't self-assured enough to say, "Hey, look, I'm still new at this game; just give me some time." Very few people show all of themselves to the public. You can't give away everything; otherwise, it's as if someone is touching you on the inside.

Once that happens, it's only a matter of time before your emotions are shredded, and then you're no good to the public or yourself.

I project cool on the court because my game demands total concentration. Once my mind wanders, the ground strokes shorten, the drop shots drift, the serves float. You can't stand at the baseline and gut out a long rally against a tough opponent when visions of a boyfriend dance through your head or you're trying to placate the public and press with gestures, trick shots and plastic smiles. My humor is dry, sometimes sarcastic. Photographers like Mel Di Giacomo, Russ Adams, Art Seitz, John Russell, Fred Mullane and others often can read my mind because their courtside lenses have been focused so intensely on me for so long. I don't have to say a word, yet my expressions tell them what I'm thinking. But there has been so much publicity about my cool side that the lighter side stays in the dark. If I had judged the British public by their accents or London's weather before, during and after my first Wimbledon, I might not have married an Englishman.

Flying to London with my mother in 1972 to play Wightman Cup and Wimbledon was more than my first foreign trip. It meant that I had worked hard enough and progressed to the point where my dad felt I deserved the chance. The 1971 U.S. Open had been my coming-out party, a late-summer bonus for a good year. Now I was getting a chance to find out what life was like on the other side of the Atlantic.

My first impressions of London were hardly positive. Edy McGoldrick, the U.S. Wightman Cup captain, picked up my mom and me at Heathrow Airport in rainy weather. It rained for the next three or four days and grew dark at four in the afternoon. For someone accustomed to sunshine, blue skies and warm weather, I was depressed. I missed my family, school friends and my boyfriend at the time, Bob Marley.

I have always felt a little awed by Wimbledon. The physical appearance of Centre Court at the All England Lawn Tennis and Croquet Club can be intimidating, even after someone plays there for ten years. It's enclosed, yet it's outdoors. You have the feeling of being in a shrine. No other place in the world can duplicate this feeling. Wimbledon is special.

The first time I played at Foro Italico in Rome for the Italian Open, I double-faulted twice on the first two points. My mother says that I served the two doubles after I saw the four huge statues of naked men around the court. It was hard for me not to look at those fifty-foot statues, especially a young American girl unaccustomed to Italian tradition. Italian crowds are the most volatile and outgoing that I have ever played in front of. At first, I was offended by the shouts of "Dai Chris, Dai Chris," because it sounded so offensive. Then I asked an Italian player what the fans were shouting and she said it meant "Come on, Chris" in Italian. I thought they wanted me to "die" on the court.

Paris is a wonderful city, and I've won my share of French Open titles. But I don't feel intimidated by Paris, and it has nothing to do with being comfortable on clay courts. I'm not intimidated by the U.S. Open either—and that's been played on three different surfaces in the last ten years.

The U.S. Open and Wimbledon are as different as their respective countries. The Open is American, where anything goes. There is no tradition at the National Tennis Center, but the challenge is awesome. Anyone who can survive sweltering summer heat, hard courts, the planes from nearby LaGuardia Airport, night matches and erratic scheduling has passed the most strenuous test in the sport.

Players treat Wimbledon differently than any other tournament. I don't know if it's the prestige, tradition or the grass courts. Everyone is polite at Wimbledon. You ask nicely for a practice court and practice balls. At other events, players just walk into a tournament office, take a can of balls and say, "I'm going to Court 13," and that's it. There's a royal atmosphere at Wimbledon, and I respect this attitude because Wimbledon is more than a sports event. It is an occasion that consumes a country.

The press plays a more visible role at Wimbledon than at any other tournament. With so many London newspapers competing for the attention of the reader, reporters are always on the prowl for stories that often have little to do with serve-and-volley or the Centre Court. Players are tracked at hotels, restaurants, nightclubs, casinos, discos. Being spotted with someone in the player's tea room may be more important than your doubles match for the day. Before my first Wimbledon, journalists interrogated me about my feelings toward Evonne. Did I know her? Did I like her? We had not played on the court yet, but what about off the court? What about our playing styles? Were there any promising young black American players on the horizon like the aborigine, Goolagong? What did I know or think about Wimbledon?

The sports sections in many British newspapers start on the back page and are easy to find. The headlines sometimes jump off the page. When your name is tossed around so freely for so long, the shock value can be disconcerting. On the first day of the 1972 tournament, Evonne woke up and saw a nude drawing of herself in the *Sun.* The caption under the drawing read "She's soft, round, cuddly like a tennis ball." What a way to start a title defense!

Some journalists will go to any lengths, even to knocking on your hotel-room door at six-thirty in the morning. "Miss Evert, Miss Evert, may we talk to you?" one reporter asked, while I was still in bed on opening day. "Is Mr. Connors there?" Reports had circulated that I had been seen with Jimmy at Queen's Club.

"No, Mr. Connors is not here," I said, refusing to open the door. "Please go away."

Jimmy wasn't in the room, but I could just see the headlines in some of the Fleet Street tabloids if he had been: "Jimbo and Chrissie Score . . . In Bed" or maybe "Chrissie Tries Luv Double With Connors."

Most people believe that Jimmy and I first met at the 1972 Wimbledon tournament, but they're wrong. I laid eyes on Jimmy for the first time at the age of ten, during the Orange Bowl Junior Championships in Florida. I don't know if Jimmy would even recall the episode, but my parents were driving home to Fort Lauderdale from the tournament one day when my father gave Jimmy and his mother a ride.

I was too young at the time to float away on romantic notions just by sitting next to a thirteen-year-old boy. But strange as it may seem, I felt uncomfortable squeezed in next to Jimmy in the back seat that day. Was it because he was simply a boy? Were there strange vibes that would intensify five years later? Or was it because our white, middle-class, Catholic families were intertwined?

My father dated Gloria Connors years before he met my mother. They practiced at the same tennis club in the Chicago area and became friends. My mother, who grew up on the East Coast, always teased my dad about Mrs. Connors because my mother's maiden name, Thompson, was the same as Jimmy's mother's.

"Oh, see Gloria there," my mom would say at the Orange Bowl, with a slight inflection in her voice. Believe it or not, I got a little worried about my dad talking to Mrs. Connors during one of my matches at Salvadore Park in Coral Gables, Florida. I was playing on the second court, and they were sitting and chatting in some bleachers. I couldn't concentrate. Watching them, my imagination ran wild, as it often did in those days.

"Gosh, I hope nothing happens," I thought, glancing from the court to the bleachers between points. "I hope my dad doesn't fall in love with her."

Of course, my fears were ridiculous. But the day my dad suggested offering Jimmy and his mother a ride, my thoughts took off again.

Jimmy was skinny at the time and not nearly as appealing as he was when I saw him again at the Orange Lawn Tennis Club in 1970. I was fifteen and had lost to Peaches Bartkowicz in the first round of the Eastern grass-court championships. Jimmy and Brian Gottfried had arrived from the 18 Nationals. Recognizing a familiar face felt good, but the familiar face was Brian's: I had known Brian and his younger brother, Larry, from Florida. Brian would ask me to practice at Holiday Park. He has a subtle sense of humor, another gentleman who seems so quiet but can be quite funny; I would be in stitches listening to him.

I told Brian how happy I was to see him win the 18-and-under Nationals. I didn't realize that Jimmy was the player he had beaten in the semifinals, and it wasn't until Jimmy started making faces at me after the remark that I put it together that he was the boy who had been sitting next to me in the car, and whose mother had dated my dad.

"I'm so sorry," I said, trying to wriggle out of an embarrassing situation. "I didn't mean that. I'm a good friend of Brian's, and I was just happy for him."

I was also flushed because Jimmy was cute. At that moment, I got my first crush on him, although I never talked to him again that week and didn't think he was interested in someone three years younger. I found out otherwise at the 1972 Wightman Cup Ball. The ball was held on the last night of the competition. The players usually went with dates, but I didn't know many boys at the time.

"Why don't you go with us?" Val Ziegenfuss suggested. Val was dating Dickie Dell, Donald's younger brother.

"I think Jimmy's going with Wendy Overton," Dickie said, "but you can join us."

I went with Bill Glaves, our coach, who felt sorry for me because I didn't have a date. Carole Graebner tried to pair me with Jimmy and have Bill go with Wendy, but it didn't work out. At the ball, Jimmy and Wendy sat at another table. I exchanged glances with Jimmy almost the whole evening and even danced with him at a disco after the ball. Back at the Westbury Hotel, I was staying in a room on the fourth floor. So was Jimmy. Wendy was in a third-floor room. As Wendy and Jimmy got off the elevator on the third floor, Jimmy turned back and whispered, "Call me."

Jimmy's blunt approach stunned me. I pushed the button for the fourth floor, all the while thinking, "Who does he think he is telling me to do that?" Jimmy had more confidence than some of the guys I went to the movies with on Saturday night in Fort Lauderdale, but I couldn't just call him, and didn't.

Because tennis is such a small society, you can usually find someone on the circuit with little trouble. I ran into Jimmy again the following week at Queen's Club, the tournament that traditionally precedes Wimbledon. Jimmy was eating lunch in the dining room with his mother. Mrs. Connors called me over, asked about my dad and my plans for the summer. Then, out of the blue, she turned to Jimmy and said, "Jimmy, why don't you ask Chrissie to play mixed doubles at Wimbledon?"

"Do you want to play mixed doubles at Wimbledon?" Jimmy said, mouthing his mother's words without missing a bite of food.

"Thank you," I said, "but I already have a partner." I had committed myself to Erik Van Dillen.

"What about the U.S. Open?" Mrs. Connors continued.

"Do you want to play at the U.S. Open?" Jimmy followed up.

"Yeah, okay," I said, uncertain whether Jimmy was serious or just trying to satisfy his mother.

I won Queen's that weekend, and Jimmy took the men's singles. On my way back to the club after Jimmy's match, Mrs. Connors saw me. "Jimmy asked me to have you stay," she said. "He's in the shower right now, but he wants to talk to you afterward."

I waited about fifteen minutes, but Jimmy did not come out, so I left the club and went back to the hotel. He called later, asked me out that night, and the wheels of romance started turning.

At Wimbledon the following week, Jimmy and I were together on the grounds one day when five press photographers bolted in front of us. Most players would have continued walking to the tea room or ducked into the clubhouse. But as soon as Jimmy saw the photographers, he playfully put his arm around me. Needless to say, the pictures made most of the major newspapers in the United States, especially the *Fort Lauderdale News* and the *Sun Sentinel*.

Because Wimbledon is such a social event, a player can wind up making news on two fronts. That's what happened to me at my first Wimbledon. Photographers and journalists wondered what was going on between me and Jimmy, and the sportswriters could hardly wait for Evonne and me to meet for the first time, even as we struggled through three-set matches early in the tournament.

Leaving the locker room for Centre Court the day of our semifinal, we walked past a pair of frosted glass doors. Over an archway between the locker room and the doors were the following words: "IF YOU CAN MEET WITH TRIUMPH AND DISASTER AND TREAT THOSE TWO IMPOSTORS JUST THE SAME." The words were from Kipling's poem "If," my father's favorite. Each time I see those words, I think of my dad and our bedtime chats.

It's not often that two players like Evonne and myself wind up meeting for the first time on Wimbledon's Centre Court. Ted Tinling, the British fashion designer and elder statesman of women's tennis, compared it to the legendary 1926 meeting in Cannes, France, between Suzanne Lenglen and Helen Wills. It was important enough to draw members of the royal family, and I wasn't shy about asking Evonne for advice on how to curtsy before the Royal Box.

"Just sort of bend your knees and bob," she said. Bud Collins reported in the *Boston Globe* the following day that our bobbing and giggling "resembled a couple of Protestants trying to genuflect at Lourdes." Not bad, since Evonne and I are both Catholic.

I took our rivalry too personally, but dealing with crowds and images, at a young age, was heavy stuff for me. Now, I can look back at our situation objectively, shrug it off and acknowledge that my meeting with Evonne in a Dallas lavatory was as important as our first match on the Centre Court.

Evonne was a moody player. If the mood struck her, she could play exquisitely, a feathery brand of tennis that no one could duplicate. There were days when she couldn't move her feet, felt pressure, and I beat her, 6–2, 6–1; other times were tension-filled three-setters. You never knew what to expect, and I learned that I couldn't put pressure on myself before playing her because it wouldn't make a difference.

I feel closer to Evonne now because we both married Englishmen, came up together and survived. But at the time of our first match, Evonne was a mystery, someone who could lose a match and still come off the court with a smile. I admired that attitude, respected her for it and at times wished I could have been as relaxed about losing as I had been at the age of ten. But I realized that not taking my losses well made me a winner; I couldn't shrug them off and say, "Well, I had a bad day." Defeat always forced me to scrutinize myself more closely.

I never resented the fact that crowds were for Evonne, but I was envious and wanted to shout, "Don't you know I'm feeling something inside?" I was tight-lipped, furiously determined and didn't crack a smile on the court while Evonne laughed at the fact that she sometimes forgot the score. She was cute, smiling, friendly. I could have catered to the crowd by grinning or waving, but I would have been a fake, it wouldn't have been me, and there's no way I can change to make people like me or root for me. It feels funny to smile on the court unless something humorous happens and the reaction is genuine. Bill Tilden once said, "Never change a winning game," and my style won for me.

Billie Jean watched my match with Evonne on the television in the locker room. Later she would tell me that I was ahead a set and 3–0 because Evonne was more concerned with trying to win the crowd. Billie Jean can manipulate a crowd. "Move your buhullas!" she will yell after a point, or she'll tell an opponent, who has just hit a winner, "I can't believe you hit that shot!" If the reaction is natural and doesn't distract, fine.

I had my chances against Evonne in the first match. If she had continued hitting without a purpose, I would have prevailed that day. But Evonne went back to some basics that Vic Edwards had stressed about playing against two-handed backhands and rallied to win, 4–6, 6–3, 6–4. Edwards had coached Jan Lehane O'Neill, another Australian, who used both hands on the backhand. His strategy to Evonne: Slice your backhand cross-court short to Chris's backhand. Low, short balls would make me work harder, limit my effectiveness to hit on the run and open up the court for volleys by pulling me out of position.

After the match, I felt as hurt by the crowd reaction as I was about losing to Evonne. "I hope they're satisfied," I said, slamming my racquets onto a chair in the locker room.

Lesley Hunt once described me as a "myth" because she said I never cried or cracked and made everyone think I was so cold. "That in itself was intimidating," Lesley intimated, "because it was like playing against a blank wall."

I have cried during matches, and the two most prominent occasions were against Lesley. The first came during a Virginia Slims event in Dallas in 1974; the second was six months later, during the U.S. Open at Forest Hills.

Lesley had played a mixed doubles tournament in Dallas and was popular in that city. Playing against her in the Virginia Slims, I won the first set, 6–0, but the crowd clapped, yelled and stomped its feet for Lesley in the second set. Even when I won a point on a passing shot, the applause for me was only token. Spectators were drinking in the box seats and raising hell. I didn't feel I had a friend in the arena; it was Forest Hills 1971 in reverse.

Usually, I can hold my emotions together during a match. But the noise and stomping swelled after Lesley won a second-set tie breaker. Finally, during the third set, the tears just came down. I held my head high, tried not to let anyone see that I was crying, won the set and the match, 6–3, and then beat Frankie Durr and Virginia Wade for the title. But it would be five years before I would return to Dallas. Nancy Jeffett, the tournament director, invited me each year and I love her dearly and felt badly for her. But it wasn't a fun city for me; given a choice of places to play, I picked those cities where I was most comfortable. Why play in a city where you feel the crowds are against you? It was psychological, and I simply developed a mental block against Dallas.

I didn't have any choice about the U.S. Open in 1974, but the circumstances were more emotional. I was on a fifty-five-match winning streak at the time that had spanned ten tournaments and six months. But instead of cheering this achievement, as spectators must have when Joe DiMaggio was on his fifty-six-game hitting streak with the New York Yankees in 1941, the fans were more interested in seeing me beaten. I was no longer the kid; I was fair game.

Serving at 5–4, 30–40, in the first set against Lesley, I faulted a first serve and then hit a second serve that appeared long. Someone shouted "out," but Lesley returned the serve. My concentration was shattered with the call, and I pushed the ball tentatively into the net. The umpire awarded Lesley the point and game.

"Didn't you call that ball out?" I asked the side linesman. He put out his hands, as if to say, "No, the ball was on the line." The linesman was about five feet away from the crowd.

"I heard somebody say 'out,' " I said, exercising my privilege to question the call.

"Will the people in the stands please abstain from calling the ball?" the umpire announced, refusing to change the call.

I thought the decision was unfair, so I went to the umpire's chair. "I'm sorry, but I heard an out call, and it sounded as if it were right from the linesman," I said. If I question two or three calls a year, it's a lot, but any injustice should not pass unnoticed.

Mike Blanchard, the referee, happened to be at courtside. I explained my situation. "All we can do is ask the crowd to be quiet," he said.

I returned to the baseline. "Evert you stink!" someone shouted. A chorus of boos followed. "Don't be a bad sport!" another voice shouted out. I got very upset. "I just question one thing," I thought, "and they start booing."

I couldn't continue playing. I walked to the back of the court and tried to compose myself. Tears dripped down my face. Most of the crowd could not see my crying because I was in a side corner, with my back turned, but I knew what was happening.

I won the match, 7–6, 6–3, coming from 1–4 down in a first-set sudden-death tie breaker. But, like Joe DiMaggio, my streak ended at fifty-six when Evonne beat me, 6–0, 6–7, 6–3, in a semifinal that was played over two days because of rain.

My loss to Evonne at Wimbledon in 1972 might have been

more traumatic if I hadn't been seeing Jimmy. We were inseparable, going out to the Playboy Club, to dinner, and dancing. Something new and exciting had taken hold. Wimbledon had not been a total loss.

6 • Growing Pains

"Chrissie . . . tennis . . . pizza . . . music . . . good
books . . . fashion . . . meeting people . . . cold
weather . . . sun . . . milkshakes . . . nature . . . food
. . . Europe . . . jewelry . . . eyes . . . curly blond
hair . . . Jimmy . . . LA . . . laughing . . . Burt
Bacharach . . . BJK

> —From *Veritas* (school yearbook),
> St. Thomas Aquinas High School,
> Class of '73

The phone rang in my bedroom, but I was too unsettled to pick up the receiver. Was it Ana, calling back to confirm our plans one last time? Was it another friend checking in, or my dad wondering if I were coming to the courts?

I nervously picked out a few blouses from my closet, tried to fold them neatly but wound up scrunching them into my suitcase. The phone continued ringing. It must be Ana. She was the only person who knew I would be home at this hour. I picked up the receiver but didn't say anything. I had to know who was on the other end of the line.

"Chrissie, is that you?" the voice said. Relieved, I recognized Ana's voice.

"I'm almost ready," I blurted. "I still don't know if it's the right thing to do."

"You don't sound too good. Are you sure you feel all right?"

"I think you'd better get over here in a hurry, Ana, before I change my mind."

"I'm on my way."

I hung up the phone and peered through the jalousie window of my bedroom, which fronted our house. No car in the driveway meant everyone was still gone. If Ana hurried, I could leave without any dramatic farewell scenes.

My mind was cluttered. Was I doing the right thing? Would I hurt my parents by secretly ducking out this way? Should I leave them a note? Would they even understand if I did?

I had called Ana the previous day in Gainesville, where she was attending the University of Florida. I had to see Jimmy, I told her. We had been apart for several weeks since the U.S. Open, I was lonely, he was in California, and my parents didn't understand what I was going through. I had to get away.

"Why don't you go and talk to my mom?" Ana suggested.

The Leairds lived only three blocks away. As a mother, Conchita Leaird might have some advice my mom couldn't give because she was too close to the situation, Ana reasoned. I agreed, spent several hours with Ana's mother and then called Ana back from her house.

"I really wish you were here," I said.

"Chris, I can't afford it. If you can pay for the ticket, I'll come home."

I was stunned. "You would do that?" I said, "You would just come home for one day?"

"Yeah, I would, if you really need me. I'll come home if you want me to." I wanted to see Ana and agreed to pick up the cost of her flight.

Ana's mother had told me to go to my parents and tell them I had to be with Jimmy because I loved him. "Honesty is the best policy," she said. Ana disagreed with her mother: Do what's in your heart because your parents may not understand, she said; if you feel you have to see Jimmy, go.

I picked up Ana at the airport after her arrival and we agonized in my bedroom. "When you're on the tennis court," she said, "you don't ask anybody. You can ask everybody what to do before a match. But when you get out there, you make the decisions. You're faced with a decision now. . . . If you ask your parents, you know they're going to say no. If you tell them, they're going to say no. But if you just get on that plane and go, you've made your point. You've said to them, 'Okay, I've done it, I'm my own person now, I love you, but I have to do what I think is best.' "

I had already called the airlines. An evening flight from Fort Lauderdale would arrive in Los Angeles that night. "I'm going to go," I told Ana. "I'll just leave them a note and hope they understand."

Ana's car pulled up near our house, but I still hadn't written the note, and now was not the time. I searched for a pen and some paper in the kitchen, grabbed my suitcase, slipped out the back door and met Ana on the street.

"God, I hope I'm doing the right thing," I moaned, sliding into the front seat and trying to scribble.

Ana tried to reassure me, but it was no use. I ripped up the first note, tried a second time but still could not make any sense. By the time we reached the airport, it was now or never, so I hastily jotted down some thoughts, handed her the note and asked if she would give it to my parents.

Aboard the flight to Los Angeles, the pilot periodically came on the intercom and reported the progress of the Billie Jean King–Bobby Riggs "Battle of the Sexes" being played that night at the Houston Astrodome. I knew how important the match was for women's tennis, but at eighteen years old, I didn't feel I had any part in it. I was involved in searching for my own freedom, and the growing pains of the last nine months had totally frustrated me.

I don't know how my mother survived Europe with me that previous spring. All of the embarrassing ills of adolescence that had been stored somewhere suddenly took over, like a game of catch-up, and an emotional tug of war surfaced, putting my mother on one side and Jimmy on the other.

Father Vincent Kelly had allowed me to graduate from St. Thomas in January because I had fulfilled my high school credits. Visiting Paris, Rome and Wimbledon as a professional for the first time should have been glamorous, but I wanted to be alone with Jimmy. Having agreed to let me play the European circuit, my parents felt I should be chaperoned.

It wasn't that they distrusted Jimmy; they liked him and respected his ability, but Jimmy was three years older, had traveled extensively, and my parents worried that I was too young to become seriously involved. I didn't speak a foreign language, was new to foreign currency evaluation and, in their minds, might be getting in over my head by traveling alone.

Like most teen-agers, I tried to tell my parents that I was responsible enough. "Don't you trust me?" I would ask when the subject was raised.

"As long as you're under our roof, you do what we ask you to do," my mother said, speaking for my dad as well. "You're not an adult yet."

"Well, I'm eighteen years old," I countered. "In some people's minds, that's an adult."

I don't know if my parents fretted about the possibility of Jimmy and me sleeping together. At the time they didn't question me about this, and I never brought it up. But they knew I was naive with men, even after a trip to Wimbledon the previous summer, and figured that a chaperone was the most comfortable bridge to adulthood.

I resented my mom's presence and preferred a younger female friend, not an authority figure. Since Mrs. Connors traveled with Jimmy, we were stifled: We held hands and kissed in public, but never in front of my mother.

I'm a very affectionate person; so is Jimmy. But at dinner with the four of us, I became cold and unapproachable, couldn't enjoy the spontaneity of people and was embarrassed to show emotion. I ignored my mother, tuned her out of our conversations or simply walked away if the discussion didn't suit me. If the clothes weren't clean or came back from the laundry with wrinkles, I blamed her. She was the reason for bad practice sessions. We argued, and she absorbed my abuse like a sponge. Once or twice, after the shouting boiled over, both of us wound up in tears.

My sour attitude spilled into my tennis. I became impatient, less determined, easily distracted and uncommitted. I fought Margaret Court in the French Open final, served for the match at 5–3 in the second set, lost 6–7, 7–6, 6–4, and it was downhill after that.

At the Italian Open in Rome, I was top-seeded, but needed three sets to beat Katja Ebbinghaus of West Germany and then went, 7–6, 6–4, against another West German player, Helga Masthoff, in the semifinals. After losing a first-set tie breaker to Evonne Goolagong, I disgustedly tanked the second set at love.

"I know you resent me being here," my mom said that night, "but your father and I both feel that it's the right thing and that somebody should be here with you."

"You don't trust me, that's all there is to it!" I snapped. "You never leave me alone, and you only go to the tournament when you know Jimmy's going to be there."

"That's not true, Chrissie. Your father and I just feel that you and Jimmy should be chaperoned when you're together."

"It's not fair!" I shouted, stalking out of our room at the Holiday Inn.

I led a sheltered, one-dimensional childhood, comforted by my parents, school, tennis, close family relationships and religion. Yet my attitudes differed from those of my parents in many areas.

My parents are strict Catholics. We went to church every Sunday, attended a religious school taught by Dominican nuns, said grace before dinner and a prayer at bedtime. We also went regularly to confession, but I was almost embarrassed to tell all my sins. The priests at St. Anthony's Church were supposed to serve in place of God, but I knew them well because they played tennis at Holiday Park. Walking into the confessional, I always felt they knew who I was because they could recognize my voice from the courts. Knowing they knew confused me. What should I tell them? What were sins and what were white lies and how much should I confess? Should I confess evil thoughts about wanting to kiss a boy or that I was angry with my parents?

As a junior player, I sometimes prayed during my matches. If I was down 4–love in the third set, I would turn around and say to myself, "God, if you let me win this match, I'll never curse or get mad at my parents again." I won a few matches after those prayers, but sure enough, the next day, I would curse or holler at someone. Was that a sin?

My parents believed that if you didn't go to church every Sunday, it was a mortal sin. They believed in the benefits of rosaries and other prayers to the Virgin Mary.

I have always had a strong belief in God and Christ. The diamond cross that I wear now is a friendship gift from Lynda Carter. She gave it to me because I wouldn't accept any money for appearing on her television special in 1981. I love it, treasure it, and never take it off because it means so much to me.

At home in Florida, I still go to church with my family. In Paris that spring, my mother and Mrs. Connors took Jimmy and me to a Catholic church for Mass and confession. Jimmy was in there for about an hour, which is unusually long. He finally came out and said he had to go back the next day because he hadn't finished confessing all his sins.

Over the years, I stopped going to church every Sunday on the tour. At first I wanted to think it was because Sunday was the day of the finals of a tournament and my mind would be on the match, not the service. Then I started to think that if my heart was not in the Mass, if I was just going to be present, it was not worth going. I didn't want to be hypocritical, and if God is just and God is there, I believed that what you did with the other six days of the week counted just as much.

You can't force faith. Some people are born with faith in God, afterlife, heaven and hell. I had to work hard at having faith. The discipline of going to church every Sunday was good for me, and when I settle down and raise a family, I'll resume going to Mass. Religion has made my parents happy, gives them peace, helped make them good people and set an example for their children. I would like to share that experience with my family.

My parents and I also differed in our attitudes regarding the double standard for raising boys and girls. Daughters are more protected by their parents than sons. Boys are told to be on their own when they are sixteen years old and prove their adulthood. Until women's liberation, society dictated that daughters go from their parents to a husband. You were supposed to look up to your parents, obey them and respect them; then you left home, got married and followed the same rules with your husband.

The rules are changing. I don't agree that the man must have the career and the woman should stay home and watch the children; it depends on the couple, and it's different for everybody. But new rules scare people; they scared my parents.

If I have a daughter, I hope to rear her to be independent, and not too reliant on me. I would go with her to junior tournaments; if she were really resentful of me at the age of fifteen or sixteen, I would let her go alone to a few and see how she liked it. I'll bet a thousand dollars that she would come back and say, "Okay, Mom, will you come with me to the next tournament?" Parents have to let their kids make their own decisions and mistakes.

I made my share of mistakes in 1973, but Jimmy was cute throughout the ordeal. "You played real well," he said with a sarcastic lilt in his voice after my loss to Evonne in the Italian Open.

"God, I played great, didn't I?" I said, mocking his biting humor that always relieved some of my tensions. It was unimportant to Jimmy whether I won or lost. He wanted me to win, but it didn't change our feelings for one another, even after I lost to Virginia Wade, 6–1, 6–2, in the semifinals of a grass-court tournament at Nottingham, to Julie Heldman, 6–4, 6–2, in the quarters at Queen's Club and to Billie Jean, 6–0, 7–5, in the final at Wimbledon.

My mom hit bottom at Nottingham. It was her birthday, and she missed my dad and little Clare, who was only five then, and the other children. She also wasn't sure how to handle my string of losses, which had never happened before. Coming from a large family, where she confided in brothers and sisters, she had been direct and open. I shut her out, yet she still let me dictate the rules because she didn't want to embarrass me.

At Nottingham she smiled, said hello to everyone and never had a bitter word. Unless you were in our room when she called home after my lackluster effort against Virginia, you would never have known anything was wrong. But she talked to Clare and my dad, cried a little and then went out, bought a seventy-dollar set of china and said she felt better. I knew otherwise, and it would be several years before my mom could shake the frustrating effects of that period. When I won Wimbledon in 1974, she later told me that she couldn't cry after the match.

"I had held in too much for too long and just couldn't let go," she said.

My mom saw I was going through a stage. She could have come down hard on me because I was unreasonable, sometimes even nasty. Whatever happened between us was my fault. It wasn't that she was hanging on me; I would have been lost without her, didn't know how to handle anything, but thought I did. We're closer than ever today as a result: She's more like a big sister than a mother, we talk all the time, trade recipes, travel together. There's nothing I wouldn't tell her, and I'm sure she feels the same way.

• • •

Tennis had similar growing pains during this period. In May of 1973, Margaret Court was lured to an outpost in the Cuyamaca Mountains outside of San Diego for a match against Bobby Riggs. Margaret had dominated the circuit that winter and won eighteen of twenty-five tournaments during the year. But on that Mother's Day afternoon, she simply took a 6–2, 6–1 licking, and "You've come a long way, baby" suddenly became "You've still got a long way to go, baby" in the minds of many men until Billie Jean routed Riggs later in the year.

Later that summer, Wimbledon proved to be an even darker time for the sport. The top pros boycotted the tournament over a suspension handed down to Nikki Pilic of Yugoslavia. The men's final wound up with Jan Kodes of Czechoslovakia beating Alex Metreveli of the Soviet Union, 6–1, 9–8, 6–3, after Metreveli eliminated Jimmy in four sets in the quarters.

Turning pro on my eighteenth birthday opened fresh opportunities for me, just as Phillis Flotow had predicted when she said, "Work now for pay back later." I collected $10,000 for winning my first tournament as a pro over Virginia Wade; my father, Uncle Chuck and Gene Rimes, a Fort Lauderdale lawyer, immediately formed a corporation, Evert Enterprises, to handle my earnings. I signed a contract with Wilson that ultimately led to my own model racquet.

I had been using various Wilson models since the age of sixteen. Over the years, I've been offered twice as much to switch companies, but there is no way I would change for any amount of money. If someone offered me a million dollars to use a racquet and I was getting $200,000 from Wilson, I might go out and practice a few times with the new racquet just to see how it feels, but all my success has been with one racquet. It would be like starting my career over with a new racquet, and I would be psyched out. I feel a loyalty to Wilson. They supplied our whole family with free racquets when I started and are not demanding. At the most, I give them one day a year for pictures and promotion; other players are required to give five to ten days a year to companies for services. If those players feel they can switch and still maintain the same level of their game, it's their choice, but I've never been tempted to change. It's tough enough for me to go out there and beat somebody, and I wouldn't want to feel guilty if I lost a couple of matches when I started using a new racquet.

Clothing is different. Very early, my mom dressed Jeanne and me in lacy tennis dresses, lacy bloomers and hair ribbons. At fourteen, I wore the clothes of Mondessa Swift, who was a

A sunny moment with Jimmy.

Jimmy, Kristien, and Ana watching me in action at the U.S. Open.

A moment away from the pressure.

President Ford explaining to me why he doesn't come into the net more often.

Jimmy and his gang, Spencer Segura, me, and Nastase.

My second Wimbledon victory. Pretty high, huh?

Jeanie Brinkman, PR director of the Virginia Slims Circuit and close friend, and I at the awards banquet.

Trying to express my innermost feelings at a press conference.

My first big splurge—a beautiful Russian lynx coat.

Yes, Stephanie, I know there's a camera aimed over this way.

Burt and I on the set of Semi-Tough.

Contemplating the future at age twenty-four.

designer in Fort Lauderdale. Mondessa and her husband, Ben, were friends of the family, and she and Mom played tennis together. Her clothes were well-made and stylish, and people always asked "Where did you get your beautiful clothes?" when I traveled to tournaments.

I like a certain style—fitted at the waist, flair skirt, and a scoop neckline so that I get as much sun as possible. I don't like tight-fitting collars, high necks, or heavy outfits that look like potato sacks. I was slim, liked my figure and felt feminine in Mondessa's clothes. What happened to her dresses? Usually, if I wore them enough, my mom gave them to school charities, church auctions, or Goodwill Industries.

After turning pro, I signed a contract with Puritan, had my own successful line of clothes for eight years, and even had a horse named after me by Carl Rosen, the president of Puritan; the filly, Chris Evert, went on to become the Triple Crown winner. I also signed a contract with the Converse Shoe Company. Few players have stayed with the same manufacturers that long, but loyalty is a virtue that our family treasures. That's why my parents agreed to pay Ana Leaird's expenses to travel with me to a tournament in Cleveland that summer, which I won.

Ana now works as the publicity director for the Women's Tennis Association, but I doubt that anything has ever been more delicate for her than delivering that note to my mother. She recounted the details to me after my arrival in Los Angeles.

"Your mom was real nice," Ana related. "She said, 'I don't hold you responsible for this, Ana. Chrissie is old enough to know what she's doing. She's made her own decision, and whether you had been here or not to drive her to the airport wouldn't have made any difference. She would have gone anyway.' "

I stayed with Jimmy and his mother, at the home of friends. After my arrival, Mrs. Connors wanted me to call my parents, but I wasn't ready. Four days after I arrived, my parents somehow got the number and called.

"We'd like you to come home," my dad said.

"I'd like to stay on a few more days," I pleaded.

"Well, if you don't come home," my dad went on, "then you'd better go straight to Columbus next week." Columbus, Georgia, was the site of my next tournament.

I agreed. We hung up, and I wondered what my parents were thinking. I very rarely went against their wishes, and sneaking out the back door was not my style. In many ways, I was a woman in a little girl's world. Part of me had to be turned free, but as long as I was living with my parents, they had the last word. Yet even if they had come in and said, "You're not leaving this house," I would have gone.

Jimmy won the Pacific Southwest Championships that week, over Tom Okker, 2–6, 7–5, 6–2. He came with me to Columbus, and I won the tournament when Margaret Court defaulted the final. But what stuck in my mind, after returning home, were my mom's words: "You hurt us very much."

I didn't want to hurt my parents, but it was a romantic period in my life. Jimmy and I were crazy about one another, I was good for him, and he complemented me. My quiet, serious nature was a source of strength for him. In Paris, he threw his racquets across the room and almost broke a lamp after losing in the first round to Raul Ramirez of Mexico. I tried to talk him through the frustrations of playing on clay courts. He helped me to stand up for my convictions.

After I lost to Margaret in the French, I wanted to tell the press that I had been proud of the way I had played. "Say it then," Jimmy told me that night, after I lamented my indecisiveness. "Say what you feel. Don't be afraid to stand up for what you believe in."

"That's just not me. I feel uncomfortable."

"You can do it," he said. "You can get away with it."

My parents have never held grudges. They were disappointed at my unexpected trip to Los Angeles but didn't stop me from going to South Africa later that year and even agreed to pay Ana's expenses for three weeks to travel with me. After checking with her teachers, Ana called her mom and dad.

"My biology teacher's going to flunk me if I go," she told

them. "But my other classes are okay." Go, they said. A three-week all-expenses-paid trip to South Africa was something she could never buy in college. If it required staying another quarter at Florida to graduate, the experience was worth the trip.

Ana and I arrived in London, en route to South Africa, on the morning that Princess Anne was to marry Mark Phillips. I was tired from the all-night flight and wanted to sleep, but Ana craned her neck from the window of our room at the Westbury Hotel, searching for a glimpse of the royal carriage as it went by.

"Can you imagine that?" she later said. "Maybe you and Jimmy will get married in a royal carriage?" I was too tired to savor Ana's dreams, but South Africa took me a step closer in that direction.

Ana and I had been invited to stay at the home of Peter Gordon in the Hyde Park section of Johannesburg. Jimmy arrived from London with a friend, Spencer Segura, several days later, and was due to stay with another family. That night at dinner, the Gordons invited Jimmy to stay at their house.

"We have five bedrooms, there's plenty of room," they said. "You're more than welcome to stay."

Jimmy liked the idea but said he was concerned about hurting the feelings of his hosts. He had already dropped off his bags and didn't want to offend anyone.

"Well, let's just get the bags back," Mr. Gordon said.

At 12:45 that night, Jimmy, Ana and I, along with the Gordons, snuck back to the house where Jimmy was supposed to be staying. We shut off the headlights, turned off the motor and coasted into the driveway, in a scene reminiscent of a movie mystery. Jimmy had a key, opened the door, ran into the house, repacked his bags and left a note: "Sorry I won't be able to stay with you, but thank you very much for your hospitality."

It was an exciting week. Ana and I stayed in one room. Jimmy and Spencer stayed in the room next to us. Every morning, the maid would wake us for breakfast. Then all of us journeyed to the courts together. At night, Ana and I would lie in bed and plan my wedding.

"You're going to be the bridesmaid," I told her. "Jeanne's going to be my maid of honor."

With everyone so happy, it's no wonder that Jimmy and I swept the singles titles that week. Jimmy beat Arthur Ashe, who was visiting South Africa for the first time and creating his own news. Evonne was top-seeded for the tournament, but I won, 6–3, 6–3. For me, however, the highlight of the week did not come on the tennis court but at a diamond factory.

South Africa is the diamond capital of the world. Selecting your own engagement ring at a factory sounded almost unreal, but Jimmy and I went and agreed on a ring with a large diamond in the middle and a sapphire on each side. He used part of his $7,000 earnings from the tournament to pay for the ring and even got down on his knees and slowly slipped it on my finger after we picked it up at the factory.

"I want to do this properly," he said.

My mom spotted the ring on my finger at the airport. "I don't think you should let your father see it just yet," she said.

"Why not? We're engaged," I said.

My mom wasn't convinced. "Don't you think that Jimmy should talk to Dad before you announce your engagement? Everybody is going to be talking, there's going to be the press. I think the nice thing to do is to have Jimmy talk to Dad."

That night, Jimmy and I waited until everyone had left Holiday Park. He stood outside the office, sweating bullets, petrified at the prospect of talking to my dad. For someone who was so fearless on the court, Jimmy seemed overly timid.

"Well, here goes," he said, sounding like Jackie Gleason preparing to saunter offstage. Jimmy walked in, they chatted quietly, and I half-expected to see Jimmy trudge out, head bowed, and beaten. I could almost see him saying something like, "Well, it won't work for now" or "Maybe we'd better wait." But after about ten minutes, Jimmy came out, all smiles, bouncing on his toes. "It's all right," he said.

7 • The Love Double

During a rain delay on the third day of the 1980 Wimbledon championships, two very nice English mums and an American woman were passing the time under their "brollies" on the top row of Court 3 at the All England Club. Their rainy-day subjects, I later learned, were Jimmy Connors and Chris Evert.

The three women had decided, after much discussion, that Jimmy was a modern-day Peter Pan—full of life, excitement, loving all the children and chasing away the Captain Hooks of tennis by making every match a new adventure. I was the perfect Wendy, they reasoned, rescued by Peter from the humdrum world of childhood, taught fun in tennis Never Never Land and totally devoted to Peter.

Anyone who sat through the 1974 Wimbledon tournament must have thought he or she was witnessing a fairy tale, as if destiny had swept Jimmy and me into Never Never Land.

I believe in destiny. While practicing and winning tournaments as a junior, I felt that I was head and shoulders above most of the girls my age because I practiced harder than they did. Something wonderful would happen if I improved, I told myself, and my temperament and determination would help me succeed. My career also seemed blessed by occasions that defied logic. I caught Margaret Court with a virus and surprised her in Charlotte shortly after she completed her Grand Slam in 1970. Then came the endless summer of '71 that wound up at Forest Hills. Bumping into Jimmy at Wimbledon in 1972 eased some of the uncertainties of traveling abroad and started us on a romantic road. But nothing rivaled Wimbledon '74 because it happened so unexpectedly. When events finally came together, who's to say it wasn't fate?

I never thought I had a chance to win Wimbledon that year. I had not beaten Billie Jean or Evonne on grass courts, I was engaged to Jimmy for seven months, but didn't know how it would affect us at a major championship like Wimbledon.

My decision to play some Virginia Slims events for the first time earlier that year boosted my confidence. I wasn't exactly chummy with the other women, but at least I rounded first base in some relationships. During 1971, 1972 and 1973, I was considered a loyalist to the USTA circuit.

After splitting the first two finals with Billie Jean—losing in San Francisco but winning in Mission Viejo—the tension seemed to ease slightly in 1974. I still wasn't "one of the girls," but playing doubles with Billie Jean bridged some troubled waters. We teamed and beat Françoise Durr and Betty Stove, 6–4, 6–2, in San Francisco, and I began to look forward to doubles as more than an afterthought. It softened the all-out pressure I exerted in singles.

In some cases, my views of players shifted as I got to know them. Betty Stove of the Netherlands intimidated me at first with her size. At 6 feet 1 inch, she was strong and rangy, with a first serve that could knock you down and an impulsive, hard-to-read serve-and-volley game. Off the court, Betty was thoughtful, practical and independent enough to have been elected president of the Women's Tennis Association. If she had dedicated herself 100 percent to tennis, she might have been one of the game's greatest players, but there were other interests that counted as enjoyment to her, and this ambivalence was probably the reason why she could be funny one day and withdrawn the next.

I won the S&H Tennis Classic final in Fort Lauderdale from Kerry Melville of Australia on an injury default. Kerry was quiet, friendly and fun loving. If you teased her, she would blush a lot; over the years, I enjoyed telling her dirty jokes just to see her face turn red.

Nothing fazed Olga Morozova, which again proved that you can't judge people by stereotypes. Soviet athletes were supposed to be intense and mysterious, but Olga was delightfully free-spirited, considerate, a better athlete than tennis player. She was married to an engineer but kept her maiden name, grew up on clay courts but preferred serve-and-volley and spoke better English than some Americans. After she beat Rosie in three sets and Billie Jean, 7–6, 6–1, at the Slims event in Philadelphia, one local writer became infatuated with her. He had watched her all week, listened to her postmatch press conference and couldn't understand how she could play so well, coming from a country that thumbed its nose at tennis.

"Are there any places to play tennis in Russia during the winter?" he finally asked.

Olga gave the writer an incredulous look. "You think we come from the moon?" she said. Everyone at the news conference roared.

Nancy Richey was my earliest nemesis because our baseline styles were so similar. On the court, Nancy seemed serious, almost grim. I had heard stories about how tough her father had been on Cliff and her—sometimes making them practice four to five hours a day. "Is Nancy as serious as she comes across?" I asked Billie Jean, the week after Billie had beaten her, 6–3, 7–5, in the final at Akron, Ohio.

"Nancy is great," Billie Jean said. "She loves to have fun and laugh a lot. You just have to know her." Sure enough, in the locker room a few weeks later, after I finished telling a joke to Billie Jean, Nancy was laughing so hard she almost fell down. Had I misjudged Nancy? Seeing her smiling and laughing made me want to know her better.

Françoise Durr made everyone laugh. "Frankie," as everyone called her, was easily the best French player in several decades, and her personality was as colorful as the crazy, unorthodox backhand that she hit with her right arm out in front of her body like a board. Frankie continually talked to herself on the court; the fact that you couldn't tell whether it was English, French or a combination made her comments more amusing.

"What did she say?" I found myself repeating, each time Frankie would curse an unforced error or bad call. Frankie never held anything inside. The structure of her face and her strawberry-blond hair and breasty figure also appealed to the crowds. In the locker room, whenever Frankie started talking, the laughs followed. Not that she would say something funny all the time: It was just the way it sounded.

"Dees game, I can't stand it!" she would shout, arms waving like those of an orchestra conductor. On some occasions, Frankie even had her terrier dog, Topspin, carry her racquets onto the court. The women enjoyed mimicking Frankie, but they couldn't match her.

Val Ziegenfuss and Ingrid Bentzer never won any major titles, but they were two of the players who first accepted me and became close friends. Val was like an older sister who could make me laugh and still offer advice. Her father had encouraged her to pursue tennis, as my dad had done, she was athletic, and we compared parental notes. An original member of the Slims tour, she enjoyed socializing after matches, and Jimmy and I often doubled with Val and her dates at different stops.

Ingrid was Sweden's No. 1 woman player. Bright, attractive and uninhibited, Ingrid said what she felt, even if it meant bruising a few toes. She also had a marvelous sense of humor, which came across in her contention that you could always tell whether a player had any sexual involvement the previous night if she arrived in the locker room with a glow. I told Ingrid that she always seemed to glow.

The sisterhood was important because the women's tour was a tough place to meet a man. On the men's circuit, there were enough good-looking girls in different cities to satisfy a sixty-four player draw, but most of the men hanging around the women's tour weren't the type you wanted to marry. One gynecologist in Chicago had a thing for Virginia Wade; he thought her deep, green eyes and dark hair were sexy and feline.

The doctor got so excited when Virginia beat Rosie in three sets in the Chicago Slims final that he begged a tournament official for an autographed picture. Of course, the official was only too willing to oblige as a public relations gesture.

"Just tell Virginia if she ever needs any medical services, I'll be happy to help in the future—free of charge," the doctor said. You can imagine the teasing Virginia took in the locker room after that story got around.

Learning to cope with peers and the adult world required adjustments for all players. Despite being ambitious and career oriented, Billie Jean was married at twenty-one. "I can't believe that I got married then," she would say, when I brought up my November wedding date with Jimmy. "But it was the pressure society put on me at the time. You know, a woman should get married."

At fifteen, after I beat Margaret Court, some members of the media already were asking how long I planned to play. I would say, "No longer than age twenty-one. Then for sure, I want to get married and have kids." But with Virginia Slims offering $935,000 in prize money for its eighteen tournaments in 1974, young players weren't in a hurry to settle down.

I came into the 1974 Wimbledon championships with a string of thirty straight singles victories that had spanned six tournaments. Two of those were the French and Italian Opens, which I had lost in 1973. This time, I beat Martina, 6–3, 6–3, in the final at Rome, and Olga, 6–1, 6–2, in Paris for my first French title.

What a difference one year made! In 1973, I was impatient, immature and stifled by my mom's presence. But an engagement romanticized Europe in the spring, and Janet Haas, an old friend, was back on the scene with her racquet and tape recorder:

Janet: "In Rome, Italy, I'm gazing upon a beautiful day with practically a pretty good crowd. I'm watching the finals between Chris Evert of Fort Lauderdale, Florida, and Martina Navratilova of

Czechoslovakia. To my left, I've got a very fine specimen of a gent, Mr. James Connors. Say a few things to my fans, James."

James: "I'm looking forward to a real fine match out there. It's a little hard for me to concentrate on the tennis when there's such, when the motion of the women moving around out there just thrills me to death. So the tennis is just secondary. Everything else I'm looking forward to very closely through my binoculars."

I don't know whether Janet, who was a fine player, secretly yearned to be Rona Barrett, Barbara Walters or Howard Cosell, but she was always in the right spot:

Janet: "Now I'm standing with Chrissie Evert, the winner of the Italian Championships. Just threw down her racquets, got her roses and her money. You got everything, Chris? How does it feel, Chris, right there in the locker room, in the showers, with all the sweat rolling off your face?"

Me: "Where? I'm not sweating at all."

Janet: "Don't you want to talk to me now? How do you think you played?"

Me: "I don't know. I'm still not comfortable on this stuff."

Janet: "You're not comfortable on clay? That's like oranges not growing well in Florida."

Sometimes Janet caught me when I couldn't get away:

Janet: "Here we are sitting in this Alitalia plane. We're on our way to gay Paree. We've just had a little snack. Chris, say a few things that we'll remember in twenty years."

Me: "Last night, I had to go to the bathroom so bad. I felt so sick. I figured I either had to go to the bathroom or throw up."

Janet: "In twenty years, we're going to remember how badly you had to go to the bathroom."

Me: "I had one hour of sleep. Jimmy said it was my nerves because the tournament was over and I was nervous, so he gave my stomach a massage. To my surprise, it didn't help. I'd just like to say that I've been eating very sensibly today. I've had six cookies, six cups of tea and three pieces of bread. I should be okay by tonight."

Janet: "I certainly hope so, Chris, because I wouldn't want to be following you all the way to the john tonight."

Wimbledon has a way of bringing everything into focus, and I could just as easily have lost in the opening round. Lesley Hunt was my opponent and we waited through the usual rain delays and then battled to 9–all in the third set before darkness forced a postponement. It was almost like a page from one of those adventure novels where the outcome is in doubt, and the story is "to be continued." The next morning, Jimmy and I had a crisp practice session, and it paid off because I broke Lesley's serve when the match resumed, held my own and won in six minutes, 8–6, 5–7, 11–9, after fretting all night.

Jimmy also had his early problems. He went four sets with Ove Bengtson of Sweden in the first round, and then outlasted Phil Dent of Australia, 10–8, in the fifth. If Wimbledon had used tie breakers then for a fifth set, who knows whether Jimmy would have survived?

It was a strange Wimbledon. The daily BBC telecasts of the tournament were periodically blacked out because of labor strikes, and it rained so long and so often that play on six of the ten days began at noon instead of two o'clock. Ilie Nastase received service one day holding an umbrella and was chastised by the umpire, but everyone thought Ilie made his point.

The wet weather didn't dampen my spirits. Jimmy and I were together, I was playing well, we tried to watch each other's matches and then Billie Jean and Evonne suddenly were out of the tournament on the same day. Was somebody on my side up there in those dark clouds? How else could Kerry Melville have beaten Evonne on grass and Olga have snapped Billie Jean's fifteen-match Wimbledon streak? It was as if the silver plate were being offered to me on a silver platter, if I wanted to fight for it.

Jimmy and I had thought of the possibility of winning Wimbledon together, but we weren't obsessed with it, and the oddsmakers had us at 33 to 1 as a "love double." Bill Riordan, who split about $20,000 with Pancho Segura from betting on

Jimmy in singles, never got around to betting on us, but others did.

"Wouldn't it be great if we could both win it?" I said to Jimmy over dinner one night in The Rib Room of the Carlton Towers. Jimmy had taken me there on our first date two years before, and we decided to celebrate anniversaries at the same spot whenever possible.

I beat Kerry in the semifinal and then had a pretty good suspicion that I could win the title after Olga ended Virginia Wade's hope of reaching her first Wimbledon final. I had never lost to Olga, we had taken the Italian and French Open doubles together, and I knew her game well. I won, 6–0, 6–4.

My dad still ranks Wimbledon '74 as the highlight of my career. When I phoned him in Florida after the match, he was sobbing, so choked up emotionally he could barely talk. To my dad, Wimbledon was the pinnacle of the sport. He had never expected his children to achieve this distinction, and his tears that day told me how much it meant to him.

Jimmy beat Ken Rosewall in the men's final, 6–1, 6–1, 6–4, and went on to his best year as a pro. "Nobody will ever have a year like I had in 1974," he has said on numerous occasions. Some people have suggested that Jimmy's success was due to our engagement, but he was far ahead of everyone that year.

Jimmy and I coordinated our schedules as much as we could to be together. Before Wimbledon, we saw each other on the average of about ten days a month. I was committed to the Virginia Slims circuit and Jimmy was on the men's tour. We would play two weeks and then have a rest week; if I wasn't playing, I tried to go with Jimmy to his tournaments, and he used his rest weeks to meet me.

I had always been attracted to outgoing types because it took that kind of man to bring out the fun in me. Jimmy brought me out of my shell and never allowed our relationship to affect his attitude. Some people saw Jimmy as outspoken, controversial and at times even vulgar with his blunt language or flamboyant gestures on the court. When we were alone, he was a quiet gentleman, someone who treated women almost as if they were fragile—opening car doors, sending flowers, writing letters. Most men are not like that, and his sensitivity may have come from his close relationship with his mother, yet few outsiders saw that tenderness; on the court, Jimmy was feisty to the end. To reveal such sensitivities, in his mind, may have been construed as a weakness.

It wasn't until after the women's final that I learned about the Wimbledon Ball. Mary Hardwick Hare, a former British player of the 1930s, told my mother about the proceedings and the first dance of the two singles champions.

"If I'm too tired, do I have to go?" I asked. My mother listened to Mary explain the tradition and ceremony attached to the affair and its importance. After Jimmy beat Rosewall, I rushed back to Kings Road, bought a dress I liked and then hurriedly found some modish stilt shoes. High heels were "in" at the time, so I picked out these shoes with skinny, six-inch heels. There's no way I would ever wear them now because they're too dangerous, but at the time, I thought they would make me look taller.

Two hours before the ball, I was informed I had to write a speech. That's when panic set in. I've always considered myself a good debater, but I'm not comfortable making speeches at formal affairs. It's much easier for me to sit in a press room after a match and mull over a question than to deliver a talk in front of several hundred people. Most of the time, the speeches at the Wimbledon Ball are little more than thanking the committee, your parents and friends. Janet Haas even wrote a few of my speeches at some tournaments. But committee members are sensitive about all aspects of a player's involvement—from conduct on the court to appearing at an awards ceremony or banquet. Jimmy learned this at Wimbledon in 1977 when the Centre Court crowd booed him after he skipped the opening-day Parade of Champions for the centennial celebration. John McEnroe also got a dose when the committee rejected his membership into the All England Club after he skipped the 1981 champions' dinner. John's absence didn't make my job any easier at that dinner, as an American champion.

Fortunately, Jimmy kept me loose at my first Wimbledon Ball. We slipped notes to each other behind the back of Sir Brian K. Burnett, the chairman of the All England Club, who was seated between us.

"Look at that blond lady over there," Jimmy wrote. "Watch her twitch when she blinks."

Before I got up to give my speech, I passed Jimmy a note that read, "I'm sweating so badly." He went into one of his impish smiles, got down with his left hand on the table and then scribbled back, "Keep cool."

I survived the speech. The band leader then asked what song we preferred for the first dance. "Play whatever you want," we told him.

The band played "The Girl That I Marry," everyone clapped, and Jimmy's boyish grin returned. If it had been a traditional fairy tale, Jimmy and I would have waltzed into the sunset and lived happily ever after, but this is a true story.

• • •

The conversation lasted from ten in the evening until four in the morning. I don't recall what the bill was for a six-hour long-distance telephone call from Denver to Los Angeles, but talking to Jimmy that September night, five weeks before our November 8 wedding date, was a lot more traumatic than losing to Evonne in the final of the $50,000 Denver Virginia Slims event.

It was not a matter of falling out of love as much as coming to grips with reality. Jimmy and I wanted to be with each other as much as possible, we were in love, our world was giving, sharing and loving. When we talked on the phone, separated by thousands of miles, there was hurt in our hearts because we weren't together. But after the Open, which Jimmy won again over Rosewall, we suddenly had to deal with different priorities. On the one hand was the marriage and looking for an apartment in Los Angeles. Then there were the future plans, like Jimmy's "Heavyweight Championship of Tennis" matches for 1975 and my Slims circuit. How could we fit all the pieces in place?

The discussions about what we were going to do with tennis after marriage were the most sensitive. Would I stop playing, have children and travel with Jimmy? Would I resume playing after children? Would we travel together or alone? How much did tennis mean to us? How would our relationship be structured? Could I be comfortable at home knowing Jimmy was on the road?

If Jimmy and I had been older and more mature, we might have been able to weed through these details. But our love wasn't secure enough to know that over the years we would be with each other for the rest of our lives, and we were only able to deal with what was happening to us now. Talking long distance only impersonalized the relationship.

"Do you think that maybe we should put this off a little bit?" I finally asked on the phone that night from Denver. It had taken me hours to summon up the courage to even bring up the subject.

"What do you think?" Jimmy replied.

I wasn't sure how to answer. If I said, "Yes, let's go on with the wedding, we can guts it out," it might be rushing in with my heart. If I said, "No, I think we should postpone it," Jimmy might take it as a copout.

"I don't know if we're ready," I stammered.

"I agree," Jimmy said. "What next?"

"Well, maybe if we could postpone the wedding for a little bit, like a month."

"I think that's a good idea."

Before leaving for Houston, I phoned my parents. My mother had planned to send out two hundred wedding invitations that day. "We called it off," I began.

My mom seemed more relieved than angry. "Your father and I didn't want to tell you, but we both thought that you were too young. Don't worry about the invitations. I haven't sent them out. You have plenty of time. If you really love each other, things will work out."

It's almost impossible to keep a secret in tennis. So much of the sport is spent with peers, on and off the court. The media are also much more intimately involved because tennis, with its country club roots, has always stressed a social side.

I stayed with my aunt and uncle, Bob and Joan Galbraith, the next week in Houston. The postponement might have slipped by unnoticed, but during a postmatch interview, a writer asked offhandedly whether the wedding was still on for November 8.

"Actually, we've postponed it," I said, trying to be honest but hoping to nullify any theatrics.

My response floored everyone. "Oh!" the writer blurted, too stunned to add anything else. Jeanie Brinkman's eyes almost popped out of her head. As the new promotional director for the Virginia Slims tour, she knew what loomed from that remark. Sure enough, the wire services leaped on the story. Ana Leaird was sunbathing at her apartment building in Gainesville when a girl walked up and told her the news. Ana had just mailed shower invitations the preceding day and couldn't believe the report until she phoned my mother.

Jeanie was more confused than shocked. She had just joined the Slims circuit several weeks before and was unprepared for this public relations jolt, but convinced me to hold a separate press conference to avoid further wild speculation.

"The media requests are getting out of hand," she said. "Let's just hold one press conference, answer questions and get it out of the way."

I reluctantly agreed. The only place Jeanie could find was a motel suite, where the decor—hot pink and dark blue— seemed more suited for a lovers' rendezvous than Meet the Press. The bed in the suite was on a pedestal, encircled by chiffon. "Cheap Las Vegas," Jeanie said afterward.

I tried to stress that Jimmy and I were only postponing the wedding, but the reporters wanted more. Did this mean the engagement was off? How would this news affect my tennis? Who fired the first shot? Would I start seeing other men? I didn't have any specific answers because I didn't know what was ahead. As far as I was concerned, the engagement wasn't over, and my tennis was still important.

Ana phoned from Florida, but I was too exhausted after the conference to say anything more than apologize for not having told her. Years later, Ana would tell me that she had sensed things were not going completely well between Jimmy and me but wrote it off as "prenuptial nerves." Janet Haas said she saw problems at Jimmy's victory party after the U.S. Open. I was at one end of the table, she recalled, and Jimmy was at the other, surrounded by Bill Riordan, Pancho Segura and Mrs. Connors. "There was never enough room for everybody at that point," Janet said.

I took off the engagement ring in Houston. Strangely enough, I won the Slims tournament that week. I don't know if the personal adversity caused me to shift my focus more to tennis, but I played purposefully. One event that shaped some of my thinking that week was the unexpected death of Evonne's father, a tragedy that forced her to default our semifinal. Hearing that news, and knowing how grief-stricken she must have been so far away from home, made me rethink my own crisis. I labored against Virginia in the final, but still won, 6–3, 5–7, 6–1.

Two weeks later, the next time Jimmy and I were together, I gave him back the ring. "I'd rather you have this since you bought it," I told him.

Postponing the marriage indefinitely and returning the ring were painful. If I had brooded over what had happened, it could have had a disastrous effect on my career. I wasn't happy, but I also knew that if Jimmy and I weren't ready for marriage, I owed it to myself to keep my mind and body moving in the right direction.

• • •

I've often been asked if I regretted not going to college and experiencing the educational and social benefits that that experience might have offered. In a sense, my college education began in January 1975 when I traveled alone on the Virginia Slims circuit.

Many kids find out more about themselves through life experiences than in a college classroom. A person who is independent must make decisions for himself or herself. Coming from a protected childhood, my parents were with me all the time and took the responsibility of handling my prize money, endorsements and practice schedules. I never went through a period when I had to sit down and say, "Okay, what kind of person am I?" Faced with answering that question, I would not have known because I had never even thought about it. But you learn about yourself when you are on your own. I had never made trial-and-error decisions because everything was done for me. I depended so much on my parents for emotional support and love and leaned on Jimmy for understanding. Starting the Slims circuit in 1975, my parents weren't with me. Jimmy and I had severed our relationship, and I was on my own. It meant going out of my way to make friends with other women on the tour, spend time with them, be giving with them, chat with them about their matches and their lives. Before, it was in and out of the locker room. I wasn't a full member of the tour, and my feelings were suppressed when sex or tennis politics were discussed.

I've always equated sex with love. I'm not in favor of one-night stands or sex just for its physical benefits. Sex is great if you really care for somebody, if you love him. But for the longest time I was shocked at off-color jokes. Even when Billie Jean and Rosie teased about Roger Taylor's good-looking legs, or other handsome players like Ilie Nastase, John Newcombe or Adriano Panatta, it took me a while to join in. But you can't hide on the circuit.

At the second Virginia Slims tournament of 1975 in Sarasota, Florida, I was in the interview room when a television reporter flashed a camera in front of me. "How do you feel about Jimmy and his new girl friend now?" she asked.

I felt like fainting. It had never entered my mind that Jimmy was even interested in another girl. I was not dating. How could he go off so soon after we had just broken up? "New girl friend?" I said. "I don't believe it until I've heard it from him."

I tried to put the episode out of my mind, but the next morning, Janet Haas and Kristien Kemmer Shaw reluctantly handed me the front page of the *St. Petersburg Times*. "You'll probably get some flak about it," Janet said, revealing the picture of Jimmy and "Mean Mary Jean," a bouncy actress, who had been featured in Dodge commercials. The article quoted her as saying they had been out on about ten dates; Jimmy had worn my engagement ring around his neck every time they had gone out, but she never thought anything about it, and they had a "very special kind of relationship."

Jimmy called later that week and said he had met her once or twice at a restaurant and that her uncle had tried to fix them up. "Don't worry about it," he reassured. "She's just trying to get publicity." Naive at the time, I believed him.

The tour became my foundation against uncertainties. I could not escape hurt and loneliness but could come out of the experience with Jimmy stronger and more mature, I told myself. If you can solve things in a tough situation and survive, your character is strengthened. I was happy with my tennis, was dedicated and single-minded enough about playing well to come from match point down and beat Evonne in the semifinals of a Slims event in Houston that spring; I rallied from being down 7–6, 5–0, 40–15 against Nancy Richey in the U.S. Clay Court semifinals that summer and from a set down against Evonne in the U.S. Open final.

I play better when I'm down because I'm more aggressive, more daring, looser. I lose matches or play my worst when I'm tentative. If I'm down close to a match point, it almost becomes a challenge. I'll say to myself, as if I'm talking to my opponent, "Okay, you have me right now, let's see you finish out the match." It might take one or two points for an opponent to hesitate or be tentative. When I can tell she is nervous, my confidence shoots up, and it's time to totally zero in.

That's what happened in the Houston match against Evonne. I had called my dad before the semifinal and asked if he could fly to Houston for the match. "I'd really like you to come," I pleaded. He agreed, but Evonne was experiencing one of her inspired days when the winners flowed off her racquet almost magically. I felt totally frustrated, fell behind, 1–4, in the third set and wanted to tank. Then, on the changeover, I looked in the stands, saw my dad and knew how nervous he must have been from the long tension-filled match. With high blood pressure, he didn't need further complications. Yet here I was, thinking about throwing away a match after I had begged him to come. "You've got to guts it out," I told myself. "You're down, but you just can't roll over."

From 3–5 in the third, I got to 6–all and then gutted out a decisive sudden-death tie breaker, 5 points to 3. Walking off the court with Jeanie Brinkman toward the press room felt almost as satisfying as winning Wimbledon. I hadn't given in to my first instincts and had fought back from match point against my toughest rival on the tour. When I saw my dad waiting for me in a corner of the press room, I broke into tears, as if I had lost the match. I'm not a crybaby, but crying is a cleansing process, an outlet that I was ashamed of as a child. I'm not ashamed anymore.

The match with Evonne finished at around eleven that night. I was so excited I couldn't fall asleep until almost two in the morning and then woke up at eight for the early afternoon final with Margaret Court. But the adrenaline was pumping so fast that I ran through Margaret, 6–3, 6–2, in the final.

I won four of the nine Slims tournaments that season and stopped Martina, 6–4, 6–2, in Los Angeles for the $40,000 first prize in the tour final. I also beat her at the Family Circle Cup and the Italian and French Opens, but my most enjoyable moments that spring came as a "coach" for the first "Ladies of the Evening" match.

You won't find the "Ladies of the Evening" results in any USTA Media Guide. For the women on the tour, however, it became as eagerly awaited as a Virginia Slims final, an event that brought out the brightest, the best and most bizarre in everyone.

The idea blossomed during the Family Circle Cup at Amelia Island, Florida, in 1975. Many people now take credit for starting it, but Rosie Casals was more instrumental than anyone in getting the two "ladies of the evening," Peachy Kellmeyer and

Vickie Berner, into a "championship match." Both were former players turned tour directors, whose after-hours reputations (Peachy with Michelob, Vickie with Dewar's Scotch) had reached legendary proportions.

Of course, Rosie could not just have Peachy and Vickie play a routine match. There had to be other conditions: On court changeovers, for example, Peachy was required to take a swig of beer while Vickie downed Scotch. Rosie also decided that everyone must be dressed appropriately, so she and Shari Barman, a friend, bought "Ladies of the Evening" T-shirts and acrylic pants. To make matters more interesting, Rosie got one-dollar donations from the crowd for prize money. Billie Jean, naturally, was the umpire, wearing two pairs of glasses, and Martina and I were designated as "coaches."

No two people ever looked less like Ion Tiriac or Robert Lansdorp. I wore an orange baseball cap with the peak backward, horizontal striped socks, hoop earrings and a T-shirt with the words "Bird Legs' Coach" across the front. "Bird Legs" was Vickie's nickname.

All of the players were involved. Betty Stove and Frankie Durr were ball girls, and others called lines. When Vickie started winning, the linesmen simply ignored her serves and called faults.

I had a great time. I bandaged Vickie's knees, toweled her off, pinned up David McGoldrick's size 48 boxer shorts, and even played bartender. We had a cookout after the match, which Vickie won, and then decided that "Ladies of the Evening" would become a permanent fixture on the circuit.

The following year, we staged it as a doubles event in Los Angeles, after the Slims final. Nobody could remember much from that party after eating Rosie's brownies. In 1977, we rented the discothèque at the Hilton Hotel in Philadelphia and put on a series of hilarious skits and dance numbers. I was the master of ceremonies at that bash, in a Groucho Marx costume. Rosie served her famous brownies that night too.

Rosie, Billie Jean, Kristien, Janet Haas and others tried to talk me into dating other people, but I had no desire. It was like, Oh, God, I have to start over again, make small talk with a guy, get to know him all over again. Even though Jimmy had seemingly bounced back well from our broken engagement, my scars were slow to heal. I went to dinner a few times with Trey Waltke, a player, but our dates were informal. I still thought I loved Jimmy, still saw potential in the relationship, but was too much of a chicken to sit in the tea room at Wimbledon in 1975, and my absence became more noticeable when Jimmy showed up for my semifinal against Billie Jean with Susan George, the actress.

Each time Jimmy made the headlines with another woman, I took it very personally. If he had any feelings or sensitivity, I would tell myself, why couldn't he be more discreet? He must know how publicity hurts. Even if he and Susan were only "friends," why the flaunt? I didn't have any claims on Jimmy, and I didn't know what his relationship was with Susan. It wouldn't have bothered me if he had used discretion, but the Centre Court was the first time people had seen them together.

There's been a lot of speculation about what happened that afternoon, and whether I suddenly collapsed after leading 3–0 in the final set and lost six games in a row after seeing them together. I never actually saw Jimmy and Susan walk into the players' section. My mom, dad and uncle Chuck were seated in the Friends Box, along with Janet Haas and Martina. It was my dad's first trip to Wimbledon. I often looked up to the Friends Box for encouragement. It was more difficult to pick out people in the players' section, which is directly behind. I remember some commotion in the area at the time, but I didn't exactly see Jimmy and Susan. Maybe I wanted to block out the notion that they were there. I thought about them during the match—yes, during the match—visual pictures and imaginative speculation about what their relationship was like. I've always been a dreamer. I may be realistic and practical about the way I live my life, but I dream a lot, and my dreams are very private and positive. When I first dated John, I dreamed about what would happen to us, physically and emotionally. I'm more aggressive than cautious in my dreams, probably because I'm not worried about winning or losing a point. If I saw myself making love to John in my dreams, it was only because I wanted it to happen.

On the court that day against Billie Jean, I was more upset with myself than with Jimmy. Did I lose the match because of him? His relationship with Susan was distracting, and I should have been able to close it out and rise above my emotional feelings. After the match, other players were more upset than I was about his grand entrance.

"How can he do that to you?" Rosie said that night at the Gloucester hotel. That the women cared was important; it was easy to take their loyalty for granted.

I didn't bother to stay for Jimmy's final with Arthur Ashe the next day. I could have played his game and taken a date into Centre Court, but what would that have proved? I was disappointed but not vindictive, and fate has a strange way of repaying dues. Jimmy lost the final to Arthur in one of the major upsets of the year.

"It served him right for dumping on you," Janet Haas tried to tell me. Janet and I listened to the match in the cockpit of a 747 flying home across the Atlantic. The pilot invited us to put on headphones and catch the BBC broadcast during the flight. I laughed each time the announcer said, "Well, there's no sign of Chris Evert in the stands."

"If they only knew," Janet said. "If they only knew."

8 · A Year to Remember

Jeanie Brinkman and I made our New Year's resolutions a few days early—in the back seat of a taxi in Washington, D.C.

"It's not going to be like last year," Jeanie promised. "We're going to spice things up this year."

"Like what?" I said, cheerful on a twenty-first birthday and eager for some excitingly fresh experiences.

"Well, let's make a list," Jeanie went on. "In all the cities we play, we'll figure out what we'd like to do and who we'd like to spend time with."

Jeanie had her Virginia Slims cities memorized. Houston, Washington and Chicago were interesting. But what could you do in Akron, Detroit or Sarasota? Jeanie could hardly wait to get to Los Angeles, the last stop. Visions of Burt Reynolds, Robert Redford, Clint Eastwood and other movie stars danced in her head.

"Robert Redford's gorgeous; but he's married," I said. The cab driver stared at us through his rearview mirror with a bewildered look. A couple of horny broads, he probably figured.

"What about Jack Ford?" Jeanie said. "Remember last year."

I wanted to forget as much as possible of 1975 except the few satisfying wins over Evonne. "Remember what?"

"When I got that call saying that Jack and Susan Ford wanted to meet you for lunch at the White House."

"Why didn't I go?"

"You mean, you forgot?" Jeanie's recall was unbelievable. She could recount whole conversations and even saved some of my handwritten notes for years. "That's when you told me you had a practice court at two o'clock in the afternoon and didn't think you'd have enough time. The White House calls, and Chris Evert is going to practice!"

I shuddered at the memory. Had I ducked that date to avoid post-Jimmy publicity? The cab neared our destination for the afternoon press conference. "Did I really say that?" I asked.

Jeanie smiled. "Listen, I made some elaborate excuse about you being tied up. Don't you remember that your sister Jeanne really wanted to go?"

"Well, maybe you can reciprocate and invite the Fords to watch the matches this year," I said.

"Would you go out with Jack if it could be arranged?"

One year ago, if Jeanie had posed that question, I would have turned her down. "Sure, why not?"

Jeanie was a first-class promotional director. The fact that she was stunning, with bright blue eyes, a slick figure and tailored clothes didn't hurt her image either. She also knew how to have a good time. The morning of the first Slims final in Houston several weeks later, Jeanie decided to throw a little brunch in her room. About a dozen of the players showed up, including Rosie, Olga and another Soviet player, Natasha Chmyreva. So did Martina and I, who just happened to be playing the final later that day.

"I don't know what I'm doing here," I announced, teasing Jeanie about the gobs of delectable food and drink she had ordered. "Usually I'm in my room throwing up before a final."

Everyone laughed and we had a joyous time. But I was never in the match against Martina and lost, 6–3, 6–4. I was so re-laxed that I couldn't bring myself to concentrate against a serve-and-volley player whose strongest surface was a Sporteze indoor carpet. Martina must have known how I felt. After the last point, we met at the net, shook hands and she said, "I'm sorry, Chris."

Jeanie also was upset. Later, she would say that she felt responsible for having initiated a party at the wrong time. I was angry, but the decision to attend had been mine, so I had to live with that choice and the knowledge that I simply couldn't divide commitments as well as others. What made the situation more touchy was that I had to return to the locker room, change clothes and play the doubles final with Martina as a partner, against Rosie and Frankie Durr.

The tension was still there. Although we were top-seeded, Martina and I were blitzed in the first set, 6–0, and lost the second, 7–5. After the match, Frankie's dog, Topspin, sauntered out to take her racquets off the court. Instinctively, Martina grabbed my racquet, put it in her mouth and walked off behind Topspin. I fell over with laughter; Martina's spontaneity had melted any ice from earlier in the day.

True to her New Year's resolution, Jeanie outdid herself in Washington. She talked to the White House press secretary and explained her plan to Jack Ford. "He understood and was absolutely charming," she reported back, confirming that Jack wanted to attend the matches and might even go out afterward.

Jeanie had thought about leaking the story to United Press International to repay a favor. But once the White House was involved, the news spread quickly enough. The day after we arrived, Jeanie received a call from the press secretary: Before the date, Jack wanted to meet me. Just routine, the secretary assured. So Jack and I huddled that afternoon for coffee after practice, got along fine and agreed that his appearance at the James Robinson Field House would probably be a bigger event than my first-round match against Kathy Kuykendall.

I never realized how much security surrounds the White House. The President of the United States obviously is well protected, but the arena that night seemed overrun with Secret Service officers pushing their little buttons and microphones. Jeanie's job was to greet Jack at the door of the arena, take him to the Virginia Slims box, sit with him during my match and relocate other box seat holders to make room for the Secret Service. The seat holders agreed to give up their places, but Jack's 1972 Jeep had conked out, so he was late and had to borrow his press secretary's car.

I waited in the locker room. Every few minutes, Jeanie ran in with reports that Jack had been in radio contact with the Secret Service and was at the junction of some highway.

"All right, he's here," she finally reported. "Perfect timing."

With such hype, how could I not be motivated? During one court changeover, I walked toward Jeanie and Jack, put my hand on my stomach and playfully mouthed the words, "I'm starving." It was hard to concentrate, but I won, 6–2, 6–1. Jeanie then told Jack that I would do a brief interview, and we could be whisked out a side door that would be surrounded by Secret Service officers. Surprisingly, Jack followed me into the interview room. Once inside, cameras started rolling and flashbulbs popped from every direction. Jack stood in the back of the room, but no one was interested in talking tennis. How had we met? Were we going out afterward, and if so, where? Would I meet the President? Did Jimmy know anything about this?

Jack handled the questions casually and comfortably, which put me at ease. He and I clowned for photographers, and then someone said, "Why don't you give her a kiss, Jack?" Of course, that picture made almost every newspaper the next day.

I quickly changed clothes and rehashed the evening's events. From a silly suggestion in a cab ride, the daughter of a tennis teaching professional was about to have dinner with the son of the President of the United States. It was the first time my world had expanded beyond the confines of tennis, and slipping on my new lynx coat added another glamorous touch to the evening. I was excited.

"Wait up for me," I told Jeanie, as Jack and I were herded out of the building. "I can't wait to talk to you."

Jeanie stayed up until one-thirty in the morning before Stephanie Johnson, a tour director, phoned her.

"I have a good friend who's in the Secret Service," Stephie explained. "We were supposed to have dinner tonight, but he just called and said he had been assigned to the Ford-Evert date, they're in the White House, haven't come out and show no signs of coming out for some time."

I slipped a note under Jeanie's door after returning to the hotel: "Jeanie, oh I'm so tired! We had a super neat dinner at a Mexican restaurant with a guy singing country music. We stayed there until 12:30!! then Jack invited me back to the White House where we listened to music. I got home at 4:00. Talk to you later."

The following month, *People* magazine reported that Jack and I "didn't agree on one thing the whole night" at Rocky Raccoon's Saloon in the Georgetown section of the city. Actually, Jack and I enjoyed each other very much that whole week. We went out almost every night, I slept until one o'clock every afternoon, practiced and then played my matches at night.

One evening, the Fords invited me for cocktails and dinner at the White House. It was just the four of us—Jack and I, and the President and his wife, Betty. We ate in a private dining room, and I remember thinking, "Doesn't the President have better things to do than dine with me?" Yet he was friendly, we talked about the women's tour and European cities. He was especially curious about the Russian players—what they were like, how they fit in on the circuit—and asked specifically about Olga.

"They travel with a coach and another man, who is probably security," I said. "There's a kind of secrecy because they have to watch what they say publicly. But Olga's something else. She belongs in our country. She's just great."

Betty Ford was very nice but didn't look well. She had undergone some health problems but never complained during our tour of the upstairs bedrooms.

Usually, Jack and I went out for dinner that week, but I saw my share of the White House. I was wandering around there after hours, in the middle of the night, while the rest of America slept. The President couldn't believe it either; you have to sign in and out of the White House so that the Secret Service can keep tabs on everyone. After the tournament, President Ford looked at the sign-in sheets for the week and told Jack: "I don't know how that girl won the tournament. When did she have time to sleep?"

Jeanie said she never saw me look so tired, but I felt great. I beat Betty Stove, Mima Jausovec, Sue Barker and Virginia Wade for the $15,000 first prize. Jack watched the final, and I overwhelmed Virginia, 6–2, 6–1.

Jack was different from any of the men I had dated. In high school, there were basically two types of guys—the ones who were attractive and played hard to get and the ones who were kind of drippy and chased girls. Jack was definitely in the first class—sensitive and picky about his girl friends. At 6 feet, with blond hair, beautiful eyes and a handsome face, Jack was a catch. For someone who had been around the political scene for so long, he was earthy, and was not embarrassed to ask questions about the women's tour.

Jack loved his father. He had the same spirited independence and intelligent nature, enjoyed the West and preferred skiing and nature to backroom politics. He also was more comfortable in dungarees and T-shirt than the formal clothes we wore to my first and probably only State Dinner.

Jack invited me to the State Dinner for Yitzhak Rabin, the prime minister of Israel, and I suddenly realized I had no appropriate dress for the occasion. Jeanie was in Philadelphia for the day, so I took the train there and bought a dress and shoes. The dress was a long, two-piece black outfit with spaghetti straps and a chiffon wrap that was blue-black and white. It cost $800, more than I had ever spent for a dress. Jack picked me up at the hotel that night with two Secret Service officers behind us, and we went in a limo to the White House. Photographers were waiting on the steps, and a guard suddenly grabbed my arm and formally escorted me inside. I looked around for Jack. He was behind, so I took his arm and we walked up the stairs. Was this really happening to me, I thought, or was Wendy back in Never Never Land again?

"Nice to see you again, Chrissie," President Ford said, nodding, as I shook hands with Mrs. Ford and him in the formal receiving line. The President smiled at Jack, and I wasn't sure if it was a Good Housekeeping Seal of Approval, a routine father-son exchange, or my imagination again getting the best of me.

Jack made me feel quite comfortable. Before dinner, he spotted Secretary of State Henry Kissinger among the one hundred invited guests. "When are you going to give me that little black book?" he asked. Kissinger, so the story went, was known as quite a lady's man as a bachelor and had kidded Jack about giving him his "little black book" after marriage.

"It's yours now," Kissinger replied, staring at me and then greeting me politely. Jack and I laughed. Kissinger was a sports fan, a soccer buff anyhow.

Jack sent me about twenty pictures from the dinner. Some of the photos taken by David Kennerly, the official White House photographer, were of President and Mrs. Ford, Jack and myself. Then there was this "darling" picture of me dancing with the President. I had trouble dancing with him, not because he was the President but because I was more accustomed to disco than waltzes and fox trots. After the President asked me to dance, saying, "Come with me, Jack doesn't dance," I had no clue as to what I was doing out there. I fumbled around, was almost embarrassingly pathetic because I couldn't catch on to the beat.

"Just follow me and you'll be all right," President Ford said, sensing that I was having problems and trying to sound fatherly. I'm certain the simple, tasteful quality of the affair was the result of the President's attitude. There were no pretensions or snobberies about him: You could see that he was a practical man with an all-American family. He actually seemed to enjoy being nice, and everyone was at ease despite the formalities.

The affair ended at about one-thirty in the morning. After the dignitaries departed and the President and Mrs. Ford left for bed, Jack and I raided the refrigerator. Actually, there were three refrigerators, but all we nibbled on were peanut butter sandwiches before going back to his room to listen to music.

The next day, around noon, I went to the White House and had breakfast with Jack and met Riva, his dog. "The most im-

portant female in Jack's life is his dog," *People* magazine later
wrote. Jack truly loved his dog, but I wasn't surprised: Riva
was just another escape from the notoriety he faced as a son of
the President. Later that day, we ran around the White House
grounds with Riva, and Jack drove me to the airport.

On the flight to New York, I was up in the clouds. How many
girls got to go to the White House except on guided tours? That
the whole affair happened at all was something of a mystery.
Jeanie called the White House after the tournament and
thanked the press secretary for the original invitation the previous year. The chance to reciprocate had worked out well, she
said.

"Chris was never invited to the White House," the secretary
stated.

"What are you talking about?" Jeanie said. "Of course she
was. I received this phone call. The man told me he was from
the White House and . . ."

"Oh, no, he's not doing it again."

"Doing what?"

The secretary then explained that a sort of semipolitical, ten-
nis-playing friend of the Fords who wanted to score points had
talked about how nice it would be to invite some players to the
White House, but that nobody had authorized any invitations
and . . .

I didn't care. The more I thought about my week in Washington, the better I felt. Jack was the first man I had dated since
high school who was completely out of tennis, who didn't know
or care about drop shots, net cords or match points. He had so
many other interests that it forced me to discuss more than who
was doing what on the circuit. Tennis players have very re-
stricted interests. I had been drawn into another world for the
first time, liked what I saw, and wanted more. My diary under-
scored this curiosity:

> *January 29, 1976*
> Last week was the most exciting week of my life. I met a very
> nice guy who made my stay in Washington fun. Not only was it fun
> but very meaningful and educating.

My newly formed friendship with Jack has added a new dimension to my life. I ended up with a special feeling for him. I really care about what he does with his life and career and if he's emotionally happy. I think he offers me so much. He's mentally stimulating and fascinating. He's really into nature and enjoys beer, country music, skiing, mountain climbing, fishing.

We communicated and talked so openly and honestly. His birthday is March 16. He doesn't want to get involved and tied down with any one girl until he can support her. He's got a girlfriend in Utah. He is a very tender, gentle person.

The whole thing started out as a publicity stunt for Virginia Slims and also because I was curious to go out with him. It didn't end up that way!

February 1
New York

Yesterday was a very mellow day for me. I woke up at 12 and found myself reading and writing, thinking and listening to music. I was really into myself and my thoughts. I enjoyed listening to Melissa Manchester. I then practiced from 3–4 and came back to read some more. We went to dinner at some small Italian restaurant with Bob Kain and his wife Muffy. Then we went to the play "Let My People Come" in the Village and left during the intermission. I had a sick, nauseous feeling in my stomach because it was so crude and they took sex and the human body for granted. The language was terrible and I didn't appreciate the quality or the theme behind it at all.

February 13
New York

As usual, I am leaving New York exhausted. It never fails, does it? I'm taking iron pills because my blood count was 12.5. Went to dinner with Jack, Kris and Rick to Andie's. The next night saw "Chicago" then went to Friday's for dinner—Jack and I sat and talked for a bit and then he brought me back.

I honestly don't know where our relationship is going. I want to get into my tennis career and not be lazy because I've been doing so many other things. There is nothing that would make me happier than to get married to someone and retire from tennis—but *not now*.

I know tennis and my freedom are the most important things to me now.

For the next three weeks, I am going to train hard, lose weight (aim for five pounds), eat good foods, (orange juice, meat, salad) in small quantities, *no* wine or alcohol, *no* smoking. I want to become thin and happy. When I get hungry—I am anxious, it is *all* emotional. I am in a weird predicament—one I've never quite been in before!! *I want to be free. . . .*

Kristien and Rick continue to be my "new family" and I love the both of them.

February 22
Detroit

I am on such a high right now it's a joke. I mean winning a tournament still gets to me, puts me in my best moods. . . .

TENNIS. I played hesitantly, cautiously, yucky all week up until Rosie. Confidence is the name of the game with me—when I'm hot, confident, no one can beat me. I find I just have to play a lot of tennis to reach my peak.

March 1
San Francisco

Another fulfilling, relieving win over Evonne in Sarasota. I think I may be getting her number. I was patient and gutty and didn't give up. . . . Played the way I love to play—aggressively. Dad and Clare came up Friday and got sick Sunday. Mrs. Ford gave me a call to wish me luck . . . Ana, Cathy and Janet all came up for the week. I must remember what a good friend Janet is.

I've never enjoyed being alone. It's not a fear of the unknown or an insecurity; I just feel more comfortable sharing things with friends and family. I come from a large family and shared a room with my sister Jeanne. Knowing someone is watching you work and supporting that effort can be a strong incentive, whether it's tennis or playing the piano at a recital.

Friendships carry certain commitments. Over the years, I've taken my share of lumps from Rosie Casals, Janet Haas, Jeanie Brinkman, Ana Leaird, Stephanie Tolleson, Lynda Carter, Billie Jean King and others. But friends are entitled to tap your conscience for not writing or calling, or for ignoring them or letting a personal date pass unnoticed.

I've always hated telephones and am not the type who will call five friends in one night and gab. To pick up the phone and say, "Hi, how are you doing?" is not my style, and not writing or returning calls is a shortcoming. Maybe it has something to do with the fact that I've never settled down. I move from city to city, and the next city is like a different part of my life. I'm much better when I'm not playing; I'll get back to people and call them if I'm not playing. But once I'm in a tournament, forget it; that's my number-one priority.

I've never wanted a great many friends, even though the opportunity was there. I'm content with the few whom I can love, trust and rely on. Fortunately, these people have also understood me, even when their advice and support weren't always what I wanted to hear.

Janet and Rosie have never allowed my status to shake their candor. During the European circuit in 1975, Janet and I spent so much time together that some of the Australian men players began teasing me about my sexual preference. Janet and I giggled through those tidbits, but I caught a poison-pen letter from her later that summer for failing to write or call.

"After being that close for two and a half months," she told me, "and then not even hearing a word from you, I'll be damned if I'm going to make the first move every time."

Friendships are not a one-way street. Janet showed up for the Virginia Slims event in Sarasota in late February 1976. We happily hashed out old and new items that week, from Jack to Jimmy, and I beat Evonne, 6–3, 6–0, in the final. After the tournament, recalling 1975, I dropped her a note:

Yes, I know, wonders never cease! I just wanted to tell you how great it was seeing you last week. Being and talking with you *always has* relaxed me and taken my mind off my pressures, so I'm not really surprised I won the damn thing. Ironically, it's YOU I always look over to and I know you understand the feelings I'm experiencing on the court, especially against Mrs. Cawley.

Now I don't want this to go to your head, but even if the selfish one here gets a little too involved with her own life to give you a call now and then, I still want you to know I value your friendship and as always *when we are together* we hit it off as great as ever.

I'm glad to see your life going so well—you deserved a break, believe me, and I think the best is yet to come for you. . . . Just be yourself because it's very appealing and honest.

I usually write funnier letters, but somehow I feel very serious. I hope we can get together more often. Definitely when I get home in a week, but this summer looks GRIM!

Thanks for coming to Sarasota, Haas—I hope it helped your frame of mind.

Love,
CE

Rosie says people who are close to me cater to me. "I don't like to be by myself either," she once said, during one of our long discussions about the loneliness on the tour. "But I know that I can. Can you?"

I can function alone. I've proved it with my discipline on and off the court, but other considerations color your attitudes. I once dreamed about being assassinated at Wimbledon. The dream was only fleeting, but the thought was terrifying enough to remain in the back of my mind for a long time. Then there was the flight from California to New York in 1976, after the Virginia Slims Championships. I'm not in love with flying—it's part of the job—but on one flight, a stocky, muscular man in a dark suit turned around in the first-class seat in front of me and began asking me questions about the trip. I was certain all he wanted was an autograph until he showed me his badge that said he was an agent for the FBI.

Was the man legitimate or a prankster? I nudged Jeanie, who was seated next to the window.

"What's going on?" she asked, reaching across and taking his badge. Jeanie knew that some men tried to bluff their way into hustling players with all sorts of schemes and lines.

"Well, I wasn't supposed to say anything," the man began, alternately glancing at Jeanie and me, "but seeing that we're on this flight now, I might as well tell you. Prior to boarding, we received an anonymous phone call that a famous person on this flight would be shot. We've gone through the list of passengers. Although there are a number of writers and directors from Hollywood on the flight, they're obviously not as well-known as someone like you."

The man stared directly at me. Later, Jeanie told me that my face turned white. I was shocked and immediately turned and glanced around the plane. Of course, everyone looked ordinary, but now these people wondered why I, a so-called celebrity, was studying them. So, of course, they stared back.

The agent tried to reassure us. "Don't worry, there are a number of agents on the plane. In fact, this happens quite often on the California–New York flights because there is every chance there will be someone well-known, although the fella who called would never have the list. He just assumes there is someone well-known."

"How often does this occur?" I asked nervously.

"About once a week."

"Do you think you know who it is?" I whispered. "Can you tell by their faces?"

Jeanie poked me. "Oh, don't be silly," she said. "You know there are people who recognize you, and that's the only reason they're looking at you."

I glared at Jeanie. "Okay, then," I said, challenging her sudden bravado. "Switch seats with me."

"There are a lot of things I would do for you," she said, "and I value your friendship greatly, but I'm not sure I'm going to give up my life for it."

Nothing happened during the flight, and I didn't expect Jeanie to give up her seat. Nor did I ever want to take advantage of her, particularly since she was in an official position on the women's tour. I tried, in whatever ways I could, to make her understand how much I appreciated her friendship.

After taking a three-week break, I returned to the Slims circuit in late March and lost my opening match in Boston to Dianne Fromholtz, 2–6, 6–3, 6–3. I had never lost in the first round as a pro and was lightheartedly casual during the match. I played without intensity, and seemed almost relieved after four straight tournament victories that winter.

"I kept waiting for the steel door to close," Jeanie said at dinner that night, "but it never happened. It was as if you didn't care if you won or lost."

"If you keep winning all the time," I said, "it's hard. I had those three weeks off, but I was only practicing an hour a day at home. I took a few too many things for granted."

I knew my first-round loss that night would ignite phone calls from everywhere. You can beg hotel switchboard operators to hold all calls, but somehow the phone will always ring at strange hours. To avoid the hassle, I asked Jeanie if I could spend the night in her suite. The next morning, I wanted to thank her, but flowers seemed too formal so I left a note:

> Thanks for letting me stay over. That was the most restful loser's night I ever had! I'll see you over at the courts. Somehow, I feel really eager to practice. Yes, I know I'm being boring now! Hope your meetings went well and you're in a good mood.

I'm not a sentimentalist. In fact, Rosie says that I'm too caught up in maintaining an image. "Who cares what people think of you? You're the one that's got to live your life," she'll argue. "They're not going to live it for you. If you want to do something or say something, say it."

Over the years, my friends have kept me on my toes, but that's what friends are for: The shots they hit pull you into reality.

• • •

It takes more than luck and talent to win a major tournament like Wimbledon or the U.S. Open. That was never more evident than in 1976, when my preparations and attitudes for those tournaments differed totally from my efforts of the past.

For one thing, winning Wimbledon became a goal, the first

time I had ever set such a lofty target for myself. I don't know whether it was a reaction to my finish on the Slims tour, but losses to Fromholtz in Boston and Evonne in Philadelphia and at the Slims final in Los Angeles (6–3, 5–7, 6–3) made me determined to remain No. 1. I returned to Fort Lauderdale, worked on my forehand with my father and became even more Wimbledon-conscious that spring with the Phoenix Racquets in World Team Tennis.

Team tennis began in 1974 and drew its share of jokes as more circus than tennis. But team tennis prepared me well for Wimbledon in 1976. I had signed a $125,000-a-year contract with the Racquets and selected Phoenix because I like the city, the weather, and had a friend on the team, Kris Kemmer Shaw, who had been traded from Denver to Phoenix the year before. Kris had positive words for Jimmy Walker, the owner, and Tony Roche, the coach.

The travel during team tennis was more hectic than on the Slims circuit. On Sunday, May 23, for example, we played a home match against the Boston Lobsters. The following day, we traveled to Indianapolis to play the Loves on Tuesday night. Wednesday, it was off to New York for a match that night against the Apples. On Thursday, we flew across the country to San Diego. Friday, it was back home to Phoenix. Saturday, May 29, we played a "home" match in Tucson against Los Angeles and then another home date with San Diego in Phoenix.

But there were also blocks of time that allowed us to practice, and about four weeks before Wimbledon, Tony sat me down and said he'd like me to win Wimbledon. It was during these periods that Tony brought the team in from ten in the morning until two in the afternoon for a mixture of two-on-one drills and doubles. Then Tony stayed with me for another ninety minutes and played sets. During that month, he taught me more about doubles than I had ever known. Most people look at my Wimbledon singles record, but anyone who checks the record books will find that I won the Wimbledon doubles in 1976 with Martina.

Tony was a great doubles player. He won five Wimbledon

doubles titles with his Australian countryman, John Newcombe, between 1965 and 1974 and knew as much about tactics
as strokes. "Why don't you mix up your returns from the forehand court?" he would harp. "Chip a few of those second
serves and come in."

I played team tennis doubles with Kristien. A left-hander,
she took the left, or backhand, court. I found that I could effec-
tively slice my forehand, chip my backhand and still come in.
Tony taught me how to poach, how to move over and not be
afraid at the net. We had serve-and-volley drills where I would
have to be inside the service line by the time I hit my first
volley. I had a tendency to take three or four lazy steps and
then hit my first volley three feet behind the service line. "You
have to be inside the service line," he stressed.

Tony's volleying technique was unsurpassed. He and I
would stand at the net and hit quick volleys to improve my
reflex and reactions. "Get the arms out straight," he urged,
showing me the proper form on the backhand volley. I was just
stabbing at the backhand volley with two hands; Tony taught
me an effective one-handed shot.

Almost all of the top women were in team tennis in 1976, and
many of the teams had Australian coaches—Tony in Phoenix,
Fred Stolle in New York, Rod Laver in San Diego and Owen
Davidson in Hawaii. Wimbledon was to be a proving ground
for their "pupils."

I arrived at the Gloucester hotel in London with confidence
after an 8–6, 6–3 victory over Virginia in the final grass-court
tuneup at Eastbourne. After beating Linda Thomas, 6–1, 6–1;
Elizabeth Coe,6–0, 6–0; Lesley Hunt, 6–1, 6–0; Betty Stove,
6–2, 6–2; and Olga Morozova, 6–3, 6–0, reaching the semis
proved easier than sitting in the tea room trying to deal with
the delicacies that can destroy you during Wimbledon. I had
shunned the tea room the previous year—too embarrassed to
face all the Jimmy talk; but my dignity was on the line this
time, and I also happened to be going out with Tom Gorman,
so I wasn't a lost lamb.

On the second day of the tournament, I was in the tea room

with Tom when a beautiful busty blonde approached our table wearing a tight T-shirt and even tighter jeans. I recognized her as Margi Wallace, a former beauty queen, who had been linked at times with such athletes as Jim Brown, Peter Revson and George Best and now supposedly was Jimmy's Wimbledon partner. Margi spotted Tom, who is one of the more handsome men on the tour, walked over and greeted him with a gaspy, "Oh, Tom, how are you doing? It's so nice to see you." She put her hands all over him, touched his shoulders and rubbed his neck. After Tom acknowledged her greeting, Margi gave me a teasingly sassy look, smiled and walked away.

I looked at Tom. "Here we go again," I said.

Tom and I enjoyed a pleasant rapport. In another time or place, if Jimmy had not come along, I might have been even more attracted to Tom. Someone once wrote that he was the "prince of players," and it's true: He's wonderfully thoughtful, low-key almost to the point of being spacey, with almost no ego at all. We went out five or six times during Wimbledon, and he was enjoyably unpredictable, a perfect outlet to the disciplined goals I had set for myself. But when it rains at Wimbledon, it pours, and not just liquid drops. No sooner had Margi rubbed my nose in the turf than Gloria Connors walked in. For an instant, I wasn't even sure it was Mrs. Connors because she had dyed her hair a different color, which Curry Kirkpatrick of *Sports Illustrated* described as "Rhonda Fleming maroon." Curry does have a way with words.

Even after Jimmy and I broke our engagement, I always felt Mrs. Connors liked me. Did she consider me the wholesome all-American middle-class Catholic alongside some of Jimmy's more flashy women, or was I still the tiny tot in the back seat of Jimmy Evert's car? I didn't know, but there she was, standing in front of me, telling me how much I had matured. After Margi, did I really need that?

Curry wrote that I "scrunched up" my nose and blushed at the meeting. If I blushed, it was because I was so shocked at what Mrs. Connors said. Here I was, discreetly dating Tom Gorman during Wimbledon, staying at the Gloucester hotel far from her world, and suddenly I had "matured."

Confidence and determination carried me through my semifinal against Martina. We had not met since our Houston Slims final, but Martina had problems earlier in the tournament, saving a match point against Frankie Durr and beating Sue Barker in three sets. At 4–all in the third set, my 14–3 career record against her at the time was reassuring; I could hold on as long as I played steadily and didn't panic. I won, 6–3, 4–6, 6–4. Evonne's 6–1, 6–2 rout of Virginia quieted British hopes and the popular press and set up the final everyone had anticipated.

I thought of asking Tom to stay for the final. But after losing in singles and doubles, he had to leave for a tournament in the U.S., and it would have been a commitment that might have generated more publicity, and I already had enough outside influences to cope with. The day before the final, Gloria Connors called to wish me good luck and then Jimmy got on the phone. At that point, I was numb from the games that had gone on during the tournament. One afternoon, Margi and I had stood separately on the patio outside the tea room watching Jimmy and Ilie Nastase in a doubles match on Court 2. Every once in a while, I looked across, and every so often she shot me a glance as if we were checking each other out. To beat Evonne for the first time on grass, I needed to channel all my energies into the final. That meant a sound night's sleep and no distractions: Wimbledon was not the White House.

I may have surprised President Ford with my energies during one week, but I could not survive on a steady diet of late nights. Without ten hours of sleep, my body tends to run down, the glands swell and the sore throat arrives. In recent years, I have supplemented my diet with Vitamin C and multivitamins to combat travel and match fatigue. But for me, nothing works as well as sleep.

The morning of the final, everyone was ready with advice. "Remember, she doesn't play well when she gets this far," Rosie said, referring to Evonne's runner-up showings with Billie Jean at Wimbledon in 1972 and 1975 and three straight losses in the U.S. Open. On the other hand, Evonne had taken the Slims title and was riding a twenty-five match winning streak.

Finals often defy logical explanations. At two-week spectaculars like Wimbledon, the U.S. Open or the French, a championship match sometimes cannot sustain the buildup. In 1973, 1974 and 1976, the men's finals at Wimbledon were settled in straight sets. From 1971 through 1975, there was only one deuce set among the women.

Reaching the final for many players is the achievement, not winning the title. Anyone who watched my 1981 Wimbledon final with Hana Mandlikova of Czechoslovakia would surely agree that Hana, at nineteen, was overwhelmed by the occasion. She had ended my season-long unbeaten streak in the French Open, stopped Martina in the semis at Wimbledon and had the classic serve-and-volley game that suited grass. But with her parents flying in from Czechoslovakia and the Centre Court studded with royalty and celebrities, without her even realizing it, the occasion took over.

Looking across the net at Evonne, I sensed a strain on her face. She had won our last two meetings—in Philadelphia and Los Angeles—owned the streak, had not dropped a set in the tournament, and was the media favorite as "Mrs. R. W. Cawley," the wife of a British subject.

It was a tense, unspectacular match alongside some of our other classics. I took the first set, 6–3, steadier off the ground, Evonne won the second, 6–4, and then opened a 2–0 lead in the third until I got back a service break and we went to 4–all. That's when I looked up in the Friends Box and saw Billie Jean and Rosie motioning with their eyes. At first, I couldn't figure out what they were trying to tell me; then it dawned: They wanted me to move in to the net and attack Evonne's second serve.

If Evonne held her serve now, it would leave me serving at 4–5; but if I broke I could serve for the match. But attacking second serves in team tennis was different than on the Centre Court of a Wimbledon final. "Never change a winning game," was a tennis motto, but if I didn't take some chances and change Evonne's rhythm, she could serve-and-volley her way straight to the title.

I didn't exactly look like Tony Roche rushing to the net in the ninth game. But my aggressiveness in chipping to Evonne's forehand threw her off enough for her to miss several passing shots. I broke to 5–4 and needed only to hold serve for a second Wimbledon title.

On the court changeover, I should have been thinking just as aggressively. Instead, I retreated, lost my serve at love and then sat back and watched Evonne carry the momentum to a 6–5 advantage.

Sitting at mid-court, I toweled off and went back to several basics: Get your first serve in, preferably to Evonne's forehand; stay keen. I looked toward Billie Jean, Rosie and my mom. Billie Jean was mouthing some words I couldn't understand, and Rosie was motioning toward the net. I shrugged almost helplessly.

Evonne helped rebuild some of my confidence. On the first point of the twelfth game, she rushed the net with an approach shot to my backhand. If I held back anything, she would be in a perfect position for a finishing volley, so I leaned forward and drove the ball cross-court with a ferocity that bordered on reck- lessness. The pace of the shot stunned her because she mishan- dled the volley, and I held serve from 15.

At many tournaments, 6–all in the third set means a decisive tie breaker. Not Wimbledon. Evonne and I would go on under conventional scoring until one of us took two consecutive games. But what strategy should I now use—stay back and try to again throw her off-balance by attacking second serves? Was 6–all in the third the time to take chances?

The game went to deuce. Evonne had chances to hold for 7–6, but I attacked and won the point with an overhead and then broke on two errors. I had served once for the match and squandered the advantage. Here I was again. At 30–0, Evonne won the next two points, but I reached, 40–30. Evonne moved in behind a forehand volley down the line. Anticipating my two-handed cross-court drive, she crowded closer to the net, leaning and waiting. Instead of the passing shot, however, I held my two-handed backhand as long as I could, and then, with the same motion as my drive, flicked a topspin lob cross-court, over Evonne's left shoulder. The ball landed a foot or so inside the baseline. Game, set and match.

I must have thrown my Wilson racquet fifty feet in the air. Pictures of that moment show my racquet almost level with the roof of the Centre Court. I was ecstatic, someone who had committed myself to winning and had done it. I saw my mother in the locker room, wept in her arms while trembling from the excitement. If 1974 was semifantasy, this time was very real, as I learned the next night when I went to the Wimbledon Ball—with my mother.

In 1974, the Wimbledon Ball was special for me. Jimmy and I were engaged, we had won singles titles, went to the ball with friends, traded notes, took the first dance together and then partied afterward. It was blissful. In 1976, I was satisfied with my victory over Evonne, and Bjorn Borg and I discoed a little at the ball when the orchestra switched the music from slow to fast during the first dance. But I left after the first dance and returned to the Gloucester; my mom went to her room and I went to mine. That's when I sat on my bed and realized that I could be No. 1 in the world, have material and personal achievements, and still be unhappy. Something was missing. I felt empty, unfulfilled. On this occasion, there was no one with whom to share my intimate feelings.

August 23,
Phoenix

Finished up the team tennis season with an inflamed tendon in right hand which prevented me from playing Fed Cup. WTT had definite plus and minuses:

Plus

> Practicing with the guys
> Learn new quick reflex drills
> Got psyched up for matches easier
> Spent the summer with Kristien
> Had my first home away from home
> Got to relax in the sun

Socialized with other players

Minus

Sometimes too much tennis
Too much travel
No break
No sleep

How my training habits and life style have changed over the last year! I am enjoying my life now. I am over Jimmy in the sense I am now open to new personalities and guys. I still cannot carry on a decent relationship with a guy because of the traveling. I am almost too vulnerable. This summer my sleeping habits were really screwed up—most of the time I felt spacey and completely out of it. I deserved to win Wimbledon because I worked hard and dedicated myself the first half of the season. I really don't deserve to win Forest Hills because I've been fooling around too much after Wimbledon.

Some dates stick in your mind more than others. December 21 is my birthday. September 20, 1973, was my declaration of independence, the night I flew to Los Angeles to be with Jimmy. August 25, 1976, was my first date with Burt Reynolds.

My initial contact with Burt began in April, almost by accident. I had gone out to dinner one night with Gene Barakat and Eileen and Jerry Ford of the Ford Modeling Agency in New York. After having signed a contract with the agency for some cosmetic and fashion layouts, we decided to celebrate with a dinner at the famous 21 Club on Fifty-second Street.

From two glasses of wine, I was feeling good. I'm no drinker, and a few glasses usually will put me under the table, especially if I start sipping on a half-empty stomach. We lingered around after dinner for a cordial or two, until the maitre d' approached our table. "I'm sorry," he began, "but you'll have to clear out by ten-thirty, because we are having the party for the premiere of *Lucky Lady* in here." I had heard about the movie.

"Oh, is Burt Reynolds coming here tonight?" I asked.

"Yes," the maitre d' said proudly.

"Can't we just stay?" Eileen chimed in.

"I'm afraid not, madame. It's by invitation only."

I was disappointed. But recalling my conversation with Jeanie in the cab in Washington, and perhaps bolder than usual from the wine, I asked the maitre d' if I could write Burt a note. Several years earlier, that thought would never have occurred to me.

The maitre d' could have been sticky and refused. But he was quite nice, a fatherly type, who recognized me, agreed to carry my message and even brought over a pen.

I wish I could say that I kept stray stationery in my purse for such occasions, but that was not the case. "I'll just write on this napkin," I said, smiling at Gene and then shrugging at my informality.

What can you say on a napkin, even one from 21? I wrote, "Dear Burt, I would like to meet you." On the back of the napkin, I wrote, "Chris Evert." That's all. Honest. Well, actually, I told the maitre d' where I was staying.

"If he's interested, this is where I can be reached," I said, giving him Kristien's home phone number. The maitre d' said okay and then gave me a rather disapproving look, as if to suggest, "Aren't you a little young for this?" I was too tipsy to worry about any moral questions.

I returned to Kristien and Rick's apartment at eleven o'clock. About twelve-thirty, the phone rang. Kristien answered. I could hear her saying, "hello," "she's sleeping in the other room," and "just a minute." Then she came running into my room and exclaimed, "I think it's him. He's got a deep voice. I think it's him." I sat there, started sweating and thought to myself, "What am I going to say to him?" After a crazy impulse at 21, I felt like a fool. But I couldn't back out, so I picked up the telephone and said hello.

"Is this Chris?" the male voice said on the other end of the line.

"Yes."

"This is Burt."

"Oh, hi."

You won't believe this. But at twelve-thirty in the morning, after leaving that unbelievably coy note, Burt Reynolds and I started talking about the garbage on the streets of New York. With the city's typical labor problems, there was garbage piled up all over the streets, and both of us couldn't get over it. I was too sleepy to recall some of Burt's funnier lines, but right away he had me laughing about the size and smell of the garbage and wouldn't it be neat just to drive a car down a street and knock over as many piles as you could?

"Would you like to go out tonight?" he asked.

You're not going to believe this either, but I said, "Well, it's a little late, and I'm in my pajamas. Do you think we can do it tomorrow?"

Burt was unavailable. "I have a flight in the morning, so I guess we can't make it this time around."

Now I was kicking myself. How many women would say no to Burt Reynolds, even at twelve-thirty in the morning? "Yeah, I guess not," I said.

"Well, what's your schedule? Will you be out on the West Coast at all?"

"I'm not sure. With team tennis, we're never in one place too long."

"That's too bad."

"Yeah."

"Well, I'll get in touch with you. We'll work it out."

"Okay. I'd like that very much."

For the next four months, about once a month, Burt called. I don't know how he found out where I was, but he tracked me down. Then, on August 25, after the team tennis season ended, he suddenly phoned one day in Fort Lauderdale. He would be in Florida for some filming on the movie *Semi-Tough* and would be staying at his home in Jupiter, which was about an hour's drive from Fort Lauderdale. Would I like to go out?

At this point, less than two weeks before the U.S. Open, I had developed tendinitis in a finger on my right hand and wore a small precautionary splint on my arm. But I wasn't about to pass up a date this time; all I had to do now was tell my parents that I was going out with Burt Reynolds.

"I have a date with an older man tonight," I said to my mom later that day, fearing Burt's image as a movie star and playboy might register some disapproval.

"Oh, who is it with?" she said, matter-of-factly, perhaps expecting some Fort Lauderdale attorney, businessman or tennis pro.

"Burt Reynolds."

My mom's mouth almost fell off in shock. "I think I'd better tell your father," she said. "I don't think you should tell him."

"Okay, you tell him," I said.

At six o'clock that evening, you would have thought the Pope was coming to 1628 Northeast Seventh Place. While I was putting on, taking off and putting on makeup, Laurie and Ana sat on the bed in disbelief. "I can't believe it," Laurie said. "I'd get a divorce in a minute to go out with him."

Laurie was kidding, of course. But my family was treating the event with high seriousness. Drew and Jeanne were hanging around the living room; John, who normally went out every night, decided he was too tired and wanted to stay home. My mom had put on a dress and a little necklace. My dad looked neater than usual.

So did the house. It was a riot: I had these three racquets on the living room bench, where they always stay. My mother wanted to move them out of the way. "No, no, leave them there," my dad said. "This is how we live, and this is what's normal for us, so leave the racquets there." My mother still felt that the racquets would be embarrassing.

Burt and I were going out with two other couples that evening. Around eight o'clock, three Rolls-Royces pulled up in front of the house, a first for our street. Burt got out of the first car and walked toward the house. In my bedroom, Laurie and Ana peaked through the jalousie, eager for any glimpse. I looked in the mirror and made one final check of my skirt and matching silk print blouse; my armpits were soaked.

Burt knocked, I opened the door, he came in and we shook

hands. Or at least I gave him my splint hand, and he laughed. Then my father stood up, my mother came into the room, along with my two brothers and two sisters. We had a full round of introductions.

"You've got a real good-looking blond brother there," Burt said on the way out to the car, probably relieved that he had survived phase one with the family. "He should be in the movies."

"John would love to hear that," I said.

No dinner with three couples can ever be romantic, even with the setting of a private dining room, which Burt requested to avoid people staring. I spent most of the evening in a friendly argument with one of Burt's friends, Alfie Wise. The topic of discussion was not movies or whether I could win the Open, but Renee Richards. Renee, who was Dr. Richard Raskind before undergoing a sex-change operation the previous year, was playing some tour events and trying to gain admittance to the Open. Alfie defended Renee's right to play the Open and the women's tour. I sympathized with Renee personally but felt that it would set a bad precedent, lead to a general acceptance of transsexuality and tempt other young men to go that route. Burt just sat there during the dinner listening to our debate, smiling at some points and nodding like a judge.

"What were you nodding about?" I asked later on the ride back to my house.

"I was just impressed that you stood up for what you believed and weren't afraid to voice your opinion," he said.

Anyone who has seen Burt Reynolds on the screen must be impressed at his good looks. But what attracted me, even before I met him, was his dry sense of humor. I enjoy people who have a good sense of humor, who can make me laugh. How many guys, the first time you talk to them on the phone at twelve-thirty in the morning, can break you up by talking about garbage?

Burt also was a gentleman. On our first date, he opened car doors, restaurant doors. I was the No. 1 female tennis player in the world, yet he went out of his way to take my hand whenever we walked into a room. You could tell that women were really special to him. And I had the feeling, when I was with him, that I was the only woman in the world at that moment. Burt didn't try to overexpose our relationship; in fact, he kept it under wraps, sensing my preference for privacy. Several years later, during an interview Burt gave to *McCall's* magazine, he was quoted as saying, "There's Chris Evert, whom the press calls an iceberg, a surgeon on the court with no emotion. When I first read those things about her, I felt if I ever saw her, I would tell her, 'I know exactly how you feel because that's not what you are.' I don't know, but I do. I finally did tell her that, and she was so touched that we became very, very good friends. She gave me her U.S. Open trophy. She's a very, very special woman."

Burt is a very, very special man. He's so different from the boisterous, confident image he projects on the screen. He's quiet, almost shy, and keeps a lot inside. Because he gives so much to the public as a performer, there were times when we were together that he seemed totally drained. I envisioned him as someone who would be totally "on" all the time, but he wasn't. Among friends, totally natural, he yearned just to ease back on the throttle. We related to one another because of our enormous mutual respect and our understanding of the pressures of being in the public eye and being on top. He was No. 1 in his field, the biggest single box-office attraction in the movies. When I added the U.S. Open title to Wimbledon that year, losing only a total of twelve games in six matches and beating Evonne, 6–3, 6–0, I was No. 1 on the computer, and I was also president of the Women's Tennis Association (WTA).

After serving one year on the board of directors as vice-president, I agreed to accept the presidency. Succeeding Billie Jean was a tough act to follow, but I enjoyed the challenge. I didn't like flying all over the country for meetings, but once I arrived, it was stimulating working with Jerry Diamond, the executive director, and others on the board.

A president must see all sides of an issue—not just offer a personal view. The players not in the top twenty were frustrated, wanted more tournaments and had strong demands for a better percentage of the prize money. Yet the promoters knew that it was the top few players who sold tickets and box seats for a successful tournament. So I was faced with a dilemma, of sorts: The leading players were making enough money and didn't need to play 40 weeks a year, but there were 150 to 200 other women who were the soul of the tour and wanted better opportunities. On many issues, I trusted my instincts and spoke up. Sometimes, the players agreed with me; on other questions, they felt I was speaking more as a No. 1 than as their president.

I could have done more work as president. But at the time, my tennis was first, and being president had to be second. I accepted the job because my presence was good for women's tennis, the women felt the media would respect me in that position, and I liked and wanted the challenge. But I know how much time and energy Billie Jean gave to the job, and I wasn't sure I could handle both for a sustained period of time without losing some intensity on the court. It's happened to almost every person who has tried to serve the WTA or the Association of Tennis Professionals, the men's equivalent. The more you commit yourself, the more is expected, but I wanted to serve at least one term.

London, November 5
2:30 A.M.

I love tennis, I love the competition, the sheer challenge of play-ing to perfection. Always striving to hit a better shot, to be more aggressive, to hit with more power. *I'm playing for myself now.*

I'm experiencing sensations in tennis I've never experienced be-fore. No pressure or nerves. Loose, aggressive, daring, gutty, confi-dent.

On the tennis court, I'm my own person. I'm expressing my inner desires and personality. I love tennis. How can I give it up? It's my life. . . .

I never get bored with winning. It's a nice, secure habit.

That December, Burt called from California. "My jeweler from Jupiter, Florida, is going to drive down to Fort Lauderdale and give you something," he said.

I was flabbergasted. What could it possibly be? Even in my

wildest fantasies, I knew an engagement ring was premature. A bracelet? Burt and I had seen each other only occasionally since the Open, but we talked regularly and he followed my tournament results. He also had a knack of reading my feelings. What had he sensed this time?

The jeweler arrived at the house and made a point of telling me that the gift was hand designed. "Something Burt felt was very appropriate," he said. I opened the small box, and it was a necklace, with a big gold No. 1, diamond studded.

You couldn't buy this gift in a store. I was saddened only that Burt couldn't give me the necklace in person. Yet he had touched me not only with his generosity, but his sensitivity. Burt knew how much being No. 1 meant. Three weeks later, I was on the cover of *Sports Illustrated* as the "Sportswoman of the Year." For the first time, I was enjoying life at the top.

9 · On the Road

February 1977

- I win because I hate to lose, not because of the thrill of victory.
- Tennis is just temporary, my potential as a person is lasting.
- I've suppressed and avoided the ability to feel as a person because I've put most of my emotional and mental energies into the right winning attitude.
- When I get bored, I don't give the best I can give.
- If you really want to achieve something in life, whatever you do to achieve the goal that you have fixed on your mind is never a sacrifice. It's something that you have to do. The sacrifice is to feel like a victim.

Martina Navratilova isn't as hard as she sometimes looks on a tennis court. In fact she's just the opposite, so honest, gracious, sensitive and candid that she leaves herself vulnerable to life's lobs.

After I won the 1981 Wimbledon singles title, Martina sent a complimentary bottle of champagne to my hotel room. She had shown the same kindness after some of my earlier U.S. Open wins, so I invited her to celebrate with John and me at Wimbledon. Even though she had a doubles final the following day, she came to our party and stayed the whole evening.

I first played Martina in 1973 when she was sixteen years old, at a tournament in Akron. I won, 7–6, 6–3, but even then her aggressive game impressed me. A big left-handed serve and her first volleys stretched me from corner to corner. As good as her serve and forehand were, however, I was more struck by her presence: At the time, Martina was about twenty pounds overweight and continually belittled herself on court. Sometimes she would be in tears; other times, she sulked and cried. Being true to your feelings is an admirable trait, but it wasn't until I knew Martina a little better—as a singles rival, doubles partner and friend—that I understood why she emotionalized so much.

Martina was born in Czechoslovakia, but she embodies the spirit and character of America. That's why becoming a United States citizen meant so much to her in 1981. After what she endured, Martina identified with the American dream at its best and worst.

When Martina was three, her mother was divorced and only made enough money to feed her daughter. At eleven, Soviet tanks took over the streets of her town, and her stepfather had to drive sixty miles on a motor scooter to pick her up at a junior tournament that weekend. At eighteen, she hid out at Jeanie Brinkman's Manhattan apartment before defecting to the United States during the 1975 U.S. Open. How many other teen-agers have dealt with so much so young?

I'm very fond of Martina. We played doubles together for several years. We split up because I found it difficult to keep a close friend and rival as a doubles partner. How could I sustain intensity for an important match against someone I cared for, someone I might be clowning with in a doubles final or going out to dinner with afterward? In 1977, a trimmed-down Martina was determined to challenge me.

The view from the top can be very satisfying. I met scores of interesting people who would not have given me a second glance if I were further down in the computer rankings. During one trip to Houston, I purchased four pairs of Calvin Klein pants at a department store at the same time that Calvin Klein himself was in the store for a promotion. He asked to meet me, and we chatted briefly. Dave Kingman, the baseball player, once phoned for a date at Jeanie's apartment. We wound up going out to dinner, along with Jeanie and Mark McCormack, the sports management representative, who was trying to sign Dave and me.

Being No. 1 carries certain responsibilities. Tournament directors depend on you for promotion. The large arenas where we began playing provided dates because women's tennis was appealing. The image of the tour was designed for an upbeat audience that included not only women but men who identified more with our game than the serve-and-volley power of the men.

Some events needed less promotion than others, like the team tennis match that was booked in Plains, Georgia, against the Russians. I teamed in doubles with Billy Carter; Billy wore jeans and played the match with a borrowed racquet in one hand and a can of beer in the other. I don't think he knew which way to swing the racquet, but he certainly swigged the beer with authority.

The exhibition was a publicity stunt for World Team Tennis. Everyone was friendly and hospitable until the match ended. Then the crowd swarmed through security guards and almost trampled me until Brenda Bricklin and I fought our way to a trailer that we had been using as a dressing room. Brenda was an official with the Phoenix Racquets who had become a good friend.

Brenda says she never saw me as frightened as I was when the crowd surged on the court and backed us into a corner. I was humped over, shaking, while Brenda tried to hold back autograph hounds with her elbows, waiting for additional security. Most of the security personnel were busy watching Rosalynn Carter, the President's wife, and Lillian Carter, his mother.

The Carter clan came out in force at the banquet-barbecue

later that night. Miss Lillian, as they called her, said she could hardly wait to meet me. She was as lively as I had imagined.

"You're my favorite girl player," she said, "And you know Jimmy Connors is my favorite boy player."

She talked for an hour about how crazy she was over Jimmy —Connors, that is—how feisty he was, how she loved his electricity when he played. Then she discussed her sons, how close she felt to them; and how proud she was. She reminded me a little bit of Mrs. Connors.

Learning to live as a No. 1 can be complex, but I was determined to remain myself among friends. It meant not only being sincere and honest but retaining my sense of humor. At a tournament awards banquet in Amelia Island, Florida, I offered to sign over my winner's check of $20,000 to Jeanie if she could spell "piña colada." Jeanie has dyslexia, a condition that affects her ability to spell correctly. I wasn't trying to embarrass her when I made the offer because she knew I would never do that, but the crowd at the dinner suddenly got silent, wondering whether I was serious or crazy. It didn't matter because Jeanie only got as far as "piña"; she muffed "colada," I got to keep the check, and everyone breathed a sigh of relief. Jeanie and I laughed about it afterward.

Then there was the time Val Ziegenfuss received a box of chocolate candy from a male admirer at a tournament and accidentally left it in my hotel room. Mischievous as ever, Jeanie and I opened the wrapping carefully, took out the candy and ate one bite from each bit of chocolate, put each individual piece back in its little paper cup, rewrapped the entire package and left it for Val. The next day, before play began, Val came into the room and asked about her chocolates.

"Oh, yeah, you left them," I said, handing her the box.

"Would you like one?" she asked.

"Oh, no, that's perfectly all right," I said. "You go right ahead. No, really."

Val opened the chocolates and started passing them around. Of course, when she opened the paper, there were forty little pieces of chocolate all with one bite out of them. If I hadn't been a friend, Val might have squished the chocolates on my head.

Watching others improved my perspective. In Seattle, Natasha Chmyreva's mother went into one of her verbal tirades during a loss to Rosie Casals. Natasha was known for her bad temper, but I didn't think there were overly aggressive tennis mothers in the Soviet Union until I saw Mrs. Chmyreva prance around the court and scream at her daughter in Russian during the changeovers. Her rantings seemed so ridiculously amusing that I walked up to Jeanie on another changeover and began spouting to her in what might be described as gobbledygook. Jeanie responded with her garble. For the rest of the winter circuit—in hotel lobbies, elevators, airports, restaurants, locker rooms and even press conferences—Jeanie and I often addressed each other, straight-faced and seriously, in this nonsensical language. It wasn't like the "IV" game that my sister Jeanne, Laurie and I had concocted as kids; this was simply garble strung together, any which way. Jeanie and I tried to incorporate it into "Ladies of the Evening" that year, but it bombed because no one could understand us. Of course, we couldn't understand ourselves.

Everyone understood the rivalry between Martina and myself, which was incentive enough for me to win our finals in Seattle, Los Angeles and Philadelphia. Los Angeles was enjoyable because, during the day, I watched some of the filming of the movie *Semi-Tough*.

Burt wasn't overly attentive during the shooting. Then again, I didn't exactly leave the court and sit in his lap when he showed up at Madison Square Garden for the Slims Championships that year. But we went out several times during that week in L.A., and I stayed on after the tournament. That's when I saw Burt at his unpredictable best.

The day after the tournament ended, Alfie Wise phoned and said Burt would have to scratch dinner because of some late dubbing at the studio. Dinner for five had been in order, with Jeanie as a fifth wheel. "I don't want to end up entertaining three women," Alfie begged, "so I've asked a friend of mine, a veterinarian, to join us. I hope you don't mind?"

What could I say? If I said no, Burt might have been insulted. Lively as ever, Alfie picked up Jeanie and me and tried to psyche us up, but going out with an animal doctor I didn't even know was hardly my favorite way to spend an evening.

"He's no ordinary veterinarian," Alfie stressed in the car. "He's one of the leading vets in the area, he's very wealthy and does some real estate. I'm sure you'll find him quite charming."

We arrived at a swanky restaurant on the outskirts of the city and slipped into a large round booth at the far end. No one recognized me without my tennis clothes, but after we were seated, everyone noticed the man who walked in about fifteen minutes later.

"May I present Dr. Burton Reynolds," Alfie announced, pleased that he had pulled off Burt's semistunt.

"I didn't know you were treating dogs and cats these days," I said as Burt joined us—all smiles.

"There's a lot of animals in our business," he countered.

Burt was darling, full of laughs and stories. After dinner, he drove Jeanie and me to see his new house in Beverly Hills, which he had bought from John Lennon. The house was stunning, with a tiered terrace and a pool that Lennon had once painted black but that Burt had repainted blue. Burt was pleasant throughout my stay—polite, eager to please, and at times so shy that I wondered whether he was putting me on. But he cared, and his appearance during the Virginia Slims Championships at Madison Square Garden added to our relationship and helped push women's tennis further into the big time. If Burt Reynolds, a symbol of the macho male, could show up for a women's tennis event, maybe it was worth checking out. We drew record crowds that week.

Having Burt there was special for me. He flew in from California, we spent time together before and after the matches, and he surprised me with a second necklace that meant as much as the first. This time, he had his jeweler inscribe the word "Babe" in gold and diamonds. "Babe" was Burt's nickname for me; he had seen me at practice one day wearing a Fabergé T-shirt with the word "Babe" across the front, the name of their latest perfume. Most men and women have special names for friends or spouses. I was flattered by Burt's nickname; it was private between us, and on several occasions people would see me wearing the shirt or necklace and say, "Oh, are you with Fabergé now?"

Burt and I had been staying at the same hotel, the Pierre, and photographers, none of whom I recognized, stalked us for days during the tournament. Gossip-type photographers make their living following the stars.

"Do you know these photographers?" I asked, as we left for the final against Sue Barker, who had upset Martina.

"Yup," he said. "I know who they are."

I've always felt comfortable with most tennis photographers. Maria Garcia, for example, is a free-lance photographer who gives me packages of M&M chocolates before my matches. After Burt and I arrived at the Garden for the final, Maria was there with some "energy."

"These are better than some of those heavy chocolate bars," she said.

In the locker room, I changed into my tennis clothes and was warmed by Maria's unsolicited generosity. I found a sheet of paper and scribbled a note to her:

> Dear Maria,
>   I, too, am sorry I haven't been able to spend more time with you—but know you understand. I want you to know I consider you a *very* loyal friend and I love it when you're cheering for me.
>
>   Love ya,
>   Chris

Maria was on court for the match but couldn't help against Sue Barker's forehand, which was devastating. I lost the first set, and Burt looked more nervous than when he was scoring touchdowns in *The Longest Yard* or *Semi-Tough*. People who are close to me say they experience a lot watching me play because they know what I go through and how much I feel inside. I looked across to where Burt was sitting and saw how uncomfortable he was. If I went down, he would feel responsible for distracting me.

I took the last two sets from Sue, 6–1, 6–1, for the Slims title and "Silver Ginny," which was awarded to the player with the highest number of points on the tour. Burt was relieved, but not half as surprised as he was several weeks later during a lunch at "21" with David Merrick, the producer.

Burt was meeting Merrick to negotiate another deal. I couldn't disturb them, but figured I owed Burt for his dinnertable gag about the veterinarian. So Jeanie and I, along with Ana and Gene Barakat made a reservation for lunch at the same time. We also brought along an eight-by-ten-inch picture of me dressed as Groucho Marx during the "Ladies of the Evening" show in Philadelphia. In the picture I wore a dark jacket, ascot, a fake moustache and glasses and a white cap to hold my hair. I was also holding a long cigar and smiling as lecherously as Groucho.

I put the picture in an envelope with an anonymous letter saying that I wanted to submit this photo to Burt for consideration in his next movie. The maitre d' handed the letter to Burt, who hadn't seen me enter the restaurant and didn't know I had planned to be there. Burt paused in the conversation with Merrick, looked around and wondered why someone was interrupting important business. An envelope addressed to him with no other imformation? He opened the envelope, looked at the picture and still couldn't understand why anyone would send him a picture of a Groucho Marx look-alike. Then he studied the picture again, and it finally dawned on him because he couldn't stop laughing. If you think some of the scenes in *Smokey and the Bandit* were gassers, he was almost on the floor of 21 with convulsions. Burt glanced around the room and then spotted me. I looked up, waved discreetly and went back to reading my menu as if nothing had happened.

Of course, "The Bandit" was a master of one-upmanship.

Several days later, Jeanie and I returned to her apartment after some Easter shopping. "There's something in your apartment," the doorman told us mysteriously. Jeanie couldn't imagine what it could be. We opened the door, uncertain of who or what was to come. Inside, we saw a five-foot stuffed rabbit and another rabbit, about three-and-a-half feet high with a little note attached: "Chris, Happy Easter, Love Burt."

$\bullet \quad \bullet \quad \bullet$

If life were all five-foot stuffed rabbits, I could have hopped along without a care. But even Peter Rabbit made mistakes and wound up sipping tea in bed to cure the cold he caught from Mister McGregor's garden. I made my share of blunders, some less serious and others where I had to live with my conscience.

Ross Case, Stephanie Tolleson and I decided on an early celebration over the Phoenix Racquets qualifying for the championship finals in team tennis. The celebration started with some champagne in the locker room and was supposed to finish at Avanti's restaurant.

Ross had a Triumph TR-7, Stephanie drove a Pacer and I had a Jaguar. Ross's car usually was in the shop, and I seldom took my Jaguar out of second gear, so Stephanie usually won our races. On this particular night, however, Ross diverted from the main road and decided to take a shortcut to Avanti's leaving Stephie and me side by side trying to figure out how and where we could cut him off. Suddenly a police car pulled out from a side street and followed us.

The three of us had made a pact during the season that if we were ever stopped by the police, the others would help. Stephie and I weren't speeding, but the police car turned on his lights and siren anyway, pulled behind my car and ordered me over to the shoulder of the road. Conveniently forgetting our pact, Stephanie drove into a small parking lot about a block away.

I had visions of being hauled in for drunk driving and making newspaper headlines. The officer approached my car, and I started talking in a frenzy trying to explain who I was, that I was innocent, had just finished a team tennis match and was simply going out for a late meal. Of course, I wasn't going to tell him that Stephie and I were tooling down the road trying to cut off Ross Case at the pass. I showed the officer my driver's license, but the car had owner's plates and belonged to the Racquets. Now it looked as if I were driving a stolen car.

Luckily, the officer turned out to be a tennis fan. He had followed the Racquets all season, was excited at how well we were playing, and could hardly wait for the playoffs. I took his address, promised him tickets for his sons and cousins and then left the scene as quickly as possible in search of Stephie. I spotted her Pacer, pulled into the parking lot and got out of the car only to have her shout, "Get down, get down." For an instant, I thought a gun would go off.

"What's going on?" I said, half-crawling and looking around for the enemy.

"You're not going to believe this," she began. "I drove into this lot to wait for you. And while I'm sitting in the car, a little guy inside that liquor store over there is watching me."

"Watching you?"

"Yeah, he's watching me from inside the door. All of a sudden, he walks over to the door, does something to the door, walks back behind the counter and drops down behind the counter."

"Are you sure you didn't just imagine this?" I said.

"I know what I saw, Chrissie. I figured he must be getting a little nervous or something, so I walked over to the door to tell him that everything was okay, that I was just waiting for my friend. But now he's locked the door, he jumps up from behind the counter and he's shouting Spanish at me a million miles an hour. Of course, I'm trying to explain that I'm waiting for Chris Evert and I'm not going to do anything to him. And now you drive up and the guy must be figuring . . ."

I looked toward the liquor store. The man had unlocked the door and was walking outside. "I call de po-leese!" he shouted. "You get out now, you no get in my store! I call de po-leese!"

I turned toward Stephie. "I've had enough problems with

the police for one evening," I said. Stephie and I darted for our cars and reached Avanti's in record time. Ross didn't believe any of our story; he thought we lost the race and couldn't accept defeat.

Ross was a person who enjoyed games—even when he was the victim. During the U.S. Open later that year, I shared a hotel suite with Brenda Bricklin, my sister Jeanne and Ana. It was a hilarious two weeks, and I sometimes wonder how I won the tournament.

Early in the first week, the Puritan people sent over some new dresses for me to wear during the tournament. Whether by choice or coincidence, one of the dresses turned out to be a pinafore with a bow in the back. Pinafores were Tracy Austin's trademark, not mine, so you can imagine how much teasing I took from my friends over that; but Brenda had other ideas. She put on the dress, braided her hair, stuck on a pair of sneakers, ran down the back hall of the Park Lane Hotel and woke up Ross in his room at two o'clock in the morning. Ross thought she was crazy, (a), because she was running around in the middle of the night and, (b), because Brenda was a stylish blonde who now looked like Little Miss Lollipop. There are pictures around of me in the pinafore, but that's as close as it got to Forest Hills.

Brenda can be fearless. The morning after her escapade to Ross's room, we were coming out of the hotel and she spotted Arnold Schwarzenegger, the muscleman, getting into a cab. "I'll give you a hundred dollars if you go over to that cab and knock on the door," I said, never figuring that Brenda would be brazen enough to try. Brenda ran over to the cab, knocked on the door and said, "I love you, I think you're wonderful." I began laughing hysterically, but Brenda didn't get her hundred dollars. Are you kidding?

On a more serious level, I mishandled a close friendship with Kristien Kemmer Shaw. We went from being doubles partners in team tennis and constant companions off the court to distant strangers. I somehow wish it were possible to replay events because now I would have handled them differently.

Kristien and I became acquainted in November 1974, after

Jimmy and I had called off our engagement. Kristien was on the tour at the time, sensed my unhappiness and reached out to me. Feeling lost and needing companionship, I reached back to her. We became good friends and learned that we shared many interests. Kristien was one of the more feminine players on the tour and enjoyed shopping, makeup and clothes. She was strong and independent; I needed strength at that time and looked to her for guidance. We had long talks about my relationships with men, and Kristien, who had just gotten married at the time, was a sounding board: why marriages work, why they don't, the hurt of dating people in tennis. Kristien had gone out with some tennis players and could relate to what I had gone through. Of all my close friends, she was the older sister I never had, someone who taught me about style, how to dress, how to apply makeup, advice about men. In college, girls can learn through sorority sisters, and boys have fraternity brothers to shape some of their values. I never learned how to project or protect myself, and Kristien, an outsider, saw things more clearly. I was too emotionally involved, she said: "Protect yourself, mix more, date other guys, don't give so much because you'll only be hurt, have a good time, don't get too involved."

I didn't play team tennis in 1975. But I visited Kristien in Phoenix, went to a week of matches and loved the concept of players cheering for each other, training and traveling together.

Kristien and I were good for each other. Practicing regularly with me, her weight dropped and she improved to the point where she qualified for the Virginia Slims finals in Madison Square Garden in 1977, was ranked eighth in the U.S. for the year in singles, and was voted "most improved player on the circuit." Steady on clay, she reached the finals of the Italian Open before losing to Renata Tomanova, 6–3, 7–6, and was a semifinalist in the French Open.

Kristien was a giving person. I needed strength and companionship, and she was there. Our playing styles were similar, so we could see the loose threads in our games and pieced them together. Phoenix finished with the best won–lost record in the Western Division of Team Tennis in 1976 and 1977.

Looking back, I have fond memories of those years. If there was a down side to my friendship with Kristien, it might have been that we lived in one another's pockets. Some players felt we excluded ourselves from everyone else and tried to build our own world on the tour. But I was her best friend at the time, and she was mine; we might have survived longer if the inevitable hadn't put us on the same court for matches.

Other players were curious to see what would happen when we finally had to play: Had Kristien improved enough to beat me? Would I carry her in a match because she was a close friend? Would I become tentative and choke because she supposedly was "my mentor"?

We played each other in the quarterfinals of a Slims event in Seattle. The morning of the match, everything seemed fine. Both of us knew there had to be a winner and loser; we would go out and try as hard as we could. Even Jeanie felt we had handled the lead-up to the match in a very mature way. But that night, I couldn't look at Kristien on the court. When I went to the net to pick up a ball, I couldn't look across the net. I had blocked her out of my mind as an opponent and won, 6–0, 6–0. Some players suggested afterward that I tried to prove a point, but it wasn't true. I went out and played as well as I could. The following week in Chicago, we met again in the quarterfinals, and the scores this time were 6–0, 6–1.

I'm sure Kristien was hurt by those two matches. She and her husband, Rick, talked it out, but she felt I tried to humiliate her. I didn't. But what could I do? If I let up and gave her a game somewhere, who's to say she wouldn't have won a second and then another? And then wouldn't I be struggling to control a situation and unhappy with myself? Where do you draw the line?

As well as I've been able to finish off matches in my career, I've flubbed some relationships. Martina was upset with me about our doubles split because she said she first read about it in a newspaper. Kristien and I abruptly parted in a similar veil of silence. I don't know whether it was a lack of guts or immaturity on my part. I should have said to Kristien, "Let's sit down and talk about our friendship and see where it's going. Let's discuss how I'm changing and how you're changing, and therefore how our relationship must be changing." But it was hard for me to take the initiative, sit down and be honest with myself and others. I wanted to pretend that the problem wasn't there, that it would disappear, and I used tennis as a vehicle to pull away. I never explained why, buried my feelings inside, hurt Kristien and myself. I still care for her and would like to renew our friendship, but time and distance don't work in your favor, as I also learned with Burt.

It was heavenly when Burt and I were together. I visited his ranch in Florida in late April, rode horses, drove his speedboat, sat in the Jacuzzi and even played touch football in the corral with him and some of his ranch hands.

Ana and Alfie Wise also came to the ranch. I was petrified of horses, but Ana said, "Follow me, it's easy." It was until the horse reared and threw Ana, and her back hit a wooden fence. The next day she was full of bruises.

My pride was hurt more than my body after the football game. Burt and I were on the same team, but any hopes he had of me as an all-pro receiver disappeared when I dropped an almost certain touchdown pass from him on our first series. Because I was a great tennis player, Burt had the impression that I was good in other sports as well. I was awful that day and couldn't catch a ball. Each time he tried to throw the ball to me, two other girls who helped with horses on the ranch would move in and intercept it.

One of the girls was trying to impress me with how good an athlete she was. Finally, after she intercepted a pass and ran for a touchdown, I got mad, and the anger must have boiled over because I almost tackled her. Burt took one look at my face and started laughing. "You're as competitive as I am," he said.

Burt and I always got along well, and there was a physical attraction. But in the back of my mind, I knew that it wouldn't go on forever. You have a feeling about any relationship—can it last? Will it grow? Is it just fun? What about potential snags? Burt and I were in different worlds. He had his career, and I had mine. I couldn't ask him to give up what he had achieved, and he knew how much my tennis meant to me, so we sort of drifted. But understanding these priorities helped us leave as close friends, just as Jimmy and I got along better at Wimbledon in 1977.

That Wimbledon had more highs and lows than any I ever played. For one thing, it was the centennial celebration, and any player who didn't get a few goose bumps during the Parade of Champions on opening day had no feelings for the sport. Just standing there on the Centre Court, surrounded by forty other past and present greats from Elizabeth Ryan to Bjorn Borg, made you understand why Wimbledon holds such a lofty place in the hearts of everyone. As the defending singles champion, I was even more honored.

For a tournament like Wimbledon, the draw can be a treasure chest filled with unexpected jewels. In the third round, for example, I was confronted by Tracy, at fourteen the youngest competitor to play Wimbledon in the modern era. The buildup for that match began as soon as the draw was made. Tracy was the latest two-handed whiz kid and had created a storm by catapulting from an Avon Futures circuit win in Portland, Oregon, to the main Slims draw. She lost her first Slims match to Linda Mottram at Houston but beat Greer Stevens in Minnesota the following week and battled Rosie, 6–3, 6–3, and 6–4, 6–4, before losing in successive tournaments. Our playing styles were so similar that our first meeting was dubbed a "looking glass war."

My friends had more fun before that first match than I did. "Why don't you hand her a bunch of lollipops when you shake hands?" Stephanie teased. "Don't start crying if you lose a game," Ana chimed in.

Before going on Centre Court, I got sick to my stomach. I was so nervous I dreaded going out there. I wanted to stay in control, but the thought of playing someone that young petrified me. I had been in Tracy's position against Billie Jean, Frankie and others but had never been on the older side so dramatically. If Tracy had been a serve-and-volleyer, someone who gave me a target, I would have been more comfortable. But with the same ground strokes and determination, I was faced with losing to my own kind. At a tournament like Wimbledon, the media would eat me alive.

The contrast was evident as we walked on court and curtsied to the Royal Box. I wore a sun dress; Tracy had on one of her light-colored pinafores.

She won the first game at 30, and you could hear the crowd buzzing with anticipation. In the third game, I slipped and fell flat on my butt chasing a ball. It was embarrassing because I had never fallen before. All of a sudden, I heard about one hundred clicks from nearby cameras and was sprawled on the grass. People didn't know how to react; I finally got up and kind of laughed it off. But I thought to myself, "What a klutz! You ought to lose a little weight."

Peter Range, formerly a correspondent for *Time* magazine, once quoted me as saying, "No point is worth falling down over." Actually, I meant that it wasn't necessary to fall down for every ball and every point. Falling down against Tracy actually helped me; I played looser after that spill and won the match, 6–1, 6–1, in forty-nine minutes.

But beating Tracy was not enough. Next in the treasure chest came Billie Jean, a player I had never beaten on grass. I may have been more determined for that match than any I ever played up to then. Nothing distracted me that day. A bomb could have hit the earth and I wouldn't have known because I had a mission to accomplish—beat Billie Jean. I concentrated the whole way, never came within a point of losing serve, played only one deuce and won, 6–1, 6–2, in forty-eight minutes.

"Have you ever seen Chris play any better?" someone asked Billie Jean in the interview room. She thought for a moment and then replied, "Actually, I haven't."

I know when I'm ready to play a great match. I feel my body will respond to my mind no matter what I tell it to do. If I tell it to run a little faster, if I tell it to go in this direction, it will respond to my mind. That's why so much of my game is mental:

If I'm not concentrating, and not determined, and take a match lightly, my body responds the same way; I don't run as quickly, I'm not as fast. It's all mind over body, and disciplining my body dispels the notion that I'm some sort of machine. Anyone who watched my Wimbledon semifinal against Virginia Wade could see the difference. I was a different person on the court that day, not concentrating as keenly and, thus, not moving as alertly to the ball.

Beating Billie Jean cleared a psychological hurdle. Off the court, another hurdle was cleared: Jimmy and I had changed the intensity of our relationship. There was no strain or competition, we were friends and companions, got along great, and there was no pressure for engagement or marriage. The night that I beat Billie Jean, Jimmy and I went out for dinner at Inn on the Park with Ana and Lorne Kuhle, one of Jimmy's friends. I don't think anyone in the dining room that night will ever forget what happened.

It began innocently enough when I teasingly poured some milk over Jimmy's ice cream. The milk looked so good on his dish that I childishly poured the rest on his head.

Jimmy looked at me and couldn't believe what I had done. So he leaned over, took a scoop of ice cream from Lorne's plate and smeared it over my face. Waiters, busboys and the maitre d' frantically converged on our table to clean up the mess and reassure other patrons in the dining room that everything was in order.

It was until we started to leave the restaurant. I walked out the door and then felt something squishing inside my blouse after Jimmy patted me on the back. I reached my arm under my blouse and pulled out a chunk of chocolate fudge. Jimmy danced out of the restaurant into the hall and ducked into the men's room. I ran into the men's room after him, realized another man was standing at a urinal and then backed out. Fortunately, no photographers were around for that scene.

Maybe I left my exuberance in the restaurant that night because I walked onto the Centre Court against Virginia for the semis and felt nothing. By contrast, Virginia was as psyched for

that match as I had been against Billie Jean. She wanted to win
the title more than ever, had trained hard for the tournament
and deserved what came her way. She played well and my
spirits weren't in the match. There was nothing wrong with me
physically; I felt great. But in many respects, losing to Virginia
that day, 6–2, 4–6, 6–1, became a turning point in my career.
Until then, I seldom had more than one or two tough matches
in a tournament. I had survived two draining encounters with
Tracy and Billie Jean; even though I won both by seemingly
easy scores, I failed a third. I couldn't handle waking up and
psyching up for a third straight day, and it was to trigger a
whole new set of thoughts for the future.

I dreaded facing reporters afterward and asked Jeanie if she
would accompany me. We walked down the long passageway
that led to the main staircase and down another set of stairs.
Before entering the press room, I turned to Jeanie and said in
a shaky voice, "I hope I don't cry." I made the conference as
painless as possible: Yes, Virginia wanted to win more than I
did; yes, maybe I had peaked too soon; I didn't feel as eager;
the thought of losing didn't bother me as much as at other
matches. At times, I was angered by the stiff tone of some of
the questions, which suggested that I had not tried.

After the press conference, I left the room, looked at Jeanie
and cringed. But it wasn't until we climbed the stairs and
reached the passageway that led to the locker room that I crum-
bled. In the middle of the passageway, I stopped, clutched my
stomach, slid down the wall, crouched over, and broke into a
painful sob.

"Are you all right?" Jeanie asked, frightened and uncertain
about what to do.

"I'm all right," I whimpered, still holding my side and gasp-
ing for air. "But don't they understand? I'm only human. I do
lose at times."

I rocked back and forth on the floor for several minutes, repeated the words, clutched my stomach and groaned. The pain
was deep in my abdomen, digging into me like a chisel. An
elderly locker room attendant overheard the noise, came into

the hall, saw my discomfort, left immediately and returned with some orange juice. Jeanie handed me the juice, sat down, draped an arm around me and encouraged me to cry. "Let it out," she said.

Anyone who saw me bent over in that dingy hallway would hardly have identified me as the world's No. 1 women's tennis player, who had lost only two of fifty-six singles matches that year. I must have looked so small, so terribly alone. "I'm sorry about your loss," a man said later, as I got into the car at the transportation desk for the ride back to my hotel. "You just weren't yourself today."

How could he know what I felt? Back at the hotel, I watched a frustrating rerun of the match, replayed the same shots and stayed in my bathrobe for several days as uncertainty settled around me. I didn't like the feeling. For the first time, my tennis was affected.

10 · A Winter of Discontent

I've never felt any physical feelings toward other women, but I have felt a lot of emotion, affection and warmth toward certain women friends. Kristien and I were very close, and I could compare what we had to having a male-female relationship on an emotional level. But that doesn't have anything to do with sexual preference, and people confuse emotional ties that women share as friends with sexual preference. When two men share a room at the Gloucester hotel for Wimbledon, it's accepted as the buddy system; two women try to defray their expenses the same way and the rumor mill starts grinding.

The rumors begin because of the way women athletes look and how they are built. Despite the progress in women's sports during the last ten years, male athletes are still more accepted than their female counterparts. A football, basketball or tennis player is considered the cream of the male crop because he is in great shape physically and has a good physique. If he is handsome and articulate, it's a bonus.

When you think of muscles, you think of masculinity, not femininity. Most female athletes have short haircuts and don't wear makeup. They have short haircuts because this is the easiest way to wear your hair when you're playing tennis or other sports. At one time, I wore makeup for matches because I thought it would make me look more attractive and feminine for the sports-minded spectator at indoor arenas. But makeup runs in about five minutes, and it's ridiculous and impractical to wear. If you're outdoors, you wear moisturizer and sun screen to prevent spots and wrinkling and to preserve your skin, but not makeup.

Being outdoors is healthier, and not just because of the sun. You play only during the day, so the evenings are free. You can go on a date, to the movies, to a show. However, on the indoor circuits, sometimes you're tied up with doubles until one or two in the morning. Then you sleep until noon the next day and your whole day is shot.

A person has the choice to live in the style he or she wants. There may be temptations or distractions, but the final choice comes to you. You have to figure out what you want to do with your life and how you want to live it. Some lesbian relationships have a better understanding of companionship and sharing than some marriages, if you look at the faltering state of marriage as an institution today.

Female tennis players are forced to reach out for companionship. The women have only two or three tournaments a year with the men, so they are forced to find someone to practice with, someone to go to cocktail parties with and to dinner. There are so many emotional highs and lows on the tour that when you win or lose, you like to share it with somebody. This attitude doesn't only pertain to sports. In many aspects of life, women are forced to be together, so the natural reaction is to seek companionship and warmth. If there are physical tendencies, then that happens too.

It's very difficult to maintain a relationship with a guy when you're traveling thirty-five weeks of the year. That's what made team tennis so appealing for many of the women; there were men on the teams and you met other male players during the matches, practiced with them and socialized together.

Other than players, the men you come in contact with on the circuit aren't "10s," or even close. When a guy comes up and asks for an autograph, the look in his eyes shows that he has you on a pedestal. If a woman player might want him in bed, she could have him. Being famous can be a turn-on, even if someone doesn't look beautiful.

It's acceptable now for women to have boyfriends on the tour, and single college girls are teased about bringing boyfriends along. "Oh, where did you pick him up?" someone will say. You don't have to hide a man anymore.

There have been rumors that some parents of young players don't want their children to dress or shower at tournaments because they fear they will be intimidated by older women. This talk is ridiculous. What bothers me even more are the innuendoes. Who are we to judge what's right or wrong? People who criticize don't understand what's going on. It's lonely staying in your room all day, practicing, waiting to play a match. "Well, why don't you go to a museum?" people will say. But if you have a match that night, you want to save your energies and emotions. It's mentally draining to walk around shopping or sightseeing, and I've lost matches that way. You have to develop a purpose to your career, and the match is the most important event for a player that day. When you're out of the tournament, you can shop and visit museums.

I'm sure many players became better-rounded individuals because of their travels. I've never been able to see all that I wanted in Rome, Paris, London, Sydney, Tokyo, Johannesburg and other large cities because I'm usually in most tournaments for an entire week.

Sponsors are concerned about the image and direction of women's tennis, but that's true in any sport. When sponsors sign an athlete for a commercial endorsement, they don't want any public scandal. They also know there is a risk, but they're willing to take the risk because the athlete has an identity.

If the public understood the root of women tennis players' relationships, why these relationships happen, they would sympathize more with what women in this sport have to endure. Most men have careers; they're not about to give up their careers to travel with a woman. The tennis career of a woman doesn't last more than five to ten years, if that long. Man is still the breadwinner, no matter what the women's libbers say; the roles are becoming more flexible, but society still wasn't ready or willing to accept Billie Jean King in 1981 after she admitted a relationship with Marilyn Barnett, her secretary.

I saw Marilyn on the circuit and always thought something was going on between them. Most of Billie Jean's friends also felt there was a relationship. But I was saddened to see how the whole affair came out. If you really love somebody, ten years later, you don't turn on them. You had some wonderful years together, and no matter how it ended, you don't seek vengeance because of jealousy or bitterness.

After the publicity broke about Billie Jean, the WTA was concerned about losing Avon and Toyota as sponsors of the women's tour. Avon is a corporation identified with women, so we checked with them many times; their people told us they were more concerned about whether the top woman would support the circuit than the lesbian issue.

Surprisingly, there is very little discussion in the locker room about sexual preference or players scoring sexually. You have dirty jokes and casual conversation about someone being seen somewhere. But nobody will come out and ask whether you slept with so-and-so, which is why the women's tour may differ from the men's. The men are open about their sexual habits; women are more sensitive about privacy. A guy can score with his hostess or a hotel chambermaid, and somehow everybody will know about it, but there isn't that kind of excitement on the women's circuit. The men are actually more catty than the women when it comes to sex.

With me, excitement usually came in the form of newspaper headlines and phone calls, like the one from the *Los Angeles Times* in late 1977 while Jimmy and I were spending time together in Newport Beach, California.

"Is it true," the caller began, "that you and Chrissie have gotten married?"

Feisty as ever, Jimmy looked at me and snickered. "I'll never tell," he said into the receiver.

"Well, is that a yes or a no?" the caller persisted.

"No comment," Jimmy replied playfully.

The next morning, wire services picked up the *Times* quotes and began speculating. Then Rona Barrett reached our hotel room.

"Is it true?" she began.

This time, I happened to be on the line. "Oh, hi," I said. "I've read some of your columns and enjoyed them."

Rona was pleased but not flattered enough to drop her purpose for the call. "What about all the marriage rumors, Chrissie?"

"No, it's not true," I said. "I don't know how it started, but it's definitely not true."

"Okay," Rona said.

How do rumors start? I don't know. Maybe someone got excited over the sign at the hotel where we checked in. It read "Welcome Chris and Jimmy Connors."

Defining my continuing involvement with Jimmy was not easy. Our problem was the strong feelings we had for each other. I had been completely obsessed with our relationship—I hadn't even looked at another man for several years—and you don't just wake up one morning, hand back a ring and say, "Well, I can't marry you because the timing is wrong, so that's it, I just don't care about you anymore."

Despite our career conflicts and differing sense of values that came from simply growing up, our feelings kept us bound together like a tightly wound yo-yo. We would be going in opposite directions when one of us, perhaps inadvertently, tugged on the string, and the other would suddenly come reeling back in, even to our surprise. Then just when everything seemed rolled up, in good shape, one of us would feel a pull from another direction, and out would go the string again.

If the public was confused about our relationship—one day they would see us together on television during a tennis match in Boca Raton, Florida, and the next day see a picture of me with a new friend, or Jimmy with another girl—many times I was just as confused about what was happening between us.

The passage of time and new relationships eventually unwound our feelings. But for about three years, there was quite a lot of yanking back and forth—not all of it timely as far as my tennis was concerned. Certainly the public display of emotions that came from living in the media fishbowl was always difficult to deal with.

That was certainly the case in 1977 when I dated Vitas Gerulaitis. Vitas and I probably had different interpretations of our relationship. To me, it was dating; to Vitas, who seldom is serious about any woman, it may have been more like a friendship. Whatever it was, we had fun together. Whenever I was in or near New York, we went out. Most of the time it was dining or dancing, touring the disco circuit. It was a different life style from tennis and training, and I had never played that game to any extent. Vitas was refreshing.

Some people are addicted to the after-hours disco scene and night life. If they miss an evening somewhere, the beat can't go on without them. My life had been spent sweating, playing matches, eating late dinners in my room and going to bed. That summer, I partied late, slept late and still won the U.S. Open for a third straight time.

An obsession with tennis or a life style at the expense of anything else can be destructive. For me, dating Vitas proved a release from the burdens of being on top. I could get away, relax. Whether it's dinner, dancing, music or a massage, you need a few diversions that completely remove you from the pressures of your profession. I was at that point. The pain I had experienced at Wimbledon after the match with Virginia revealed the depth of the pressure.

It never entered my mind that Vitas would be marriage material. He was an appealing, charismatic person, with a great personality. He could tease me about moving faster on the court or the fresh blond streaks in my hair. He could say it with a laugh and twinkle in his eye. I liked him, he liked me, we enjoyed being with one another; there was definitely an attraction, but we just lived day by day. The future was now, it was the first time I had experienced that sort of relationship, and I wasn't as anxious as I had been with Jimmy. It didn't matter whether we were going to make it or what was ahead and how we would get there. The men I dated and girl friends I developed strengthened my security. I didn't have to rush into relationships; I was fine by myself, I liked myself more.

It should have been a glorious November in San Francisco that year. I beat Billie Jean King at Mission Hills in the finals of the Colgate Series, 6–2, 6–2, ending her eighteen-match winning streak. The Wightman Cup gave me another chance to settle my Wimbledon score with Virginia, but not even a 7–5, 7–6 victory could lift my spirits. The glamour was gone. I had squeezed all the enthusiasm and eagerness out of myself. After playing tennis almost nonstop for eighteen years, no amount of money or revenge excited me.

• • •

It was a picturesque summer night, ideal for a romantic stroll even with a Wimbledon final to be played the following day. "What about a walk in the park?" John Lloyd suggested politely, after we had returned to Inn on the Park from a dinner date at Newton's.

"Sure, why not?" I said, more eager to spend time with a new, exciting friend than go to my room and fret over facing Martina Navratilova on Centre Court.

We crossed one of London's busier intersections and headed toward Hyde Park. The park was deserted, and the pitch-dark sky sent a slight chill through me. I have always been afraid of the dark and never sleep in a totally dark room. Growing up in Fort Lauderdale, I always left on a light in the closet at night and slept in the bed nearest the door. I would close the door but could still see the sliver of light underneath. That sliver assured me that I was not going to be kidnapped. If I heard any noises, I usually crawled under the covers or climbed into my sister Jeanne's bed.

Jeanne still teases me about the unidentified flying object that was allegedly sighted in Fort Lauderdale. The news flashed on all the radio stations one night, and everyone was driving around town trying to find it. Jeannie and I went with Ana Leaird in Ana's Mustang to track it down. Ana drove, Jeanne was the copilot, and I was the navigator, listening to the radio and hanging out the car window. Of course, we found nothing, but it was exciting to be in on a "chase."

Walking with John was fun too, until we saw this strange-looking man swinging from tree branches in the park, screaming obscenities and coming toward us. "Is he drunk or what?" I said, tightening my grip around John's arm.

"I don't know if he's drunk," John said, picking up the pace of our walk, "but I don't want to find out."

The man staggered closer, still shouting words that I only used in dirty jokes. I wasn't sure if he had a gun or a knife because of the darkness. At the last instant, as John and I braced for the worst, the man turned away and continued his rantings in a different direction. I looked at John and smiled in relief. "Life with you so far certainly hasn't been dull," I said. It had been our second date.

John rushed into my life after I first saw his picture in one of the English newspapers. I was in Eastbourne for the traditional pre-Wimbledon tournament; even after a four-month layoff from mid-November to March, my heart had not returned to tennis.

"Nobody understands what it's like," I lamented to Stephanie Tolleson after losing the Eastbourne final to Martina. "I'm No. 1 in the world and I'm unhappy."

I had expressed some of these same feelings to Lynda Carter several months earlier following a team tennis match at The Forum in Los Angeles, where I was playing for the Strings, but my arguments weren't convincing. On the one hand, I was tired of tennis, wanted to settle down, meet someone and have a baby; in the next breath, I told Lynda that Jimmy and I had broken up because I didn't want to quit, have children and simply follow him on the tour. I was confused, and Martina's thirty-seven-match winning streak that winter, along with her comeback, first from 2–4 and then from match point, in the

third set at Eastbourne demonstrated her determination to un-
seat me.

My preparations for Wimbledon lacked the intensity of previous years. But then, who could prepare seriously when your
coach was Ilie Nastase? Life with Nasty on the Strings was the
equivalent of a three-ring circus. On court changeovers, I
would listen to Stephanie try to talk strategy. Meanwhile, Nasty
was more concerned about line calls and umpires. "Good girl,
Chrissie," he would say. "Keep going. Good girl."

No team with Nasty as coach could be well disciplined. We
practiced at the Riviera Country Club, and Nasty sometimes
preferred hitting with Cheryl Tiegs, the model, than with us. I
guess I couldn't blame him.

Our matches were events for the wrong reasons. If calls went
against us, Nasty threatened the officials, fans, even other players. "My team, we leave!" he would shout. "We no play here."
Of course, while Nasty was telling the umpire we were leaving,
I informed Nasty that I was not about to walk out. Bad calls
were a fact of life I had learned to live with; for Nasty, they
were a curse, delivered from some supreme tennis being out to
destroy him. Thus, his arms frequently gestured to the heavens,
alas, in vain.

Nasty nicknamed Stephanie and me "The Blondies" for obvious reasons. Vijay Amritraj and Ashok Amritraj, two other
members of the Strings, were his "Black Horses," also for
obvious reasons. "Anybody bother you, Chrissie," Nasty
would lecture in the locker room, "I sic my Black Horses on
them."

Nasty's humor is hardly subtle, as tennis audiences are well
aware. But he couldn't grasp my sense of humor. Stephanie and
I would playfully pass him dirty letters on an airplane, the type
that you buy in a novelty store and then fill in the four-letter
words. We would add our bits to the letter, and he didn't know
what to do. "You serious or not?" he would ask, passing the
notes to others on the team for inspection.

Traveling with Nasty, the Amritrajs, trainer Bill Norris and
Mitch Oprea, Nasty's friend and adviser, was an all-star, any-

thing-goes experience. But our lively, unpredictable troupe could not hide the fact that I seemed destined to spend another drab, lonely fortnight at Wimbledon.

John had revealed some of the same feelings about the loneliness of the circuit in a newspaper article that week. There were so many groupies on the men's tour, he said, that he just wished he could meet somebody he could fall in love with, who would travel with him and share his life. What he said struck a sensitive chord in me. I had been feeling the same way for some time. One of the pictures of John in the paper showed him shirtless, hugging a girl who was topless. John was tall, handsome and intriguing.

The following week, with Wimbledon under way, Stephanie and I were in my hotel room watching the matches on television. Stephanie was glued to the screen, about two inches away, when I walked into the room.

"What are you doing so close?" I said. "It's bad for your eyes."

"Look at him," she replied, fixed to the set.

I looked at the TV. In living color, John Lloyd, the British Davis Cupper, was playing at Wimbledon.

"I think I'm in love," Stephie said.

"Yeah, he sure is great looking," I confirmed.

Stephanie always teases about that day, insisting she spotted John first. Actually, I watched John play the first match on Centre Court at Wimbledon in 1975, but my interests were with another player at the time, Jimmy Connors, the defending champion.

If it weren't for another friend, Ingrid Bentzer, I don't know whether John and I would have hooked up at Wimbledon that year. Ingrid and I had been practicing during the tournament. After several days of remarkable restraint, I had to pop the question: Did she know John Lloyd?

"He's a great guy," she said. "Really different from the other men. Really nice, sweet and very shy."

"Can you introduce him to me?" I asked boldly.

Ingrid has a deliciously sneaky smile when she knows what's

on your mind. "Well, what I'll do is mention your name the next time I talk to him," she said.

In the tea room the next day, Ingrid and John were having a conversation on the other side of the room. The way Ingrid tells the story, out of the blue, she said to him, "Why don't you go over and talk to Chrissie?"

"Pardon me," John said, stunned more by the subject than Ingrid's candor.

"Why don't you go over and talk to Chrissie?"

"Well, why should I do that?"

"Because she's a nice girl. And I think you should go over and talk to her."

Ingrid would not relent. Finally, John said, "Listen, I'm playing an exhibition at Queen's tomorrow. Why don't you and Chrissie come along and we can have lunch?"

She agreed. By the time we got to Queen's, however, his match was over, and he had gone. I wondered if we could ever get together before the tournament ended.

The next day, I noticed John eyeing me in the tea room. By accident, Ingrid, John and I happened to be standing in front of the transportation office waiting for rides later in the day. Ingrid introduced us and then, in her fashion, corralled John into meeting us at The Tramp disco later that evening.

Stephanie, Ingrid and I went to The Tramp and waited for John after I had beaten Virginia, 8–6, 6–2, in the semifinals. He arrived at about ten, we talked and danced. Stephanie then excused herself. About thirty minutes later, Ingrid decided she was too exhausted from a weekend trip to Amsterdam, so she also left. John and I were alone.

John didn't know what to expect. Nor did I. He had an image of me from what he had read in the papers, and it wasn't terribly favorable by British standards. "I just really didn't know," he would tell me later. "But within an hour, you and I were on the same wave length."

The Lloyds and the Everts are tennis families. John's father didn't take up the sport until he was eighteen years old, but he loved it and reached Wimbledon qualifying standards. His mother never played but finally realized she had to learn or would never see her husband; so she went to their club on weekends and wound up a good first-team player.

"My father was a great fighter on the court," John told me. "He didn't have a serve-and-volley game, but he learned how to play purely by himself. He could get the ball back all day, had a big topspin forehand and was very gutsy. I don't think there's anybody in the world who loves tennis more than he does. That's how David got involved."

David, John and Tony are as different as the Evert brothers and sisters. David, the oldest, was fiercely intense and loyal whether he was playing soccer, tennis or dominoes. John saw himself as more middle-of-the-road. "If you fused the two of us together," he said, "we would have been a lot better in tennis than one of us individually." The consensus was that Tony, the youngest brother, had more ability than David or John but was painfully shy, perhaps comparable to Drew. John's sister Anne wanted nothing to do with tennis although she married a sportswriter, Bob Hammond.

Because of his good looks and tennis ability, John's name was linked romantically with assorted women. At nineteen, he was engaged to Isabel Larsson, a Swedish player, and their relationship sounded a little like my early involvement with Jimmy.

"It was one of those things you do when you're young," he said. "Everybody tells you it's wrong and won't work out, but you don't care and you do it anyway. If we had gotten married then, it would not have lasted more than six months. We were from two completely different cultures, we both liked completely different things and there's no way it could have worked."

John never saw himself in the social spotlight. He went to the discos occasionally with friends, he said, but didn't like trying to pick up someone he had just met. "When I did go out with anybody, it obviously got around a little bit more and then was blown out of proportion."

Even though I have been characterized as careful and cautious on the court, my feelings for John were spontaneous and instinctive. Again, timing is important, on and off the court, and the time was right for us. John had traveled extensively and wanted to settle down. He had admired me from a distance, he said, but the occasions were never right for approaching me. Either I was dating Jimmy at the time—at least, John thought that the case—or he and I were never in the same place at the same time. Even when the men and women are together for tournaments like Wimbledon, the U.S. Open or the French, it's not as if you sit around the tea rooms or player lounges waiting to meet someone. If Wimbledon didn't have so many rainy days, there would be even less time for socializing.

Being with John took priority over everything else. On the eve of the women's singles final, we went out for dinner. "I'll find you a place that's discreet," he promised, realizing that I was still being linked romantically with Jimmy.

That night, John booked a corner table at Newton's. After dinner, over coffee, we heard this booming voice in the restaurant, looked up and saw a parade of people tramping down the stairs, led by Lennart Bergelin, Bjorn Borg's coach. Borg wasn't with the group, but there were about fifteen members of the Swedish tennis association, and John recognized some of them.

We looked at each other. "Oh, my God," John said, sensing that the news of our being spotted by the Swedes would certainly spread all over the tea room the next day. Somehow, though, they walked straight past and didn't even notice us.

The incident in the park later that night was further disconcerting, and I woke up the next day thinking more about John than winning a third Wimbledon crown.

I should have beaten Martina. I led, 4–2, in the third set. Sitting in the stands, John turned to his friend, Martin Hill, and said, "She's going to win it. It's going to be great."

If I had been hungry, the match was mine. But Martina's confidence was keen from our long Eastbourne three-setter, and she wanted Wimbledon as badly as Virginia had in 1977. She swept five of the next six games and the match, 2–6, 6–4, 7–5. I didn't feel badly about losing; in fact, I didn't feel anything. I walked to the net, shook hands with Martina and actually was happy for her. In the last four games, all I could think about was going out with John. Something fresh and wonderful was happening to me.

If my attitude sounds illogical, consider the past: In 1976, I won a second Wimbledon but crashed because there had been no one to share it with; in 1977, I beat Tracy and Billie Jean and then lost to Virginia, mentally drained.

"It was obvious to me that your mind wasn't on the game," John would say of that final. "But I had no idea that I was the distraction. To think that a Wimbledon title went because of that."

Looking back, it's easy to say that I should have been more committed. To come so close? Yet what mattered most at that moment was happiness. I could not buy happiness with another title. If Martina had folded quietly or exploded, I might have backed in, but she showed courage and determination.

In the tea room afterward, I joined Tony Roche and Fred Stolle at a table. They talked about the match, how close it had been. Just a matter of a shot here or there!

"How about a beer?" Fred asked. Australians live on their lager.

"I hate beer," I said.

"Okay, what about a shandy?" Shandy was a mixture of beer and Seven-Up; I nodded. Turning Fred down again would have been an insult.

Dianne Fromholtz and Mike Lupica, a columnist for the *New York Daily News*, stopped by the table and wished me well. Then my mom came over and wondered when to order a car. I could see John off in another corner, perhaps too concerned about my defeat to ask whether I wanted to go out. Later he would tell me that he really didn't know what to say because everything seemed so out of place. But he finally walked over and said hello to my mom, whom he had never met.

"Do you still want to go out tonight?" he asked. "Because I can completely understand if you don't."

"You've got to be joking," I said. "I really want to go out."

My instant response took John by surprise, but I wanted him to know how important I viewed our relationship. Maybe a Wimbledon title was lost because of it, but I had won something far more important.

11 • The Team

The first time the key turned in the door, I shrugged off any fear. It was the room next door, I reasoned, and not worth concerning myself in the comfort of a hot bath. Then the key rustled in the door a second time, and the noise sounded as if it were outside my door. But who would have a key to my room at the St. Moritz hotel, and why would anyone be hanging around at eleven-thirty at night? I squirmed uneasily in the tub.

I had arrived in New York City earlier in the day for the 1979 Avon Championships finals at Madison Square Garden. John was to meet me the next day, so Ana Leaird and I had room service in my suite before she left for her hotel at eleven o'clock.

Soaking in the tub has always been a form of relaxation. I sleep better and feel more relaxed. But I could hardly unwind after suddenly seeing a man I didn't know walking through the living room of my suite into the bedroom. Lying in the tub, I could feel my heart pounding. I was frightened. All I could blurt out as the man moved toward the bathroom was "Can I help you?" The words seemed inappropriate when the thought of being raped flashed through my mind.

The man looked about fifty years old, wore a rumpled suit and weaved slightly as he walked. I studied him more closely and sensed that he might be drunk. The zipper on his pants was down.

"Is that you, honey?" he said, reaching the door of the bathroom, which was half-open.

Blurry visions passed through my head. He was older, so maybe I could beat him up if he tried to attack. Where were my tennis racquets? Did he think I was his wife or girl friend? Why my room? Did he know me from tennis?

"Wait a minute," I said, still too nervous to stand. "Just stay there and let me get out of the bathtub."

I waited for his reply. Would he ignore my words and walk in? Had he even heard what I said? "Oh, okay, honey," he said.

The man turned and walked back through the bedroom into the living room. I stood up in the tub, reached for a towel—accidentally pushing three others into the toilet—wrapped it around me, tiptoed into the bedroom and peeked through the door. The man was eating off my room-service table. I quietly closed the door in the bedroom, nervously picked up the phone and dialed the front desk.

"Hello, there's a man in my room," I whispered. "This is Chris Evert, and there's a man in my room. Please send some security up right away."

The clerk sounded startled, so I repeated my name several times, hoping it might speed the request.

"What room are you in?" he said.

I gave him the room number. "Do you think you could please hurry?"

"We'll send somebody up right away."

I stayed in the bedroom, wishing John had been there and wondering how something like this could happen. Was this one of those bizarre New York experiences you read about? The bedroom door opened, and the man stood in the doorway staring at me. Panic set in.

"What are you doing in here, honey?" he muttered, stumbling toward me.

"This is my room," I said, trying to sound authoritative without being testy.

I didn't know what to do. Would he grab me? Did he even know where he was? Where was security?

The man walked past me toward the bathroom. "Can I use your bathroom?" he asked. I was almost too startled to say anything other than "Sure."

When he reached the bathroom, I ran into the living room, opened the door of my suite and prayed he would take several minutes to relieve himself. I glanced toward the elevator and waited hopefully. A light flashed on the elevator. Three men stepped out.

"He's in the bathroom," I said. The men rushed through the bedroom and into the bathroom. They frisked the man and found nothing.

"You don't know this guy?" one of the security guards asked, standing in the living room, while the others were interrogating the man in the bathroom.

"I never saw him before," I said. "I was sitting in the bathtub when he walked in with his zipper down. I don't know how he got in or where he came from."

The security men brought the midnight visitor back into the living room. My heart was still beating like a drum. "Listen," the man said, trying to explain, "I had a key, I had this room last night. . . ."

"Did you check out this morning?" one of the security men interrupted.

"Well, yeah."

"Why didn't you turn in your key then?"

The man had no answer. He half smiled out of the corner of his mouth, a cynical look from someone who probably was too drunk to realize what he had done and yet was still sober enough to think that, well, nobody had been hurt in the affair, so it wasn't really all that bad, was it?

My mind and heart weren't into tennis. I had won a fourth consecutive U.S. Open singles title the previous summer, taken the National Indoors and Colgate Series championships and finished the year with a thirty-two-match winning streak. But while writers debated whether Martina or I deserved to be No. 1 for the year, the only No. 1 in my life was John. From the time we first went out at Wimbledon, there was something more between us than just an occasional friendship. We clicked together, liked each other's company. By October, after I returned to London for the Wightman Cup, John and I went out every night and talked seriously about marriage.

John's proposal wasn't one of those down-on-the-knees versions. We both wanted marriage, talked enough about it and agreed it was just a matter of how and when. John and I still tease about the first time we said we loved each other. John says he first told me at the U.S. Open in September, which may explain why I was so overjoyed during that tournament. I told John during the Wightman Cup in London the next month. We formally announced our engagement on my twenty-fourth birthday, during a press conference in Hollywood, Florida, for an Avon tournament. George Liddy, the promoter and a longtime friend, had bought a large birthday cake for the occasion.

I walked into the conference that day wearing the engagement ring. Jim Martz of the *Miami Herald*, Craig Barnes of the *Fort Lauderdale Sun-Sentinel* and Jim Sarni of the *Fort Lauderdale News* were all there. They started with the usual tennis questions about who was No. 1 and what my plans were for 1979 until someone spotted the ring.

"Is that something new on your left hand?" A hush went over the room, I blushed and looked down at my hand.

"It's called a ring," I said.

"Could you tell us about it?"

I paused. "It's an engagement ring."

"Anyone we know?" someone asked coyly from another side of the room.

"John Lloyd."

All that week, before the conference, John had suggested that I call Jimmy to tell him about the engagement before he heard it from the press first. I remember those times when the press first informed me of Jimmy's wanderings. John knew that Jimmy always phoned on my birthdays. "I think you should do it," he told me. "You owe him that courtesy."

John was right. But for some reason, I was a little uncomfortable and was afraid of having to tell Jimmy. What do you say to someone in those circumstances? "Hi, guess what, I'm engaged"?

Sure enough, after the conference, Jimmy called. "I want to wish you a happy birthday," he began. "Is it true what I heard over the news?"

I was too embarrassed to tell him I wanted to call but couldn't. "About what?" I said.

"About your engagement?"

"Yeah."

"That's great. Congratulations."

"Thanks."

Gloria Connors then got on the phone and congratulated me. Talking with her reminded me of that era when the Connors and Evert clans rode in the same station wagon to and from the Orange Bowl Juniors.

My dad never had a clue that John and I were serious enough to consider marriage. About a week before the announcement, he wanted to talk to John about the marriage. Like Jimmy, John couldn't bring himself to meet with my dad. "It's no big deal," I would tell John, "but you've got to do it." John would say, "I will, I will." But for days he was hanging around, trying to pick the right time and place. One night, he was watching television and my dad came into the room. "Is it any good?" my dad asked.

"It's pretty good," John said.

"I think we should have a word now," my dad suggested.

"Oh, yeah, good idea," John said. They went into another room. My sister Clare was watching TV. As soon as John left the room, she laughed her head off because she knew what was going to happen.

Clare fell in love with John. So did my dad. After their "meeting," my dad teased John about the wedding. "You sure you don't want to use a ladder?" he would say, laughing as he talked. "I'll give you the money to buy a ladder."

John and I wanted a wedding—to bring over his family from England to share our closeness and to celebrate with our friends. As far back as 1975, Ted Tinling had even asked about being able to make my wedding dress.

No one knows more about women's tennis than Ted, and not simply because he dressed almost all of the top players since Suzanne Lenglen of France. One of Ted's laments was that he had not been able to dress me. My loyalty to Mondessa in the beginning and then the Puritan contract prevented any other agreements. With Ted, designing was a matter of pride.

"Do you realize how sad it is for me that you broke my daisy chain?" he once told me over breakfast in Washington during the 1975 Slims tournament. "Since Maureen Connolly," he continued, "you're the first champion that I haven't dressed ever. Why don't we have a guess wager that I will make your wedding dress?"

"You've got a long time to wait," I said, floundering from the broken engagement with Jimmy.

Anyone who knows Ted will tell you he can recall the color of Suzanne Lenglen's dresses from matches in the 1920s. Two years later, he asked me the same question, and I gave him the same answer.

For the Federation Cup matches that were to be played in Australia in December 1978, I asked Ted if he could make me some halter dresses for the competition. Ted was outfitting the United States team but there was almost no time to make the dresses before I left for Australia and no means of measuring me because I had to leave from the West Coast, and Ted's offices were in Philadelphia. Trouper that he is, Ted made three dresses in a day on sheer guesswork and brought them to Australia. I tried them on and they fit beautifully, except for one problem: I don't wear a bra with halter dresses and Ted's dresses were too sheer to be worn without a bra.

"Leave it to me," he said. Ingenious as ever, Ted chopped up six Christian Dior handkerchiefs his staff had given to him for the trip and sewed portions of the handkerchiefs into the bodice of the dress for a lining. By the time he finished the second dress, he had only one whole handkerchief left, so he took the Christian Dior symbol, made it into a "T" and sewed it onto the chest of the dress. I played in the dresses, and we won the Federation Cup. The night of the banquet in Melbourne, Vickie Berner, our captain, asked if I would sign Ted's last handkerchief. He sent it over with a waiter, and I wrote, "Thank you for the lovely dresses, but don't forget you owe me the most important dress of all."

It must have been the first and only time Ted had ever received an order for a wedding dress on a handkerchief, but I knew how much he wanted to make the dress, and it seemed like a wonderful way to surprise him.

John and I settled on April 17 as our wedding date for several reasons. Spring was a refreshingly happy time of the year, it would not interfere with any commitments we had made for winter tournaments, and it would allow us a relaxed honeymoon in Bermuda and still enough time to prepare for Wimbledon.

The plans for the wedding dominated my time that winter. Whenever I was on the court, thoughts would flash about fittings for the dress, the ceremony, invitations, pictures. I lost to Greer Stevens in the first round of a tournament in Hollywood, Florida, and went down, 6–3, 6–1, to Sue Barker in Boston on the night that friends threw a bridal shower for me. Things did not improve in New York. Tracy beat me for the first time, 6–3, 6–1, in the Avon finals, and I dropped a 6–3, 6–3 match to Dianne Fromholtz the next night that eliminated me from the championships. After the loss to Fromholtz, I skipped the postmatch conference for one of the few times in my career. Instead, I gave Ana a statement that read, "I don't feel the media has been sensitive enough to my personal situation. I searched for my competitive fires, but they weren't there. I promise you this summer I'll be tough and eager."

Tennis seemed so secondary. During the Avon finals, Ted came to New York for the final fitting, and I could hardly wait.

Years before, dividing my time during a series championship would have been a no-no.

The only person in the room that day, aside from Ted and Margaret Krigin, his longtime associate, was Ana Leaird. As soon as I saw myself in the dress, I knew that Ted had achieved what I wanted—a single column satin dress, chantilly lace, pearls, long tight sleeves, fitted at the waist, low neckline, lifted overskirt in the front.

"I'm sorry to keep you so long," he said, fidgeting with the dress and realizing that I had a match that night.

"I don't ever want to take it off," I said.

Ted was very happy with the dress. In his mind, the lace expressed the femininity that I wanted to convey as a person and the two thousand pearls stood for durability. To me, the dress was stylish yet traditional.

A wedding is a very personal and private event in someone's life. John and I planned ours to distinguish between the public and private side of our lives. On Friday the 13th, there was a pool party for friends, a relaxing day, perhaps the only time John and I would be able to bring everyone together. The following afternoon was a bridesmaids' luncheon; that night, everyone went to a soccer game.

At the wedding rehearsal, friends recounted events from the past, and I realized how important their love, kindness and consideration had been over the years. Of course, not all stories during the rehearsal were sentimental, especially when people like Ingrid Bentzer, Stephanie Tolleson and Laurie Fleming Rowley were involved.

Laurie recalled the time we played in this 14-and-under tournament at North Miami Beach. A monastery, brought over brick by brick from Spain, was close to the court, and visitors could pay fifty cents to tour the building. However, between matches tennis players would sneak through the woods into the monastery, dare each other to ring this huge bell and then escape before the monks caught on.

One day, Laurie and I were alone in the woods. I dared Laurie to go up and ring the bell five times.

"You go first," she challenged.

Faced with putting up or shutting up, I ran about one hundred feet, climbed a small stone wall, pulled the rope attached to the bell five times, jumped down and scampered back.

"Now it's your turn," I told Laurie, who had been hiding behind a bush. Of course, by now, with the bell having been rung, Laurie worried about being caught. She ran down the walk, jumped up on the wall and rang the bell five times. But before she could get away, a monk stood in her path, angry at having been harassed all week by players from the tournament.

"Stop where you are," he yelled at Laurie. "Come with me."

She walked with the monk to the main office, all the while looking for me. "Is there anybody else with you?" the monk asked. Laurie shook her head and went into the office. The monk reproached her, said he would call the police the next time it happened and wondered when the tournament would be over.

Laurie told everyone at the rehearsal that she left the office crying. "I went out and called out, 'Chrissie, Chrissie' but I didn't hear anything so I went back to the tournament," she said. "There was Chrissie, watching the matches, sitting in the crowd, just sitting there. She just forgot all about me. As soon as I got into trouble, she just ran and acted as if nothing ever happened."

Believe it or not, the Evert family had three weddings in 1979. My brother Drew married Terri Cox on March 10. My sister Jeanne married Brahm Dubin on November 29. Somehow, my mom and dad survived all three.

No wedding comes off perfectly, and mine was no exception. The day of the wedding, someone telephoned a bomb scare to St. Anthony's Church. I didn't learn about the threat until after the wedding, from my dad. On the ride to the church, about fifty people had gathered outside our house. The limousine went about a block when I discovered I had forgotten my floral bouquet, so we hastily returned to the house, and I had to search for my bouquet while all these people stood outside wondering whether I had gotten cold feet at the last minute.

About nine hundred people were in front of the church, including dozens of photographers and members of the media that I recognized. Leaving the limo, I bunched a portion of the train to my dress underneath my arm to avoid falling on my way into the church. That fall would have made even more newspapers than when I landed on my butt against Tracy on Wimbledon's Centre Court in 1977.

From the back of the church, all my bridesmaids kissed me and wished me good luck before they walked down the aisle. My sister Jeanne was the maid of honor, then came Clare, Laurie, Ana and Stephanie Tolleson. Stephanie, who was the last, gave me a kiss, said "good luck," turned and then tripped over the carpet and fell flat on her face. As serious as the occasion was supposed to be, I couldn't stop laughing. Maybe it was because Stephanie and I always seemed to be in and out of mischief over the years. She got up, her hair was in shambles, and she limped down the aisle. What Stephanie didn't realize at the time was that her misfortune relaxed me.

My dad downed a couple of drinks before his walk down the aisle. He may have been more nervous than anybody that day, and not simply over the bomb scare. He gets claustrophobic and faint in rooms with a lot of people, which was another reason why he preferred a small wedding. There were only about one hundred and twenty-five people in the church.

Some moments you remember more than others. I'll never forget the ceremony and how wonderful it was sharing it with John. At the altar, I was shaking like a leaf, but John took my hand, squeezed it, and I felt his strength. The first dance at the reception was also appropriate: "We've Only Just Begun." And there was a final moment at the reception, between John and his brother David, who had been best man, that was especially touching.

After all the guests had gone, when only a few of us remained, he and David sort of hugged each other and broke into tears. It was a sentimental way of expressing joy, of saying perhaps that things might never be the same again, but that things would always be close between them. Seeing them together, sharing brotherly love, moistened my eyes. I was about

John plays a mighty good game himself.

*My bridesmaids—Laurie, Stephanie, Ana, Clare, and Jeanne,
my maid of honor.*

Bennett Yell

Our wedding portrait.

*Our first trip to
Hawaii together.*

Art Seitz

John and I, Lynda and Ron having a little toast.

Art Seitz

Concentrating.

John and his parents and I at a Florida tournament.

My father, who still acts as my only coach and sometime ball boy when I'm practicing.

Bjorn Borg and I receiving our awards for being selected "World Champion" of our respective sexes for 1980.

My fifth U.S. Open victory, over Hana Mandlikova. I was twenty-five, and everyone had counted me out. Tsk, tsk. . . .

Luigi E. Serra

*The 1981 American Wightman Cup Team, consisting of
Pam Shriver, Andrea Jaeger, me, and Tracy Austin,
parading through Chicago to promote the event.*

*Holding up the plate
one dreams about
holding.*

Art Seitz

to embark on a new life, but I too would never relinquish my love for my family.

• • •

Of all my achievements in tennis, I'm probably as proud of my record on clay courts as any of my Wimbledon, U.S. Open or French singles titles.

When I started, at the age of six, I practiced every day on clay courts. At seventeen and eighteen, I worked out more on cement courts, but until then, my indoctrination to tennis was on clay.

My father's philosophy, when working with me, was "Be patient, be steady, let your opponent make the error. The player who makes the least amount of errors will eventually win the match." That's where I developed my concentration, because you have to concentrate on clay. You can't be loose and allow yourself the luxury of distraction. Rallies with Laurie Fleming and my sister Jeanne usually wound up with twenty to thirty hits.

Many players find clay a very frustrating surface, but it never frustrated me. I felt as if I could go out there and play a physically stronger opponent or more aggressive opponent or someone who had more weapons and still win. Clay was an equalizer, a place where I could move well, slide, retrieve and utilize my patience and mental strengths. Some of my earliest national titles were achieved on clay courts. I would like to think my clay-court winning streak between 1973 and 1979 contributed to an appreciation of clay as a competitive surface.

Record-keepers like Steve Flink of *World Tennis* magazine and Bud Collins always pointed out that my streak began the week after I lost to Evonne Goolagong, 6–2, 7–5, in the finals of the 1973 Western Championships in Cincinnati. Interestingly, Evonne started her career in Australia on clay courts and then gradually developed a grass-court game.

I didn't become conscious of my clay-court streak until after it reached one hundred. If the media hadn't harped on it, I probably wouldn't have been aware of it at all, but after one hundred victories in a row, every time I went on the court for a match in a clay-court tournament, it seemed like a new piece of history.

It was ironic that my clay-court streak ended at 125 in the spring of 1979, at the hands of Tracy Austin, in the semifinals of the Italian Open. The Italian was only the second event after John and I returned from our honeymoon in Bermuda. At the Federation Cup in Madrid, I struggled before beating Dianne Fromholtz of Australia, 2–6, 6–3, 8–6.

My confidence still had not returned in Rome. I handled JoAnne Russell (6–1, 6–2) and Janet Newberry (6–2, 6–1) in my first two matches but needed three sets against Ivanna Madruga of Argentina (3–6, 6–1, 6–4) in the quarterfinals. That brought me face to face against Tracy in the semis, two months after the Avon Championships.

I went into the match afraid to play her. I had respect for Tracy's game and knew how tough she could be, the only player who was a threat to me on clay. Against Martina, Evonne, Billie Jean and Virginia, I was quite confident on that surface. But with Tracy's game, when we played, the deciding factor became determination: who was more determined on that day.

It was a very emotional match for me. Tracy was fearless, hitting out with nothing to lose. I returned balls, but played more defensively than purposefully. I lost the first set, 6–4, won the second, 6–2, and led, 4–2, in the third. But there was never a point where I thought I was going to win. I've played very few matches where I've thought that I was going to win and wound up losing. I can usually trust myself. If I think I'm going to win a match, ninety-nine out of one hundred times, I'll win that match. Against Tracy that day, I was shaky and uncertain. I was threatened, and Tracy played with no nerves. From 2–4, we went into a third-set tie breaker, and Tracy took the playoff, 7–4. Usually in tight situations, I've been able to come through; that's when I'm at my toughest. But on that day, disappointed as I was about seeing my streak ended, Tracy beat me. The last set was 7–6, the first time I had ever lost at that score. But I had known that if someone was going to end the streak sometime or somewhere, it probably was going to be Tracy. Her game and temperament suited the surface.

My streak would not have gone on forever. Bjorn Borg has lost matches on clay courts. I was proud of my ability to rebound in Vienna and the French Open in the following weeks. Those victories started me on another clay-court streak that reached sixty-four in a row before I lost to Hana Mandlikova in the semifinals of the 1981 French Open.

I can't quibble with 189 victories in 191 matches on clay. Steve Flink produced some interesting statistics on my record during the 125-match streak: 71 of the 258 sets—or 28 percent —were 6–0 sets. Only 8 of the 125 matches were three-setters.

• • •

They say absence makes the heart grow fonder. I don't feel absence helps a marriage when you're away, traveling to different tournaments. It's not two careers I'm questioning because they can work beautifully. But I don't like being away, growing apart. You need to share things. You have to be independent for your own good or you'll be miserable away from your spouse, but you can sometimes grow too independent. If I'm away from John for three weeks, for several days after we're together again, it's awkward. It's as if we're rediscovering each other, and I don't think that's good.

Before we were married, trying to be together as often as we could meant sacrifices. In 1978, John had been playing well. But after we met at Wimbledon, as he later told me, if he won another round in a tournament, it meant he had to wait a day before flying to see me. "I felt as if I was a winner either way, whether I won or lost," he said.

The travel wasn't good for either of us. We wound up flying across the country and then flying back again for another tournament. Since John spent more time traveling with me, he suffered more in trying to maintain his sharpness and conditioning. It was easier for me to benefit from practicing with him than it was for John to find suitable practice partners on the women's circuit.

My competitive urge also faltered in 1979. A few matches challenged me, like the 7–5, 5–7, 13–11 final with Martina at Eastbourne. But at Wimbledon, after having taken Evonne, 6–3, 6–2 in the semis, I lost to Martina, 6–4, 6–4, in the final for a second straight year.

The rest of the season was equally indecisive. I gutted out a three-setter over Tracy (6–7, 6–4, 6–1) in the final of a tournament in Bergen County, New Jersey, the week before the U.S. Open. She and I met again in the Open final, the day that John had to leave for a Davis Cup commitment in Italy; I lost 6–4, 6–3. After that loss, I made John promise never to leave me during a Wimbledon or U.S. Open, but even this assurance didn't solve losses to Wendy Turnbull, Martina, Virginia and Tracy again later in the year.

I was mellow on the court, an ominous sign. I like to fire up, to feel the adrenaline flowing; that's when I play my best. But in those losses, I kept thinking, "Big deal, if I don't win this match, I've got other things in life. I've got a great marriage, a great husband." I dismissed defeats and was torn between playing my tennis and going with John.

The scheduling also scared me. I didn't want to play twelve months a year and be separated from him for so many weeks, and was uncertain about how long I could continue playing. "Maybe in a year or two, you'll stop playing and have a family," I would tell myself.

Both of our careers suffered. Neither of us wanted to be away, and neither was motivated to do the work that we had to do to remain competitive.

John is a fine tennis player. He was Britain's under-16 champion in 1970 and a junior champion in 1972. In 1977, he beat Roscoe Tanner at Wimbledon and reached the finals of three Grand Prix tournaments, including the Australian Open. He was Britain's No. 2 player in 1978, but if you asked anyone in Britain who was their favorite British tennis player, John Lloyd was far and away No. 1.

John and I have always thought of ourselves as a team, but we each knew that work required individual effort. With John, he lost self-confidence and had written off his talents as a player before giving himself a full chance. "I've let things slide a little bit in terms of not working hard," he would tell me. "It's my own fault."

I tried to encourage John when he lost some early-round matches. Watching him became more emotional than if I had been on the court. There were periods of anger because I had flown all the way to be with him and then he went out and tanked. But then, I felt some sympathy because maybe our marriage had put some of that pressure on him. Maybe he felt he hadn't lived up to my standards of what a competitor should be or the standards I had set for myself. I began to second-guess myself.

"The pressure for me is to achieve what I've achieved before," he said. "But I've got to do it for myself. I can't worry about playing for other people."

John's low point was Wimbledon 1980. He had trained long and hard for the tournament and saw beating Buster Mottram, his first-round opponent and British countryman, as the opportunity to put himself back in the picture again. But he lost, 6–4, 6–2, 6–2.

"I was really keyed up," he later told me, "but I froze."

John was devastated that night. I had never seen him so depressed. He doesn't take his losses out on anybody but himself and becomes real quiet, but I was devastated too. I feel so much for John when he plays.

It would have been easy for John to write himself off. His ATP computer ranking had slipped into the hundreds, and it meant battling through pretournament qualifying, which can be more cutthroat than main draws, but he fought back. At Wimbledon one year later, he gutted out a five-set victory over Phil Dent of Australia in the opening round. Back on the Centre Court, he played well against Jose-Luis Clerc, the No. 9 seed, and lost a close four-setter in the second round. That match showed John he was capable of being as competitive as he wanted to be with the top ten players.

Uncertainties over our tennis did not affect our marriage. In fact, John likes to say that both of us were surprised at how easily we adjusted to being husband and wife. Elizabeth Wheeler, a writer friend, once wrote that it would be easier to be married to John Lloyd than to be married to Chris Evert. John saw these early pluses and minuses.

Although he was engaged to Isabel, John always envisioned himself being married to an Englishwoman, living in England and maybe opening some sports shops there. Living in the United States for eight or nine months a year was an adjustment for him, a period of feeling his way culturally. In England, John would have been a big fish in a little pond because of his popularity and identity. In the United States, he is a big fish in a bigger pond.

I love spending time with John. At our home in Palm Springs, we don't go out that often. I'll cook dinners for us— chicken and rice or lamb with vegetables—and we'll watch television or go out to movies. John loves to tape-record movies on television and play them back; he could watch and analyze movies for eight hours a day and would make an excellent critic; he reads *Variety* and other show business magazines, and Ron Samuels believes John would be a first-class producer because he has such a positive way with people. John teases me about my "thing" for "General Hospital," but I know I'm not alone. I've been watching that soap opera for about six or seven years; one year, I even tried to arrange my practice sessions in order not to miss the show. John says the plots are rubbish, but for one hour a day, I let myself unwind and deal with other people's problems instead of my own. During this time, John will either practice or bury himself in a novel by Ken Follett or Irving Wallace.

We have a flat in Wimbledon and a condominium in Amelia Island, Florida, where Drew is a teaching pro. My mom and dad built a second-floor addition to the house in Fort Lauderdale that can be used by any of their children. It's a nice feeling for John and me to know that we have so many "homes" where we can be comfortable.

Some people have said it's impossible for us to have a traditional husband-wife relationship because of our schedules. But John and I agree that I may not be playing much longer—whether it's two, three or four years—and he feels it wouldn't be right for him to say, "Hey, I want you to come with me every week," or to have me say the same thing to him. John knows I'm a career person, that I still want a career. He has said that even after we have children, and I'm out of tennis, he figures I'll want to set up a boutique or stay involved in sports through television.

Our situation is much different than that of Evonne and Roger Cawley, for example; Roger doesn't play so he can travel with Evonne all the time. The same was true with Margaret and Barry Court.

We never tried to model ourselves after any tennis couple. We're very close and honest with each other yet need times to ourselves. If we're in England, John will wander off to a soccer match with friends and I'll go shopping with the girls. We're not possessive, but we share the same values. The family is important, and loyalty is important. I enjoy being unselfish with John.

Tennis is a selfish profession, but anything he needs or wants to make him happy is my first priority. I enjoy giving so much to John because I know how much he cares. He has allowed me to be myself, and I want John to feel good about himself.

John and I hate arguments. It's just wasted energy and emotion so we avoid it. As I write this book, we've never had a fight in our marriage. Some people might feel this is unhealthy, but we talk over things. We never fight, scream or argue. We're waiting for that time to happen, but so far it hasn't.

In 1979, I played 22 tournaments and 107 matches, equaling my total for 1974, despite my marriage. The 1980 Avon circuit was a survival test that I lost. I guess I used more of my emotional reserves because the year began badly at the Colgate Series finals in Washington, with two straight losses to Tracy. Then came a third defeat within ten days to her, 6–2, 6–1, in the Avon final in Cincinnati. When Martina buried me, 6–2,

6–4, at another Avon final tour stop in Chicago, I had bottomed out.

I didn't want to play Chicago, after having announced in Cincinnati that I would leave the tour. All week, I conveyed negative impressions to Ingrid Bentzer, who was living in Chicago. "I'm nervous, tense and cringing out there," I told Ingrid during lunch at her apartment. "And every time I come off the court, I feel like I'm going to break into tears."

Ingrid watched the final against Martina. After the match, she came into the locker room, saw how upset I was and volunteered a ride back to the hotel. The weather was cold, damp and dreary as John and I made our way out of the arena. John held his arm around my shoulders for reassurance, but the wind from Lake Michigan left a chilling reminder of the conditions and my state of mind.

In the car, he tried to cheer me up. "Lovey, listen, it's not the whole world," he began. "You really played well, and it was only a couple of points, and you might have won that one. It will be all right."

I know what John was trying to do, but at that moment, his words were hollow to me. I gritted my teeth, turned and stared at him, tears on my face. "That's not the point," I said. "I don't care if I win or lose. I care about doing my best, and I didn't do my best. I couldn't produce my best, and that's the whole point."

Later, Ingrid said that she got goose pimples from the intensity of the situation. "I have never seen you so vulnerable," she said. "I looked in the rearview mirror, and it seemed like fire was coming out of your eyes, but your face was absolutely white and drawn. You had nothing left."

I played Seattle the following week. Two of my first three matches, against Lucia Romanov and Sylvia Hanika, wound up shortened by injury defaults. By the time I reached the semifinals against Virginia, I was too drained to continue and I myself defaulted. I had nothing left. If a break from the tour turned out to be permanent, I would have to accept the inevitable, but retirement now sounded more inviting than leaving my emotions in a lonely locker room.

12 · Coming Back

I've been blessed with great friends. Not just "let's-get-together-for-coffee" types, but friends who have given time, energy and support when it counted.

I could have just as easily walked away from tennis in the spring of 1980. I had won every major title, was financially secure and knew that John and I were a solid couple. In Cincinnati, I told John that my heart wasn't into tennis, that I didn't want to be on the court anymore, and he was totally supportive.

"You've had such a great career," he said. "If you don't want to play now, you shouldn't let anyone pressure you into playing."

John was confident we could be happy away from tennis and that I didn't need tennis as a crutch. I got similar feedback from Craig Barnes, a journalist, who explained how Jack Nicklaus had successfully defined his priorities after many years on the pro golf tour.

I never realized how much I wanted to get away until I finally threw up one morning in Seattle and actually made myself too sick to play for the first time. "It's not worth it, love," John said when I asked whether I should try to play the match that night against Virginia.

The following week, in Palm Springs, I felt as if a load had been lifted off my shoulders. It was total freedom; I didn't have to answer to anybody. I also didn't know what to do with myself. I woke up and made breakfast for John, he went off to practice and I watched TV, made calls or just walked around the house. It was a strange feeling, to have time on my hands and not worry about rushing off to a practice court.

Sitting around the house gave me an opportunity to think about past, present and future. I wanted to help John in his career because he had been so understanding. I also knew that I would only come back on my own terms and would never, ever, let anybody persuade me to play. I had to make my own decision, with John's help, and play by my rules.

"If you don't feel 100 percent," John would tell me, "don't worry about whether you want to play."

Many of my friends, like Ron Samuels and Lynda Carter, said leaving tennis then might be a mistake I would regret.

Lynda spent hours talking, listening and crying with me over whether I should go back or settle down. She harped on the idea that it was normal and natural to feel the way I did. "When you realize that another person feels the way you do," she stressed, "you don't feel as if you're such a bizarre creature."

I've never felt self-indulgent around Lynda and Ron. Neither would let me. "How did two dogs like us ever get two gorgeous things like John and Lynda," I once teased Ron.

"Speak for yourself, Chrissie," Ron replied.

I cherish Lynda's camaraderie. On one occasion, I saw a pair of beautiful diamond hoops at the Marvin Hime jewelry store in Beverly Hills. I asked Lynda how she liked them; she said they were stunning, so I bought a pair and brought them back to Lynda's house.

"Show Lupe what you bought," Lynda said, rushing to tell her housekeeper.

I had my own ideas, however, took the box from the bag, stuck it about three inches from Lynda's face and said, "Here."

"What are you doing?" she asked.

"I just decided to get you something."

Lynda was so shocked and touched she had to sit down. "It's the first time in my life that anybody besides my own husband has ever bought me anything like that," she said, almost teary-eyed.

"It's okay, Lynda," I said, pulling another box from the bag. "I bought myself a pair too."

Lynda has tried loaning me some of her clothes. It would have worked out perfectly, but her blouses are a little big—for obvious reasons. That didn't stop Lynda from trying to change my hairdo. She felt I should cut some tiny sideburns because they would give my face a little cheekbone line and could be used as attractive spit curls. Lynda proceeded to cut my sideburns, all the while telling me how they would add softness to my face.

"What you want to do," I said, "is make me look like you."

"No, no," Lynda pleaded. "It'll be your look."

After Lynda finished, I checked out the sideburns. They looked interesting and different. "Okay, would you cut mine?" she said.

What could I say? I got the scissors and trimmed some of the edges. "Try a little bit shorter," she said.

"Are you sure?" I asked. Lynda nodded.

I took the scissors and fingered strands of Lynda's hair. But instead of cutting the hair, I lost control and poked the scissors into Lynda's earlobe. Blood dripped all over her neck; she jumped in the air. That was my last experiment as a beautician.

Lynda tells me I'm one of the most sensitive women she has ever met. "For someone who always seems in control of things," she says, "you feel hurt very easily."

Lynda and Ron understood the dilemma of the career-oriented woman. Ron was involved in managing the acting careers of Lindsay Wagner, Jaclyn Smith and Susan Anspach, in addition to Lynda's. We had intense conversations about my career, and Ron never minced words.

"I'm going to tell you something," he began one day, "and believe me I'm not saying it in a flippant way or without the most careful thought about what I'm telling you. I really believe this from the bottom of my heart and as a person who loves you and cares about you, as much as my own family. If you don't go back and play, ten years from now, you're gonna never know or realize what your potential was. Granted, you've accomplished a lot of things in what you've chosen to do. But it's not something that's just a business with you. It's obviously something that you enjoy doing, something you've done all your life. When you're not working, we even go out and play tennis together, so you must enjoy playing."

"I do," I said. "But I just don't know if I have the desire to go out there week after week. It's just not enjoyable."

Ron smiled. "Your perspective is wrong," he said. "You don't have to play every week on the tour, you don't have to stay out there and grind like that. You should develop other interests in your life, but it doesn't mean you cut off tennis completely."

I tried to explain my rationale for not playing. The girls were tougher; I didn't know if I wanted to go back and hang around as a No. 3 or No. 4.

"If you think there is anything that you have lost by being a little bit older, you've gained as much by being smarter," he said. "You're a better player today than you were a year ago. You're thinner, quicker, more intelligent than anyone. I can parallel Lynda's career. She came out wearing a red-white-and-blue flag as Wonder Woman and then had to prove herself as an entertainer. She went over to London at the Palladium, broke all the records and got a fifteen-minute standing ovation. This is a person who was running around jumping over buildings. Everybody wants to put down somebody who is successful. For your own sake, you have to cut all that out and not deal with what other people say. You do it for your own satisfaction. You play because it was what you were trained to do. It's what you enjoy doing. You'd never realize your full potential if you quit now. It will affect your husband and your marriage. If you're not happy with your life, you're not going to be happy in your marriage."

I valued Ron's advice. Standing on the court inside Louis Armstrong Stadium at the National Tennis Center for the semifinals of the 1980 U.S. Open, I recognized Ron's voice from the stands shouting, "Okay, the match is just starting now!" He was trying to pull me together from 0–4 in the first set against Tracy.

I turned toward Ron and Lynda, who were in a courtside box. Ron was standing, shaking his fist, talking as positively then as he had months before. I smiled to myself. He and I were thinking alike: "Now is the beginning."

I broke Tracy's serve for 1–4, and then broke it a second time. Serving at 4–5, 30–40, I saved one set point with an overhead. The next point turned out to be the most important of the match.

The point began with one of our long baseline rallies. I went for the drop shot, low and angled, but Tracy recovered and hit an unbelievable cross-court forehand, a great shot that no other player would have hit. I lost the point and the set, but the momentum had shifted; I was prepared to play.

In the first game of the second set, I broke Tracy at love with a backhand cross-court winner off another drop shot. She broke back, but then I swept the next five games, losing only eight points.

There were no cheap points. Once again, the drop shot and lob were effective weapons. Both are shots that I have always been comfortable with but that other players seldom use enough in their games. Growing up on clay, the drop shot was one of the first shots my dad taught me, a stroke that requires touch, feel, timing. Not everyone can master the drop shot. You have to know how much underspin and backspin to put on a ball. It's not just a flat shot. How deep to hit it, and when and how are equally as important.

For players raised on hard courts, the drop shot has less relevance. Hard courts yield a high, true bounce that makes the shot easier to cover and less effective. But for a change of pace, bringing someone to the net, or as an element of surprise, the drop shot can be valuable on any surface. Once an opponent senses that you're not afraid to try the drop shot, it forces them to concentrate on another aspect of your game.

That's what happened with Tracy. My drop shots took her

out of a groove and changed the tempo of our rallies. I was taking the ball on the rise, stepping into my shots, thinking forward, adjusting speeds. Breaking her from deuce for the second set allowed me to serve the opening game of the last set, which can be an advantage when you're faced with 4–5 or 5–6. The first game went to deuce before I held with a backhand down the line that forced her into a forehand error. Just stay in the match, be keen, eager, don't think about the benefits, don't think of the outcome, just stay up emotionally, mentally and physically, I told myself. In the back of my mind, this match was another turning point.

Tracy held serve at love for 1–all, I held at 15 for 2–1 and then she reached 40–15. But her netted forehand and my backhand pass down the line brought the game to deuce. An overhead gave me the first break point of the set, and when Tracy sliced a forehand cross-court wide after a long rally, I had my first breakthrough, to 3–1.

The first shot that will go with Tracy when she is under pressure is her forehand. It's a stiff, flat, mechanical shot, not natural, and anything mechanical can break down. The pressure was on her this time. She had beaten me the last five times and was the No. 1 seed on the Open. The five losses had been a shock for me because Tracy was giving me a dose of my own medicine, drubbing me the way I had beaten all the other women for so long. But in my heart, I still felt I was a better player. I had lost because she was stronger mentally, but stroke-wise, I was technically better and wanted to play her when I was at my peak.

Although Tracy and I had played each other many times over a period of four years, it was hard to get close to her. Perhaps Tracy and I are too competitive with each other to be close. Interestingly, we have the same playing styles, were brought up by tennis families in warm-weather climates, traveled with our mothers as teen-agers and have other parallels in our lives. But our personalities are different. I don't know if Tracy wants to be by herself or feels more comfortable with her mother, attorney and coach.

That's one of the joys of looking at younger players like Tracy, Andrea Jaeger, Pam Shriver and Kathy Rinaldi. They're all so different. Although only sixteen, Andrea already is her own person. You've got to go through her if you want to deal with her; she's totally spontaneous. Pam's sense of humor is closer to mine, but she leaves her emotions all over the court, which can be good and bad. At fourteen, and already a pro, Kathy has a head start on all of us; how she develops as a player and person will depend on her attitude. She is stronger physically than Tracy, Andrea or I were at the same age.

Attitude played a key factor in the third set of my match against Tracy at the Open. Serving at 3–1 in the third set, I reached 30–0 with an ace and then double-faulted on the next point. But my double fault was long, not into the net, which meant that I was still playing aggressively, not tentatively. In my earlier losses to Tracy, I had lain down and said, "Okay, run all over me. You play the aggressive game, and you dominate." But in the second and third sets, I played a different brand of tennis. I was taking the initiative. All my experience and confidence peaked. Tracy drove a forehand service return long and then I put away a bounce smash from the service line that ended a moon-ball rally for a 4–1 lead.

Everything came out during the next two games. Shots that I had worked on for years but seldom used flowed out of me: volleys, overheads. I practiced my volley forty-five minutes a day, loved hitting overheads and almost never missed them. A running forehand pass down the line off Tracy's forehand volley gave me 15–40 on her serve, and I broke her again with a forehand lob after a drop-shotted return lured her in on a second serve.

Preparing to serve for the match, I felt I could play whatever shot I wanted and still win the point. This feeling is rare among tennis players. John McEnroe discovered it during the eighth game of the third set against Bjorn Borg in their 1981 U.S. Open final. McEnroe had been tentative, almost uncertain during the early stages, dropping the opening set. Then, he suddenly crunched two backhand cross-court passes and two winning topspin forehand lobs, and he was flying. McEnroe's attitude buried Borg. I felt the same way. As long as I didn't panic, the match was mine. If I made a mistake by inches, I had to keep going forward aggressively.

Experience is important in major championships like Wimbledon, the U.S. Open or the French. The player who uses experience to his or her advantage is the player who survives these long tournaments. It is easier for someone to psyche up and play relaxed and challenged against me than it is for me to become motivated against them. But at the Open, I didn't worry about age or whether Tracy hit the ball harder than I did. Serving for the match, I said to myself, "Close it out, just keep going." Her forehand drifted wide. 15–0. A backhand volley off my forehand drop landed wide. 30–0. A forehand drop shot winner. 40–0. A netted backhand off another forehand drop. Game, set and match.

I felt wonderful. I didn't jump up and down or throw my racquet in the air, but my emotions were overflowing. I looked across at John, my mom, Ron and Lynda. They were elated. I left the stadium, my mom and I hugged each other and we both started crying. Then Lynda began crying.

Before entering the press interview room, I went to the referee's shed and made one telephone call. "Dad, I won!" I said, after hearing his voice. Everyone thinks my dad is so serious, but his voice cracked a little when he said, "That's great."

After Wimbledon, we had talked about his role in my career. I told him then that I wished he could have enjoyed my success more. Don't worry, I've enjoyed everything, he reminded me. When I asked him at the time if he would come to the Open, he said, whenever I needed him, all I had to do was ask.

"Can you and Clare come up tonight or tomorrow?" I said, hoping he could fly up for the Open final.

"Yeah, we'd love to."

After the match with Tracy, John and I agreed it was a satisfying victory, but no time for celebrations. "You can really celebrate after the tournament," he said. "But you've got to mentally prepare yourself to play Hana because if you don't you're going to lose and you'll regret it."

Both of us recalled what happened at Wimbledon: I had beaten Martina in a highly emotional semifinal, played Evonne the next day, had a letdown and lost the first set, 6–1, in about fifteen minutes. Just when I seemed in the match, I dropped a second-set tie breaker. "Don't let the same thing happen to you that happened at Wimbledon," John stressed.

Too many players celebrate after a big victory and lose sight of what's ahead the next day. As a result, they are drained emotionally before they even walk on the court. I was ecstatic after beating Tracy. But once the handshakes, phone calls, press conferences and locker-room rituals were over, John and I went back to the hotel, and I told myself, "Okay, calm down, relax, save your emotion and energy for tomorrow's match." We ate an early dinner, made no phone calls to friends, read none of the telegrams or even looked at the cards in the floral arrangements that arrived after the match. I wanted my feet on the ground.

Sometimes the emotions from one match can sustain a player over a period of days. Manuel Orantes was down two sets to love, and then 0–5 and three match points in the fourth set against Guillermo Vilas in the semifinals of the U.S. Open. He won in five sets and then stayed on the high the following day and beat Jimmy in straight sets. The same thing happened to John McEnroe in the 1980 Open: He outlasted Jimmy in a fifth-set tie breaker in a long semifinal and then beat Borg in a five-setter the next day.

I don't know if men sustain their emotions better than women or simply stay at a physical peak. Each person knows how much energy he or she needs, and I wanted to be as keen as possible for Hana. That meant nutritionally and physiologically. I try to eat three to four hours before a match because I can feel food jumping around my stomach if I eat an hour or two before. Some players eat closer to a match because they want the food to serve as energy in a long match. I need more time for the food to digest.

Growing up in Florida helped my endurance. Florida has to be one of the hottest places in the world in the summer. At the ages of six, seven and eight, I played four, sometimes five hours a day when it was 95 degrees with 100 percent humidity. In the summer, it only takes me two or three days to adjust to 100-degree weather, and supplementing my fluid intake with Gatorade or a time-released salt tablet replenishes the three or four pounds of water I may lose in a match.

About thirty minutes before the final, I went into the trainers' room and began stretching exercises. I always stretch before matches now, and after a strenuous three-setter against Tracy, stretching was even more important to keep the muscles flexible.

When I first played the Open in 1971, few women stretched before matches. Maybe some of the players bounced around in the locker room, tried a few deep knee-bends or loosened up shoulder joints for serves. But Connie Spooner got me into the habit of slow, deliberate stretching before every match.

You don't notice how beneficial stretching can be until your body reacts adversely. I first noticed a difference when I had to switch from an indoor court to a cement court to a clay court —three different surfaces—within three weeks. Each surface affects specific areas of the body: On a grass court, you feel it in your rear and lower back; on a cement court, the stress is in the shins; with a synthetic carpet, I feel it in the middle of my back.

The exercises are more like yoga than jumping jacks. I will stretch the calf muscles, thighs, hamstrings, lower back. You especially stretch out the problem areas. Many players have one area where they have recurring injuries; if you stretch out that area every day, chances are you'll avoid an injury. It usually takes me about ten to fifteen minutes for my exercises; knowing how much I would have to run against Hana, I made certain my muscles felt loose.

In the final, once again, I lost the first set and then just settled down and said, "Okay, the match is just beginning now." Too many players lose a close first set and are resigned to believing a match is over. I've always taken the opposite approach: I've lost the first set, so I'll just have to win the next two. I looked across to where my dad was sitting and knew that I wanted this one.

For most of my life, my incentive had been to play for other people—my mom and dad, Jimmy, Jack Ford, Burt, Tony Roche, John. Even after I won my first U.S. Open, I gave my Wilson racquet to Mel Di Giacomo, a photographer.

I didn't pick up a tennis racquet on my own. My father introduced me to the sport. If I didn't have someone pushing me a little bit, I might not have achieved my level of success. I look at players like Billie Jean, Jimmy or Tracy and see special qualities that make them tick. I don't have their intensity, but other qualities have driven me. For example, I played for my family. Knowing how happy my dad was and the hard work he had put into my career motivated me.

If I threw away a match or didn't play my best, I was letting him down. It wasn't because he wanted us to win so much. He only asked us to try, but knowing that someone cared about how I did was the bottom line. Tony Roche cared whether I won Wimbledon in 1976; he never took my success for granted, and winning Wimbledon was my way of paying him back for the time he spent with me that spring.

The 1980 Open was different. For the first time, after beating Hana, 5–7, 6–1, 6–1, I won something for myself. You can go through life and not know yourself, dream and think, "Well, this is what I should do and this is what I shouldn't do." But I wanted to win the 1980 U.S. Open. It was important because I made it important. Win or lose, I wanted it for myself, and I got it.

13 • Being There

"Who's that?" Hana Mandlikova asked, staring at a picture on the wall.

"Maureen Connolly," I said. "Haven't you ever heard of her?"

"No," Hana replied.

At nineteen years old, Hana Mandlikova was too young to appreciate Maureen Connolly's three Wimbledon singles titles in 1952, 1953 and 1954. But any student of tennis knows that "Little Mo," as she was called, ranks among the great women players of all time. Sitting with Hana in the Players' Waiting Room before our 1981 Wimbledon singles final, I couldn't help but wonder whether any of today's young pros could develop an attachment or appreciation for the achievements of players in the past. The game dances to a different beat these days.

As someone who had won two Wimbledons and was runner-up four other times, the half dozen pictures on the pale blue walls of the Players Waiting Room were significant to me, especially the photo of Virginia Wade with Queen Elizabeth at the 1977 centennial celebration. Virginia had beaten me in the semifinals that year before going on to win the final against Betty Stove.

The Players Waiting Room at Wimbledon sounds lavish, but, in fact, it has a chilly, impersonal atmosphere and is no more than ten-by-twelve-feet large. Players are brought to the room before going onto the Centre Court or Number 1 court for a match, and it's doubtful if more than four players can sit in the room without feeling cramped. Four green velvet chairs and a hard green couch are remnants of other eras. Peter Morgan, who traditionally escorts players to the room, says blankets are stored there for cold or snowy days. There is also a "notice" of another Wimbledon trademark: "Clothing which displays any form of advertisement (other than one manufacturer's small logo) is not permitted to be worn on the courts. Players are also reminded that all clothing must be predominantly white."

The committee gave Martina some flak about some of her multicolored outfits during the 1981 tournament. But the rules are more lenient now than they were when I first played "The Championships" in 1972.

Losing three consecutive Wimbledon finals made me more committed than ever in 1981. Sitting with Hana, who had beaten me in the French Open semis the previous month, only put circumstances in a clearer perspective.

When things go right at a tournament, it can work to your advantage in many ways; you feel positive, on top of things, as if no shot or match is too difficult. In Paris, I was more concerned with how my opponents were playing than with pre-paring myself, and I allowed other distractions to unsettle me.

My dad had to cancel his planned trip to Paris because of his high blood pressure. John was involved with a tournament in England, playing well, and also unable to be with me, so I invited Clare; but the tournament came during her eighth-grade graduation.

"Would you rather go to graduation or come to Paris?" I asked.

Clare is too much. "Can I think about it and call you back in two days?" she said.

"Forget it," I replied, figuring Clare would be jumping for

joy and ready to grab the first flight. "You know, the men are playing here, too."

There was a long pause on the line. "Oh, really! Is John McEnroe playing?" Clare asked.

I knew what was rummaging around in Clare's mind. She had a huge first crush on John McEnroe, adored him and thought he was so cute. During an Avon tournament earlier in the year at Boston, I saw John, told him about Clare's crush and asked if he could send her some pictures. One week later, two giant colored pictures autographed by John arrived at the house. One of the pictures read, "Dear Clare, I feel the same way about you as you feel about me. Love, John." I was pleasantly surprised: John was busy, traveling all over the world, yet was considerate enough to take the time to make certain that pictures were sent to a thirteen-year-old girl. Again, it was a side of John that the public never sees.

When Clare heard that John was in the French Open, Paris seemed much more interesting than eighth-grade graduation. Unfortunately, her presence couldn't stop a succession of room changes for me at the Hilton hotel, after Saudi Arabian royalty moved into the next suite with an entourage of birds, animals and people.

I didn't see any camels, but the birds began chirping about six-thirty every morning on an outside balcony. Wanting as much sleep as possible, I complained to the manager. The manager informed me that the birds and animals belonged to the brother of the king of Saudi Arabia, and there was no way he could change his room.

"You are not the only player to complain," the manager said. "Bjorn Borg has been having problems too because there is another king in the hotel, and the king has had belly dancers in his room every night. The room is directly over Mr. Borg's."

The French is a well-run tournament, even if it is not as familiar to Americans as Wimbledon. On the second Tuesday, the International Tennis Federation has its annual championship dinner. John was still in England, so I went to the dinner with my mother, Clare and Susan Mascarin, a promising young American player from Grosse Pointe, Michigan.

I didn't leave after the first dance this time. In fact, I sent one of my playful "love notes" to an old friend, Ilie Nastase, during the dinner: "Dear Nasty," I wrote, "I don't have a date tonight. Since you have one, can Bambino be mine?" Bambino is Nasty's well-known, 260-pound, Italian-born bodyguard, Raul Belluci, who looks more like a menacing character from a James Bond novel than a popular regular on the tennis circuit.

Minutes later, a note arrived at the head of the table. "Bambino says he will be right over." Sure enough, the dancing started, Bambino came over, took my hand, kissed it and said, "Would you like to dance?" I got up, we walked onto the floor and about ten photographers quickly hustled into position for pictures. That surely was a first for them—and me.

Bjorn Borg and I were honored as the federation's champions for the year. Photographers asked us to pose for pictures, and while we were standing there, jokingly I said to Bjorn, "Are you going to take off three or four months as I did last year?"

"I think I should take a year off," Bjorn said, in a half-kidding tone. Right then, I could tell that Bjorn was thinking about a layoff. I had followed his success closely because many people, especially Ingrid Bentzer, had always suggested that our careers paralleled each other. I wondered after five consecutive Wimbledon titles whether Bjorn could sustain his motivation and goals. After awhile, if you're a human being and not a machine, the pressure has to settle in. When Bjorn announced later in the year that he would be taking a five-month break totally free from tennis, I recalled our conversation and was not surprised.

Bjorn won a sixth French Open title despite the belly dancers and his doubts. But my bid to preserve an unbeaten record for the year and win a fifth French championship was stopped by Hana, who handled Sylvia Hanika of West Germany in the final.

You develop certain feelings about players in certain tournaments. At the 1981 U.S. Open, for example, John and I weren't worried about Hana or Tracy as much as Martina, and Martina played wonderfully against me. In the French, Hana was playing very well. I watched one of two of her matches; she seemed eager to practice and was in a good mood. The morning of our match, I was tense, nervous, inhibited and felt as if she were going to dominate. At times, Hana reminded me of some of my earlier matches with Evonne; I found myself watching her hit the ball. She was steadier, hit winners, served well, played an almost perfect match and won, 7–5, 6–4. The reason I lost was not because of my own indecisiveness; Hana simply played too well that day.

Before we walked on Centre Court at Wimbledon, Fred Hoyels, the tournament referee, stopped by the waiting room and wished us luck. I wondered whether Hana had given any deep thought to this match. I attach a great deal to mental preparation before a final, and Wimbledon demands even more understanding. Hana seemed filled with energy, perhaps because it was her first Wimbledon final and her parents had flown in from Czechoslovakia. But she looked like someone who was thinking, "Well, I'm going to go out, and if I play well, great. If I don't, well, okay." The look of determination that I saw in Paris was missing.

The omens were with me at Wimbledon. Having lost to Hana in Paris, there was no pressure of carrying a perfect record into Wimbledon. I also withdrew from a grass-court tournament in Surbiton, England, because of a strained tendon attached to the tibia, and the withdrawal became a blessing in disguise. I rested and then practiced for about ten days with John, Dennis Ralston, Roscoe Tanner, John Sadri and Pat DuPre. I spent four hours a day working out—playing two-on-one drills with John and Pat, playing sets with Dennis—and went into Wimbledon feeling eager. Mima Jausovec's upset of Andrea Jaeger eliminated Andrea as a possible quarterfinal opponent. Then Pam Shriver beat Tracy for the first time in the quarters; I respected Pam's serve-and-volley game on grass, but Tracy would have been a more difficult opponent in the semis. As it turned out, Pam played our semi with a slight groin pull that inhibited much of her net game.

Anyone who doesn't believe that draws and destiny can influence the outcome of a tournament isn't realistic. At the 1981 U.S. Open, Tracy had only one strenuous match en route to the title—the three-set final against Martina. Her lower half of the draw went wide open when Andrea, nursing a torn rotator cuff in her right shoulder, lost to Andrea Leand, an amateur, in three sets. The upper half had Martina, Hana and myself; I beat Hana in the quarters, lost a close three-setter to Martina in the semis, and then Martina, after taking the first set easily from Tracy, lost the next two in tie breakers. Beating me was Martina's match of the tournament instead of continuing another step, just as Hana used some of her best finishing shots at Wimbledon in the semifinal against Martina.

If our 6–2, 6–2 score lacked any drama, I was excited at having won a third title. Even if Hana had played superbly, there was no way I wasn't going to win. I had worked for six months, Wimbledon was my goal, and I knew that when I put in that much time and emotion, I could win it. After the match, I didn't want the awards ceremony to end; I just wanted to stand on the Centre Court, hold up the Challenge Trophy, and enjoy. "Just feel this, enjoy it, don't think about the press conference or anything else," I told myself.

Hearing the crowd clapping at Wimbledon makes you want to hold the platter even higher. It's the greatest feeling; you've won it, you're showing people your trophy, you're proud of the moment, you're the best woman tennis player in the world and everybody would like to be in your shoes. For me, a disappointed runner-up for the last three years, holding up the trophy in front of my husband, family and friends and seeing their joy meant even more. In seven matches, I had lost only twenty-six games, the first player since Billie Jean in 1967 to win Wimbledon without dropping a set.

The presence of the Duke and Duchess of Kent, along with Lady Diana Spencer, made the victory even more satisfying. After the ceremony, I asked Air Chief Marshal Sir Brian K. Burnett (that's his official title), the chairman of the club, if John and I could meet Lady Diana, who was to marry Prince Charles later in the month.

"I'll see what I can do," Sir Brian said. Following my press conference, he told me that Lady Diana was having tea and would love to meet us in the members' enclosure.

I was not dressed to meet royalty. In the excitement of the match, ceremony and the anticipation of going to the members' enclosure, I wore only a yellow warm-up suit. John and I waited in the bar area adjacent to the members' enclosure, and he tried to explain some of the royal protocol that went with such events. For example, he said, if a waiter offered the Duke or Duchess biscuits or pastries, none of the other people sitting with them would eat or accept food until they took their portions.

"Why doesn't Lady Diana come over and meet us?" I asked, noticing that she was finished with her tea.

"She can't," John said. "She's got to wait for the Duke and Duchess first. They must leave first."

The Duke and Duchess of Kent are wonderful tennis fans. You can always find them in the Royal Box during Wimbledon, and they have become as synonymous with tennis as Queen Elizabeth is identified with horse racing.

The Duchess seemed especially pleased to see me. "I love your sweater, it just looks beautiful," she said pointing to my yellow Ellesse tennis sweater. I almost felt like saying, "Well, I'd like to send you a sweater," but then I worried, "Would it be proper to send a gift to the Duchess of Kent, and where would I send it?"

Lady Diana followed. She was tall, with a great figure and prettier in person than her pictures. Her dainty white skin and rosy cheeks sparkled. "I'm so happy you won," she began. "You played a really good match."

"Thank you," I said. John was standing next to me, speechless. I thought to myself, "Oh, John, we're finally meeting Lady Diana and you're speechless!" Later John would say he couldn't believe how casually I took meeting royalty. Being born and raised in Britain, for someone like him to meet royalty was a thrill. I guess I would feel equally speechless if I had met the Pope.

"How long do you have to go before your wedding?" I asked.

"Three weeks," Lady Diana replied.

"Are you nervous about it?"

"Actually, no," she said. "I haven't thought about it at all because I've been so busy every day."

I wasn't sure how my next question would go over but decided to ask it anyway. "I'm very annoyed," I began, "because I heard that your fiancé doesn't come to Wimbledon and doesn't like tennis."

Lady Diana didn't flinch at all. "Oh, yes," she said. "Sometimes he acts like a little boy and can't sit still when we go to these matches."

"Well, tell him that he had better come next year to Wimbledon."

Lady Diana smiled, "Okay, I'll tell him." she said.

I wish Prince Charles and Lady Diana had been at the Wimbledon Ball. Then the notoriety it received probably would have been different. John and I reached the dinner at about nine o'clock, but we didn't start eating until eleven-thirty because the committee had hoped John McEnroe, the men's champion, would appear.

McEnroe had infuriated the committee with several temperamental outbursts during the tournament, drawing several fines, reprimands, threats of suspension and tons of headlines. But he wound up beating Borg in four sets in the final, and thus was entitled to attend the ball if he wanted. The committee said they had invited him—McEnroe's father said the invitation had never been received. Whether that is the case or John simply preferred to spend the time with friends was not my business. But when he did not appear, the show had to go on, even if everyone at the Savoy hotel was seething.

I sat down next to Sir Brian, and everyone moved down one seat at the head table because they didn't want to leave a seat empty next to Lady Burnett.

"I can't believe he didn't show up," John said to me. "There's so much tension in this room."

You could feel the heat, as if the ball was incomplete.

"Should I crack a few jokes and loosen them up a little bit?" I asked John, trying out a few lines.

John laughed. "Yeah, that would be good."

"Are you sure?" I went on. "McEnroe is going to be so mad at me. Are you sure it's okay?"

John grabbed my shoulders. "Sure it's okay," he said. "Listen, love, you're saying it in good humor, and there is so much tension in this room anyway that you have to make the best of it. This is your Wimbledon, too."

But McEnroe was the focal point. Before introducing me, Sir Brian noted, "Unfortunately, the men's champion is not present with us. He might be out having his own celebration."

I went ahead anyway. "Sir Brian Burnett has informed me that I must make two speeches," I began, "one for myself and one for what's his name. Unfortunately, I don't have the same vocabulary as he does."

Looking back, my lines may have been a bit saucy, but the crowd laughed, and it seemed to break the tension in the air. Then I talked about how much more winning Wimbledon meant this time and the role that my John and Dennis Ralston had played. Toward the end of the speech, I also apologized for John McEnroe not being there. I never meant to put him down, but to totally ignore his absence would have been equally ridiculous. So often, I've had to watch what I say, and I've been very sensitive about not criticizing people openly. I've tried to treat people the way I would want to be treated and to put myself in their position. I wouldn't want to open the paper and read how Chris Evert Lloyd had criticized me. I meant nothing ill toward McEnroe, and I guess he felt that I should have stayed out of it and minded my own business. But in a way, the tension in the room detracted from the whole affair. Should I have been overlooked because people were more concerned about McEnroe not being there?

Tennis is changing in more ways than in the behavior of the players. Women's tennis is in a very critical position. Until now, the strength of our game has been that the players have stuck together. On the men's circuit, for many years, many of the top pros were not even members of the Association of Tennis Professionals; they remained unconcerned and uninvolved with policies and direction. Not so among the women. We were divided over whether to stage a separate U.S. Open in 1981, a move that I opposed and that was finally rejected by the association, but at least we spoke at the finish as a group. The men will be more fragmented than ever in 1982.

But the women's game has grown so rapidly that we may be spreading ourselves too thin. More tournaments, exhibitions and special events are added to the schedule each year. Yet the top women are not fulfilling commitments to these tournaments.

With the stress of travel and tournaments, I don't see a woman playing more than ten years. How can you keep an Andrea Jaeger or Kathy Rinaldi motivated for ten years when they're likely to be worn out as teen-agers? Women's tennis also needs spokeswomen for the future, leaders who are willing to take over for Billie Jean, Martina and myself. If the average age of the top players is seventeen or eighteen, and they haven't finished high school, you're not going to have educated women talking to the press and trying to build the game. Diane Desfor, who was elected as the new president of the Women's Tennis Association, is a Phi Beta Kappa from the University of Southern California. She is a college graduate and psychology major who can contribute as a player and a leader. But someone who turns pro at fourteen might drop out of the tour or lose interest in it just when she might reach the top ten and be able to make her most significant contribution.

It's not necessary or, for that matter, even good, for the few top players to face each other every week. If Borg and McEnroe played every week, the glamour and excitement of their rivalry would wear off completely; there wouldn't be any mystery about who would win. If the top women—whoever are No. 1 and No. 2—meet four or five times a year, that's plenty. If these meetings happen to be at Wimbledon or the U.S. Open, where the television and press coverage are exceptional, so much the better. The Avon and Volvo circuits are great for the women and men to earn a living, but it's Wimbledon and the Open that broaden the popularity of tennis and make people want to come out to their local tournament.

To be Number One, you have to think about yourself. As a child, playing with my brothers and sisters, I was totally aware of their feelings and wants. I wasn't that demanding. Then on the tour, I discovered that I had to learn to say no, and that saying no would hurt people's feelings. I hate turning down a request for an interview. I look into the eyes of the person asking and see a man or woman trying to earn a living, and this interview might be his or her break. Most of the time, I have to say no because a succession of interviews will drain me during a tournament.

I've also been cold in other personal situations. There were times when my sister Jeanne played a match at nine o'clock in the morning, and I had a match that evening. To be at my best for my match, I needed to sleep until ten or eleven and rest, so I might miss her match, she would lose, and then I'd feel terrible.

Where do you draw the line? One week, I might see Martina crying in the locker room after our match and my heart would go out to her. So I felt sorry for her, and the next week she knocked my block off. And now I don't feel sorry for her; now I say that I reacted vulnerably to the situation. That's probably why I haven't tried to make friends with every single player. I have friends, but don't feel as if I have a lot of best friends on the tour.

The tour is much tougher now. Eight years ago, even five years ago for that matter, I would win matches 6–0, 6–1 until the semifinals or final. Then I would have a relatively strenuous final. Now, if you look at the tournament results, the scores are closer and you have to prepare yourself mentally unless you want to burn out. Physically, you need more rest periods, more breaks. My decision to take a break in 1978 started other players thinking: If I wasn't afraid to risk my ranking, maybe they too could lay off and come back refreshed?

What made me a champion? My father's coaching, training

and persistent encouragement paved the way. But it was something more—a mental strength, belief in myself, guts and the ability to never give up. I was consistent over a long period of time because I never looked back, never dwelled on my defeats. I always looked ahead. Why? Maybe fear of losing control of the winning flow. I wanted to be in control and always thought of myself as a chess player. I never won by overpowering opponents, but by outthinking them and maneuvering them around the court. I tried to make them play my game instead of theirs.

Some players are satisfied with winning one Wimbledon or U.S. Open and don't care about their results for the rest of the year. That would be enough for them. I have used my results in smaller tournaments to build up for the long run. When a player who has lost two tournaments in a row faces someone who has won two in a row, the difference between them still may be so minute that it might come down to how much confidence each feels at that moment. It took a year of being Number Three in the world to appreciate what being Number One means. I had my back up against the wall, almost everybody had lost faith in me. I put myself on the line, was determined and wasn't afraid of failure.

I liked the idea of competing with another person, where someone wins or loses. At least you know where you stand, and it gives you a goal, something to strive for. If you're Number Three, you know you must work hard to be Number One, and when you're Number One you can reap the benefits.

Barbara Potter, a bright, thoughtful player and former valedictorian of her school class, once described concentration as the ability to live only in each moment—not one second in the past or one second in the future. I agree. You are born with certain instinctive traits. I'm not a great natural athlete, as I learned in that touch football game with Burt, but I was born with natural concentration. Developing these traits depends on the individual. To overcome my shyness, I turned to concentration. It may have hindered me initially, particularly in relationships. I never wanted anything to come between my tennis and me and wasn't ready to risk losing for anybody. My heart was on the court, and I believe that's where I made my greatest contribution to the game.

Money aside, tennis opened my eyes to reality. It put me in situations that tested my strength as a person. Thinking back to all my press conferences over the years, my strength was tested more when I lost than when I won. After I lost, I had to learn to accept defeat and the negative feelings inside. Tennis also helped me to deal with people. Learning how to answer questions in front of five hundred people, signing autographs, making speeches, traveling to different countries and just being friendly tested my patience. It was an education.

But there are other qualities that go with being a champion. I cried after losses, was more emotional than the public ever knew, but also gave my opponent credit for a victory. I've had to work at being gracious because there were times after losses when I wanted to walk off, go home and not deal with the media and my opponents. I just wanted to be sour about it. But after thinking about the consequences a second time, I remembered what my dad said: "You've got to take the bad with the good; you've won so much and if you lose three or four times a year, don't be a bad sport about it, just be gracious."

Women's tennis badly needed a young, fresh face, someone removed from the stereotyped woman jock. If I added youth, femininity and consistency and gave young players hope, I achieved something. At the same time, I felt a responsibility not to let myself down. I had pride, but even more important, it was a challenge to reach Number One and remain there. To regain it became the ultimate challenge.

Tennis has been my life since I was six years old. I channeled my mental, physical and emotional energies into the game. Maybe I missed out on some of life's more subtle joys, but I can't put less than 100 percent into a successful effort. Now older, I realize that tennis, or any other sport, is not the total key to happiness. Being able to compete hard in a sport I love and still cook a meal for John or take a long walk with him in Hyde Park is equally important. I don't have to put all my eggs in one basket, nor do I want to. After tennis, I hope I will always have a challenge in life, something at which I can work hard and feel fulfilled. When I lose my inspiration and incentive, I begin to worry.

I hope some of my achievements have reached beyond the tennis court. Perhaps there are people participating in sports now who realized, from watching me, that everyone can find an enjoyable playing level, if each uses his or her mind. Being gracious in defeat as well as victory and keeping success in perspective are important to a balanced life. The real world appreciates the simple things in life.

Perhaps the most important thing, though, is something I proved to myself: Whatever your goal in life, try to do it to the best of your ability but stay happy. Wherever you set your sights, don't get discouraged, and be proud of every day that you are able to work in that direction. Most of all, along the way, don't forget to stop and smell the roses.

A Statistical Record

Chris Evert Lloyd Career Highlights
Compiled by Steve Flink

1971

Tournaments Played	9
Tournaments Won	7
Finals Reached	0
Semifinals Reached	1
Record	31–2 .939
U.S. Ranking	No. 3
Season Highlights	Semifinalist U.S. Open
	Won Eastern Grass Court Championship (South Orange, New Jersey)
	Won Virginia Slims Masters (St. Petersburg, Florida)

1972

Tournaments Played	11
Tournaments Won	4
Finals Reached	3
Semifinals Reached	3
Record	47–7 .870
World Ranking	No. 3
U.S. Ranking	No. 3
Season Highlights	Won Virginia Slims Championship
	Won U.S. Clay Court Championship
	Semifinalist Wimbledon and U.S. Open

1973

Tournaments Played	21	
Tournaments Won	12	
Finals Reached	5	
Semifinals Reached	3	
Record	88–10	.898
World Ranking	No. 2	
U.S. Ranking	No. 2	
Season Highlights	Won Virginia Slims Championship	
	Won South African Open	
	Won U.S. Clay Court Championship	
	Finalist Wimbledon, French Open, Italian Open	
	Semifinalist U.S. Open	

1974

Tournaments Played	23	
Tournaments Won	16	
Finals Reached	5	
Semifinals Reached	2	
Record	100–7	.934
World Ranking	No. 1	
U.S. Ranking	No. 1	
Season Highlights	Won Wimbledon	
	Won French Open	
	Won Italian Open	
	Won U.S. Clay Court Championship	
	Finalist Virginia Slims Championship	
	Won 10 straight tournaments and 56 straight matches between April and September.	

1975

Tournaments Played	22	
Tournaments Won	16	
Finals Reached	2	
Semifinals Reached	3	
Record	94–6	.940
World Ranking	No. 1	
U.S. Ranking	No. 1	

Season Highlights	Won U.S. Open
	Won Virginia Slims Championship
	Won French Open
	Won Italian Open
	Semifinalist Wimbledon
	Won 35 straight matches and 8 tournaments to close season.

1976

Tournaments Played	17	
Tournaments Won	12	
Finals Reached	4	
Semifinals Reached	0	
Record	75–5	.938
World Ranking	No. 1	
U.S. Ranking	No. 1	
Season Highlights	Won Wimbledon	
	Won U.S. Open	
	Finalist Virginia Slims Championship	
	Won 36 straight matches and 6 tournaments in a row between April and November.	

1977

Tournaments Played	14	
Tournaments Won	11	
Finals Reached	1	
Semifinals Reached	1	
Record	70–4	.946
World Ranking	No. 1	
U.S. Ranking	No. 1	
Season Highlights	Won U.S. Open	
	Won Colgate Series Championship	
	Won Virginia Slims Championship	
	Semifinalist Wimbledon	

1978

Tournaments Played	11	
Tournaments Won	7	
Finals Reached	3	
Semifinals Reached	1	
Record	56–3	.949
World Ranking	No. 1	
U.S. Ranking	No. 1	
Season Highlights	Won U.S. Open	
	Won Colgate Series Championship	
	Won U.S. Indoor Championship	
	Finalist Wimbledon	
	Closed season by winning 32 straight matches.	

1979

Tournaments Played	22	
Tournaments Won	8	
Finals Reached	6	
Semifinals Reached	4	
Record	92–15	.860
World Ranking	No. 3	
U.S. Ranking	No. 2	
Season Highlights	Won French Open	
	Won U.S. Clay Court Championship	
	Finalist Wimbledon, U.S. Open	

1980

Tournaments Played	15	
Tournaments Won	8	
Finals Reached	3	
Semifinals Reached	3	
Record	70–5	.933
World Ranking	No. 1	
U.S. Ranking	No. 2	
Season Highlights	Won U.S. Open	
	Won French Open	
	Won Italian Open	
	Won U.S. Clay Court Championship	
	Finalist Wimbledon	
	Won 59 of last 62 matches of the season.	

1981

Tournaments Played	15	
Tournaments Won	9	
Finals Reached	3	
Semifinals Reached	3	
Record	72–6	.923
World Ranking	No. 1	
U.S. Ranking	No. 1	
Season Highlights	Won Wimbledon	
	Won Italian Open	
	Won WTA Championship	
	Finalist Australian Open	
	Won 32 straight matches and 6 straight	
	tournaments between March and June.	

1971–1981 Summary

Tournaments Played	180	
Tournaments Won	110	
Finals Reached	41	
Semifinals Reached	24	
Record	795–70	.919
World Ranking		
Summary	Ranked No. 1 1974–1978, 1980–1981.	
U.S. Ranking		
Summary	Ranked No. 1 1974–1978, 1981.	

SPECIAL NOTE: Chris Evert began entering selected women's tournaments in 1969 at the age of fourteen, and at fifteen in September of 1970 she produced her first big victory when she toppled Margaret Court, 7–6, 7–6, in the semifinals at Charlotte, North Carolina. But because she did not begin to compete on a frequent basis in women's events until 1971, her complete record is listed in this statistical evaluation beginning with that year.

Chris Evert Lloyd Wimbledon Record

1972 (seeded fourth): d. Val Ziegenfuss 1–6 6–3 6–3; Janet Newberry 6–3 6–0; Mary Ann Eisel 8–6 8–6; Julie Anthony 6–3 6–2; Patti

Hogan 6–2 4–6 6–1; lost semifinal to Evonne Goolagong 4–6 6–3 6–4.

1973 (seeded fourth): d. Fiorella Bonicelli 6–3 6–3; Judith Goyn 6–0 6–1; Julie Heldman 6–3 6–1; Janet Young 6–3 3–6 8–6; Rosie Casals 6–2 4–6 6–2; Margaret Court (the No. 1 seed) 6–1 1–6 6–1; lost final to second-seeded Billie Jean King 6–0 7–5.

1974 (seeded second): d. Lesley Hunt 8–6 5–7 11–9; Isabel Fernandez 6–1 6–1; Mona Schallau 7–5 6–1; Helga Masthoff 6–4 6–2; Kerry Melville 6–2 6–3; Olga Morozova 6–0 6–4 in the final.

1975 (seeded first): d. Chris O'Neil 6–0 6–2; Elly Appel 6–0 6–1; Kazuko Sawamatsu 6–2 6–2; Lindsey Beaven 6–2 6–4; Betty Stove 5–7 7–5 6–0; lost semifinal to third-seeded King 2–6 6–2 6–3.

1976 (seeded first): d. Linda Thomas 6–1 6–1; Annette Coe 6–0 6–0; Hunt 6–1 6–0; Stove 6–2 6–2; Morozova 6–3 6–0; Martina Navratilova 6–3 4–6 6–4; Goolagong 6–3 4–6 8–6 in the final.

1977 (seeded first): d. Ruta Gerulaitis 6–0 6–3; Winnie Wooldridge 6–0 6–2; Tracy Austin 6–1 6–1; Greer Stevens 8–6 6–4; King 6–1 6–2; lost semifinal to third-seeded and eventual champion Virginia Wade 6–2 4–6 6–1.

1978 (seeded first): d. Helena Anliot 6–1 6–0; Laura DuPont 6–1 4–6 6–0; Kerry Melville Reid 6–3 6–4; King 6–3 3–6 6–2; Wade 8–6 6–2; lost final to second-seeded Navratilova 2–6 6–4 7–5.

1979 (seeded second): d. Marita Redondo 6–4 6–2; Andrea Whitmore 6–1 6–2; Kathy May Teacher 6–4 6–3; DuPont 6–2 6–1; Wendy Turnbull 6–3 6–4; Goolagong 6–3 6–2; lost final to top-seeded Navratilova 6–4 6–4.

1980 (seeded third): d. Christiane Jolissaint 6–0 6–1; Lindsey Morse 6–1 6–4; JoAnne Russell 6–3 6–2; Andrea Jaeger 6–1 6–1; top-seeded Navratilova 4–6 6–4 6–2 in semifinal; lost final to fourth-seeded Goolagong 6–1 7–6.

1981 (seeded first): d. Chris O'Neil 6–3 6–0; Yvonne Vermaak 6–1 6–2; Lele Forood 6–2 7–6; Claudia Pasquale 6–0 6–0; Mima Jausovec 6–2 6–2; Pam Shriver 6–3 6–1; Hana Mandlikova 6–2 6–2 in the final.

Wimbledon Summary

Tournaments Played	10	
Tournaments Won	3	
Finals Reached	4	
Semifinals Reached	3	
Record	57–7	.891

Chris Evert Lloyd U.S. Open Record

1971 (unseeded): d. Edda Buding 6–1 6–0; Mary Ann Eisel 4–6 7–6 6–1; fifth-seeded Françoise Durr 2–6 6–2 6–3; Lesley Hunt 4–6 6–2 6–3; lost semifinal to top-seeded Billie Jean King 6–3 6–2.

1972 (seeded third): d. Laurie Tenney 6–1 6–1; Marita Redondo 6–1 6–2; Julie Heldman 6–1 6–2; Olga Morozova 3–6 6–3 7–6; lost semifinal to ninth-seeded Kerry Melville 6–4 6–2.

1973 (seeded third): d. Rayni Fox 6–3 6–3; Redondo 6–2 6–2; Julie Anthony 6–4 6–4; Rosie Casals 6–1 7–5; lost semifinal to top-seeded Margaret Court 7–5 2–6 6–2.

1974 (seeded first): d. Gail Chanfreau 6–1 6–1; Helen Gourlay 6–1 6–1; Pattie Hogan 6–2 6–2; Hunt 7–6 6–3; lost semifinal to fifth-seeded Evonne Goolagong 6–0 6–7 6–3.

1975 (seeded first): d. Hunt 6–1 6–0; Natasha Chmyreva 6–0 6–3; Wendy Overton 6–0 6–1; Melville 6–2 6–1; Martina Navratilova 6–4 6–4; Goolagong 5–7 6–4 6–2 in the final.

1976 (seeded first): d. Greer Stevens 6–1 6–0; Glynis Coles 6–0 6–0; Sue Barker 6–1 6–0; Chmyreva 6–1 6–2; Mima Jausovec 6–3 6–1; Goolagong 6–3 6–0 in the final.

1977 (seeded first): d. Sharon Walsh 6–1 6–0; Pam Whytcross 6–0 6–0; Helena Anliot 6–2 6–2; Nancy Richey 6–3 6–0; King 6–2 6–0; Betty Stove 6–3 7–5; Wendy Turnbull 7–6 6–2 in the final.

1978 (seeded second): d. Donna Ganz 6–0 6–4; Caroline Stoll 6–1 7–5; Regina Marsikova 6–4 6–1; Tracy Austin 7–5 6–1; Turnbull 6–3 6–0; Pam Shriver 7–5 6–4 in the final.

1979 (seeded first): d. Iris Riedel 6–0 6–0; JoAnne Russell 6–0 6–2; Renee Richards 6–2 6–1; Sherry Acker 4–6 6–0 6–2; Goolagong 7–5 6–2; King 6–1 6–0; lost final to third-seeded Austin 6–4 6–3.

1980 (seeded third): d. Kim Sands 6–0 6–0; Peanut Louie 6–3 6–1; Wendy White 6–1 6–1; Russell 6–2 6–1; Jausovec 7–6 6–2; top-seeded Austin 4–6 6–1 6–1; ninth-seeded Hana Mandlikova 5–7 6–1 6–1 in the final.

1981 (seeded first): d. Kathrin Keil 6–1 6–1; Kate Latham 6–0 6–1; Alycia Moulton 6–3 6–0; Bettina Bunge 6–2 6–0; Mandlikova 6–1 6–3; lost semifinal to fourth-seeded Navratilova 7–5 4–6 6–4.

U.S. Open Summary

Tournaments Played	11	
Tournaments Won	5	
Finals Reached	1	
Semifinals Reached	5	
Record	59–6	.908

Chris Evert Lloyd French Open Record

1973 (seeded second): d. Margot Tesch 6–1 6–0; H. Goto 6–0 6–1; Renata Tomanova 6–2 6–3; Helga Masthoff 6–3 6–3; Françoise Durr 6–1 6–0; lost final to top-seeded Margaret Court 6–7 7–6 6–4.

1974 (seeded first): d. Regina Marsikova 6–1 6–4; Virginia Ruzici 6–2 6–3; Victoria Baldovinos 6–2 6–2; Julie Heldman 6–0 7–5; Masthoff 7–5 6–4; Olga Morozova 6–1 6–2 in the final.

1975 (seeded first): d. Carmen Perea 6–2 6–2; Mima Jausovec 6–2 6–3; Tomanova 6–3 6–2; Kazuko Sawamatsu 6–2 6–2; Morozova 6–4 6–0; Martina Navratilova 2–6 6–2 6–1 in the final.

1979 (seeded first): d. Kate Latham 6–1 6–0; Laura DuPont 6–3 6–3; Ivanna Madruga 4–6 6–2 6–3; Ruta Gerulaitis 6–0 6–4; Dianne Fromholtz 6–1 6–3; Wendy Turnbull 6–2 6–0 in the final.

1980 (seeded first): d. Caroline Franch 6–0 6–0; Pam Teeguarden 6–1 6–1; Bettina Bunge 4–6 6–4 6–3; Kathy Jordan 6–2 6–0; Hana Mandlikova 6–7 6–2 6–2; Virginia Ruzici 6–0 6–3 in the final.

1981 (seeded first): d. Claudia Kohde 6–3 6–2; Claudia Casabianca 6–4 6–0; Eva Pfaff 6–3 6–1; Virginia Wade 6–3 6–0; Ruzici 6–4 6–4; lost semifinal to third-seeded and eventual champion Mandlikova 7–5 6–4.

French Open Summary

Tournaments Played	6	
Tournaments Won	4	
Finals Reached	1	
Semifinals Reached	1	
Record	34–2	.944

Chris Evert Lloyd Federation Cup Record

1977: d. Sabbine Bernegger (Aust) 6–0 6–0; Annemarie Ruegg (Switz) 6–3 6–0; Françoise Durr (Fr) 6–1 6–3; Brigitte Cuypers (SA) 6–1 6–1; Kerry Melville Reid 7–5 6–3 in final round.

1978: d. Hanh Yoo-Ja (Korea) 6–1 6–0; Judy Chaloner (NZ) 6–1 6–1; Brigitte Simon (Fr) 6–2 6–2; Virginia Wade (GB) 6–2 6–4; Wendy Turnbull (Aust) 3–6 6–1 6–1 in final round.

1979: d. Sylvia Hanika (Ger) 6–4 6–2; Simon (Fr) 6–0 6–0; Morozova (USSR) 6–4 8–6; Fromholtz (Aust) 2–6 6–3 8–6 in final round.

1980: d. Brenda Perry (NZ) 6–1 1–0 ret.; Olga Zaitseva (USSR) 6–0 6–2; Renata Tomanova (Czech) 6–1 6–2; Fromholtz (Aust) 4–6 6–1 6–1 in final round.

1981: d. Duk Hee Lee (Korea) 6–1 6–3; Carmen Perea (Sp) 6–2 6–0; Virginia Ruzici (Rom) 6–1 6–2; Petra Delhees (Switz) 6–2 6–2; Sue Barker (GB) 6–2 6–1 in final round.

Federation Cup Summary

Singles Matches Played	23
Singles Matches Won	23
Winning Percentage	1.000

Chris Evert Lloyd Wightman Cup Record

1971: d. Winnie Shaw 6–0 6–4; Virginia Wade 6–1 6–1.

1972: d. Wade 6–4 6–4; Joyce Williams 6–2 6–3.

1973: d. Wade 6–4 6–2; Veronica Burton 6–3 6–0.

1975: d. Glynis Coles 6–4 6–1; Wade 6–3 7–6.

1976: d. Wade 6–2 3–6 6–3; Sue Barker 2–6 6–2 6–2.

1977: d. Wade 7–5 7–6; Barker 6–1 6–2.

1978: d. Barker 6–2 6–1; Wade 6–0 6–1.

1979: d. Barker 7–5 6–2; Wade 6–1 6–1.

1980: d. Barker 6–2 6–1; Wade 7–5 3–6 7–5.

1981: d. Wade 6–1 6–3; Barker 6–3 6–0.

Wightman Cup Summary

Singles Matches	
Played	20
Singles Matches Won	20
Winning Percentage	1.000

Chris Evert Lloyd 125-Match Clay Court Winning Streak

1973: U.S. Clay Court Championships (d. Pat Bostrom 6–0 6–0; Isabel Fernandez 6–3 6–4; Pat Pretorius 6–2 6–1; Linda Tuero 6–0 6–0; Veronica Burton 6–4 6–3 in final); Columbus, Ga. (d. Janet Haas 6–1 6–0; Françoise Durr 6–0 6–2; Laurie Fleming 6–4 6–0; Rosie Casals 6–3 7–6 in semifinal; won by default from Margaret Court—defaults not counted as matches in the streak); Virginia Slims Championships, Boca Raton, Fla. (d. Kristien Kemmer Shaw 6–2 6–3; Karen Krantzcke 6–0 6–0; Julie Heldman 6–2 6–4; Kerry Melville 6–1 6–2; Nancy Richey 6–3 6–3 in final).

1974: Fort Lauderdale (d. Fleming 6–1 6–2; Wendy Overton 6–0 6–3; Betty Stove 6–3 6–4; Casals 6–0 6–1; won final by default from Melville); Sarasota, Fla. (d. Carrie Meyer 6–1 6–2; Sue Stap 6–1 6–1; Betty Stove 6–0 6–1; Olga Morozova 6–2 6–0; Evonne Goolagong 6–4 6–0 in final); St. Petersburg, Fla. (d. Bostrom 6–0 6–1; Glynis Coles 6–1 6–3; Krantzcke 6–7 6–0 6–0; Helga Masthoff 6–1 6–1; Melville 6–0 6–1 in final); Family Cup Circle, Hilton Head, S.C. (d. Kerry Harris 6–1 6–2; Wendy Overton def.; Stove 6–2 6–3; Casals 6–1 6–0; Melville 6–1 6–3 in final); Italian Open (d. Lita Sugiarto 7–5 6–2; Marie Neumannova 4–6 6–1 6–4; Kazuko Sawamatsu 6–1 6–1; Morozova 6–1 1–6 6–0; Martina Navratilova 6–3 6–3 in final); French Open (d. Regina Marsikova 6–1 6–4; Virginia Ruzici 6–2 6–3; Victoria Baldovinos 6–2 6–2; Heldman 6–0 7–5; Masthoff 7–5 6–4; Morozova 6–1 6–2 in final); U.S. Clay Court Championships (d. Helle Sparre 6–0 6–0; Roberta Stark 6–2 6–2; Ruzici 6–0 6–1; Meyer 6–1 6–2; Gail Chanfreau 6–0 6–0 in final); Canadian Open, Toronto (d. Maria Nasuelli 6–1 6–2; Chanfreau 6–0 6–2; Laurie Tenney 6–0 6–0; Sawamatsu 6–0 6–1; Heldman 6–0 6–3 in the final).

1975: Family Circle Cup, Amelia Island, Fla. (d. Meyer 6–0 6–0; Casals 6–1 6–0; Durr 6–2 6–0; Goolagong 6–1 6–1; Navratilova 7–5 6–4 in final); Italian Open (d. Rosalba Vido 6–0 6–2; Sue Barker 6–1 6–3; Fiorella Bonicelli 6–1 6–3; Mima Jausovec 6–2 6–0; Navratilova 6–1 6–0 in final); French Open (d. Carmen Perea 6–2 6–2; Jausovec 6–2 6–3; Renata Tomanova 6–3 6–2; Sawamatsu 6–2 6–2; Morozova 6–4 6–0; Navratilova 2–6 6–2 6–1 in final); U.S. Clay Court Championships (d. Paulina Peisachov 6–0 6–2; Coles 6–2 6–0; Donna Ganz 6–1 6–2; Richey 6–7 7–5 4–2 ret. Evert recovered from 7–6, 5–0, 40–15 down to win this match and keep the streak alive at 73 matches; Dianne Fromholtz 6–3 6–4 in final); Rye, N.Y. (d. Chanfreau 6–2 6–1; Jausovec def.; Mona Schallau 6–0 6–4; Court 6–3 6–3; Virginia Wade 6–0 6–1 in final); U.S. Open (d. Lesley Hunt 6–1 6–0; Natasha Chmyreva 6–0 6–3; Overton 6–0 6–1; Melville 6–2 6–1; Navratilova 6–4 6–4; Goolagong 5–7 6–4 6–2 in final); Orlando, Fla. (d. Janet Newberry 6–1 6–2; Fernandez 6–1 6–4; Linky Boshoff 6–2 6–2; Casals 6–0 6–2; Navratilova by def. in final); World Invitational, Hilton Head, S.C. (d. Casals 6–0 6–1; Goolagong 6–1 6–1 in final).

1976: Family Circle Cup, Amelia Island, Fla. (d. Wendy Turnbull 6–2 6–1; Tory Ann Fretz 6–0 6–0; Stove 6–4 6–4; Mary Struthers 6–0 6–0; Melville Reid 6–2 6–2 in final); U.S. Open (d. Greer Stevens 6–1 6–0; Coles 6–0 6–0; Barker 6–1 6–0; Chmyreva 6–1 6–2; Jausovec 6–3 6–1; Goolagong 6–3 6–0 in final).

1977: Family Circle Cup, Hilton Head, S.C. (d. Bunny Bruning 6–0 6–3; Turnbull 6–1 6–0; Kathy May 6–0 6–1; Jausovec 6–3 6–3; Billie Jean King 6–0 6–1 in final); U.S. Open (d. Sharon Walsh 6–1 6–0; Pam Whytcross 6–0 6–0; Helena Anliot 6–2 6–2; Richey 6–3 6–0; King 6–2 6–0; Stove 6–3 7–5; Turnbull 7–6 6–2 in final).

1978: Family Circle Cup, Hilton Head, S.C. (d. Beth Norton 6–1 6–0; Jausovec 6–0 6–1; Renee Richards 6–4 6–3; Tracy Austin 6–3 6–1; Reid 6–2 6–0 in final).

1979: Federation Cup, Madrid (d. Sylvia Hanika 6–4 6–2; Brigitte Simon 6–0 6–0; Morozova 6–4 8–6; Fromholtz 2–6 6–3 8–6); Italian Open (d. JoAnne Russell 6–1 6–2; Newberry 6–2 6–1; Ivanna Madruga 3–6 6–1 6–4; lost semifinal to Austin 6–4 2–6 7–6).

Career Head-to-Head Records with Leading Rivals (Complete Through 1981)

9–4 vs. Margaret Court
16–7 vs. Billie Jean King
29–16 vs. Martina Navratilova
24–13 vs. Evonne Goolagong
38–6 vs. Virginia Wade
22–0 vs. Betty Stove
13–0 vs. Françoise Durr
15–0 vs. Olga Morozova
13–0 vs. Mima Jausovec
6–0 vs. Andrea Jaeger

20–0 vs. Virginia Ruzici
16–1 vs. Wendy Turnbull
7–9 vs. Tracy Austin
10–2 vs. Hana Mandlikova
10–0 vs. Pam Shriver
6–5 vs. Nancy Richey
17–1 vs. Kerry Melville Reid
22–1 vs. Rosie Casals
15–3 vs. Dianne Fromholtz
5–0 vs. Sylvia Hanika